# SWIFTER THAN REASON

The Poetry and Criticism of Robert Graves

*"We never could have loved had love not struck*
*Swifter than reason, and despite reason."*

*"Under the Olives"*

*"Few self-styled poets have experienced the trance;*
*but all who have, know that to work out a line by*
*an exercise of reason, rather than by a deep-seated*
*belief in miracle, is highly unprofessional conduct."*

*The Crowning Privilege*

CHAPEL HILL
THE UNIVERSITY OF NORTH CAROLINA PRESS

# SWIFTER THAN
# REASON

The Poetry and Criticism of

ROBERT GRAVES

By

DOUGLAS DAY

TO FLOYD STOVALL

# Acknowledgments

I wish to express my gratitude to my colleagues, Professors Floyd Stovall, Robert Scholes, Robert Langbaum, and George Garrett, who have been more than generous with their time and their advice; to Robert Graves and Mrs. Laura Riding Jackson, for their helpful correspondence with me; to the staff of the Alderman Library of the University of Virginia, for making so many research materials available; to the Rare Book Division of the Library of Congress, for permission to work with their collections; and to my wife, Mary Hill Day, who has served as critic, proofreader, and child-silencer throughout this undertaking.

I wish to thank Mr. Graves also for reading the proofs of this work and for correcting my more grievous factual errors. I am grateful to him also for permission to quote from his works.

# Contents

# Introduction

You, reading over my shoulder, peering beneath
My writing arm—I suddenly feel your breath
    Hot on my hand or on my nape,
So interrupt my theme, scratching these few
Words on the margin for you, namely you,
    Too-human shape fixed in that shape:—

All the saying of things against myself
And for myself I have done well myself.
    What now, old enemy, shall you do
But quote and underline, thrusting yourself
Against me, as ambassador of myself,
    In damned confusion of myself and you?

For you in strutting, you in sycophancy,
Have played too long this other self of me,
    Doubling the part of judge and patron
With that creaking grind-stone to my wit.
Know me, have done; I am a proud spirit
    And you forever clay. Have done.[1]

1. "The Reader over My Shoulder," *Collected Poems, 1961*, p. 99. (Complete references to all of Graves's works cited in the footnotes will be found in the first part of the Bibliography at the end of the book.)

There has never been a full-length study of the poetry and criticism of Robert Graves, and, whatever Graves may say about the reader over his shoulder, there needs to be one.[2]   His irascible attitude toward critics of his work is entirely understandable when one considers that, in the forty-six years that Graves has been publishing poems, perhaps seven or eight writers on contemporary literature have taken the trouble to examine his work carefully and objectively at first hand.   Most scholars (especially those on this side of the Atlantic) have persisted in linking him with such lesser fry as Edmund Blunden, Walter de la Mare, W. H. Davies, and the other contributors to the volumes of *Georgian Poetry* edited from 1911 to 1922 by Edward Marsh.   That Graves, like D. H. Lawrence, did not tarry long in the Georgian camp has not apparently registered very strongly in academic circles. One hopes that Graves's recent election to the Professorship of Poetry at Oxford will do something to awaken American interest in him; and, indeed, there have since appeared at least three indications that this might be the case: the *Atlantic Monthly* (June, 1961) had Graves's portrait on its cover; *The New York Times Book Review* (July 16, 1961) devoted prime space to a review by Horace Gregory of Graves's *Collected Poems, 1961;* and even *Life* (June 24, 1963) has done a close-up of him.   But most American scholars of contemporary literature still seem to regard Graves as primarily a poet of the Twenties.

A large measure of the misunderstanding of Graves has also been caused by the tendency of literary historians to concern themselves only with those poets whom they can more or less neatly classify as members of readily identifiable "groups" or "movements."   Graves has studiously avoided any such associations—has, in fact, been emphatic in his denunciation of them—and has been quite willing to be thought of as an aloof and somewhat eccentric escapee from what is usually called "the mainstream of English poetry."

2. The most extensive studies of Graves to this time have been two pamphlets: Martin Seymour-Smith, *Robert Graves*, Writers and Their Works, No. 78 (London, 1956); and J. M. Cohen, *Robert Graves*, Writers and Critics, No. 3 (Edinburgh, 1960).

Graves's poems *are,* of course, quite different from everyone else's; and they have one peculiar quality which has thrown more than one critic off the track: the ideas and emotions in them are, while not especially unusual, so unconventionally expressed that would-be explicators have turned in desperation to considerations of their formal aspects. Here there has been little trouble, for Graves has almost always been a perfecter, not an innovator. Hence his reputation as a clever and diligent craftsman, a real "poet's poet"—that dimmest of accolades which is given by critics to poets who seem to have little to say, but who say it with a certain prosodic facility.

Since the mid-Forties Graves has drawn much of his poetic subject-matter from his own particularly arcane storehouse of mythology; and critics who have cheerfully read *From Ritual to Romance* and even all twelve volumes of *The Golden Bough* for Eliot, and *A Vision* for Yeats, have not cared to do Graves's poetry the necessary favor of reading *The White Goddess* or *The Greek Myths.* Of his Goddess, Graves has said, "Unworthy as I am, I am her man";[3] and his single-minded devotion to her has caused his later poetry to be inextricably bound up with his obscure and fugitive investigations of her nature. The reader who makes no attempt to understand what the Goddess means to Graves cannot hope to understand his best poetry.

There is a final obstacle between Graves and the critic, and it is a large one: the matter of texts. Periodically throughout his career Graves has gone through his poetic corpus, suppressed those poems which have seemed to him inferior, and drastically revised those which he has chosen to retain. Thus a poem originally published, say, in *Over the Brazier* (1916) might reappear, its structure and diction markedly altered, in *Poems, 1914-1926,* only to be dropped from the contents of *Collected Poems, 1938*— and then turn up again, its face once more lifted, in *Collected Poems, 1955.* Such thorough and ceaseless pruning has been almost invariably beneficial to the poems subjected to it (Randall

3. From a conversation of Graves with Kathleen Nott, cited by Seymour-Smith, *Robert Graves,* p. 16.

Jarrell has said that Graves is "the best re-writer and corrector of his own poetry" that he knows[4]); but, commendable as it may be, this habit has created no small textual problem for the critic. Good as the poems in Graves's collection of 1961 are, they must not be taken as representative of anything more than the sort of poetry Graves chose to write in 1961. To see what he was like in 1916, one must read the volume that was published that year. Unfortunately, his critics have seldom done this, with the result that Graves has generally been described as a man whose poetic technique and attitudes toward life have remained almost unchanged and without development from the beginning of his career to the present. This notion is, of course, an absurd one, and is easily dispelled if one takes the trouble to read more of Graves than the latest volume of his collected poems.

Graves has himself often seemed almost eager to lead his critics into misconceptions about his poetry. In the foreword to his *Collected Poems, 1938,* for instance, he gave an account of his poetic development which seems on the surface to be a valid one. That volume was divided into five sections, each of which was supposed to illustrate one stage of his career; and of these stages he wrote:

The first stage is that of being strongly moved by poetic urgencies but attempting to identify them with the impulses of romance.

In the second stage the discrepancy between romantic and poetic values becomes painfully felt; and the spell of poetry is seen as a protection against the death-curse in which humanity seems entailed.

In the third stage the poetic self has become the critic of the divided human self. Poetry is not a mere mitigation of haunting experiences: it is an exorcism of physical pretensions by self-humbling honesties.

In the fourth stage the criticism is turned outwards upon a world in gloom: poetry is seen not only as a saving personal solution but as a general source of light.

4. "Graves and the White Goddess," *The Yale Review,* XLV (Winter, 1956), p. 309.

In the fifth stage comes a more immediate sense of poetic liberation—achieved not by mysticism but by practical persistence.

Unhappily, however, Graves's stepping stones to "poetic liberation" are not likely to appear from this somewhat cryptic description as clear to the reader as they perhaps did to Graves when he set them down; and we must distrust it even more when we realize that his arrangement of the poems into five categories is only partly based on chronology—that he has in fact included several of his 1938 poems among those that were supposed to illustrate his first stage, and that many of the poems in the final two stages were actually written as early as 1923.

A careful reading of Graves's poems as originally published, however, will in fact show that there *has* been a very distinct pattern of progress in his career, and that there have been in reality four more or less sharply delineated periods into which his work may be divided.

In the first period, which runs from 1916 to 1923, we find Graves jolted out of his whimsical and banal Georgianism by the shock of the First World War.  After 1918 we see him in what he has called his "anodynic" phase, when he believes poetry to be a therapeutic measure for the many psychological disturbances the war has brought him; when he seeks, through the composition of self-consciously childlike and bucolic poems, to escape from the turbulent and potentially destructive emotions aroused in him by the war into an ultra-romantic world of fantasy.  This mood passes, and he begins, by 1921, to write poems which are more aggressive and self-disciplinary in spirit, impelled not by escapism but by anger.  By 1923 he has tired of such emotional intensity, and is sliding, almost imperceptibly, into the semi-detached, analytical poetry of his second major period.

The volumes of poetry which belong to the first phase are *Over the Brazier* (1916), *Fairies and Fusiliers* (1917), *Country Sentiment* (1920), *The Pier-Glass* (1921), and the first section of *Whipperginny* (1923).

The poems of Graves's second period are marked by his determination not to become emotionally involved in his work.

He announces at the outset that he will no longer cater to "those who demand unceasing emotional stress in poetry at whatever cost to the poet,"[5] that his poems will from now on examine coolly and abstractly a series of problems in religion, psychology, and philosophy.  The poems of this period are, in fact, less intense than their predecessors had been; but they give way too often to a somewhat flippant cynicism and display a frivolous lack of purpose which indicates that Graves is at this time trying to deal with matters for which he has little real sympathy.  To write most effectively, he has always needed to be emotionally involved in his subject; and here his attitude is frequently much too negative to allow him to be more than clever and occasionally amusing.

In this period are the poems from the second section of *Whipperginny,* and from *The Feather Bed* (1923), *Mockbeggar Hall* (1924), *Welchman's Hose* (1925), *Poems, 1914-1926,* and *Poems, 1914-1927* (substantially a reprint of the 1926 volume, with nine new poems added).

The third period of Graves's career opens in 1926, with the arrival in England of Laura Riding, the American poetess who came to visit the Graves family, but who remained to teach him a great deal about the toughness and discipline necessary to the composition of good poetry.  The influence of Laura Riding is quite possibly the most important single element in his poetic career: she persuaded him to curb his digressiveness and his rambling philosophizing, and to concentrate instead on terse, ironic poems written on personal themes.  She also imparted to him some of her own dry, cerebral quality, which has remained in much of his poetry up to the present.  For eleven years Graves and Miss Riding, having exiled themselves to Majorca, thumbed their noses at the outside world.  As it does in *Poems, 1914-1926,* the satiric mode predominates during most of this period, although one notices now a growing tendency in Graves toward a serious and direct treatment of the themes to which he was ultimately to give his complete attention.  The poetry of Graves's third period is difficult and frequently obscure, but there can be

5. *Whipperginny,* p. v.

little doubt that some of his best work to date was done during the years of his literary partnership with Laura Riding.

Six volumes of poems appeared during this period: *Poems, 1929, Ten Poems More* (1930), *Poems, 1926-1930, To Whom Else?* (1931), *Poems, 1930-1933,* and *Collected Poems, 1938.*

After an interim period of six years, during which Graves composed only fourteen new poems, the fourth period begins with the publication of *Poems, 1938-1945,* and has continued to the present. The poetic discipline to which Graves had subjected himself in his third period had, by 1938, made him the master of a poetry of restraint and metrical subtlety, in which his characteristic attitudes toward love, nature, and society could find their most effective expression. By the end of the Second World War, Graves had become a poet able to write with technical perfection over a somewhat narrow range of subject-matter. He still lacked the one quality that all poets must possess if they are to be more than competent craftsmen: a vision of the universe which informs and unifies all their work, a way of going beyond themselves into something larger, more universally meaningful— in short, a religious attitude. Graves's poetry up to this time had been essentially negative; by nature cynical and rationalistic (though from almost the beginning of his career he has consistently and vociferously held that reason has no primary function in poetry), he had not since the age of fifteen been able, intellectually or emotionally, to accept any ecclesiastical system.

This unifying vision came to Graves in 1944, when he began his study of the Triple Goddess, the ancient Mediterranean deity who, attacked by worshippers of new patriarchal religions, had gone underground one thousand years before the birth of Christ. For reasons I shall discuss later, this Goddess caught and held Graves's imagination as nothing else had been able to do; and he immediately became, poetically at least, her ardent devotee. For eighteen years she has, in all her manifestations, been his poetic inspiration; and, while continuing to believe that "the main theme of poetry is, properly, the relations of man and woman,"[6] he has caused the Goddess to become the woman for whom his poems must express his love. In a more practical sense, she has, like Yeats's familiars, brought him metaphors for poetry; and his best poems have been constructed about the ancient myths in which she played a central part. Even in the poems in which she does not actively figure, the Goddess is almost always in the background, enhancing the poems by her awesome and mysterious presence. If Graves occasionally writes poems which are not inspired by this single great theme, he is careful not to call these "true" poems: they are instead "satires" or "grotesques." He still writes light verse, but he never treats his Goddess lightly: *her* poems are, as is fitting with religious invocations, always intensely serious.

Thus far, nine volumes of poems have appeared in Graves's fourth period: *Poems, 1938-1945, Collected Poems, 1914-1947, Poems and Satires* (1951), *Poems, 1953, Collected Poems, 1955, The Poems of Robert Graves, Chosen By Himself* (1958), *Collected Poems, 1959, More Poems, 1961,* and *Collected Poems, 1961.*[7]

Most of Robert Graves's critics have used his admirable autobiography, *Good-bye to All That* (1929), as a way into his poetry, but for reasons hard to determine they have neglected to make more than passing reference to any of the eight books of criticism Graves has written, or to the numerous essays and talks on poetry he has produced over the past forty years. Each of his four main periods has in it at least one critical work that serves as a valuable commentary on the nature of the poetry of that period: in the first period there is *On English Poetry* (1922); in the second, there are *Contemporary Techniques of Poetry* (1925), *Poetic Unreason* (1925), and *Another Future of Poetry* (1926); in the third there are *A Survey of Modernist Poetry* (1927) and *A Pamphlet Against Anthologies* (1928)—both written in collaboration with Laura Riding—and the "November 5th Address" to the Teachers' Union in London (1928); and in the fourth period there are, in addition

6. *The White Goddess* (rev. ed., New York, 1958), p. 501.
7. A tenth volume, *New Poems, 1962,* has just been released by Cassell.

to *The White Goddess*, *The Common Asphodel* (1949), *The Crowning Privilege* (1955), the essays on poets and poetry collected in *5 Pens in Hand* (1958), *Steps* (1958), and *Food for Centaurs* (1960), and the *Oxford Lectures on Poetry* (1962).

Here is God's plenty for the student who is willing to ferret it out, and his task will be lightened considerably by the fact that almost all of these works have no small intrinsic worth. There is little of the objective, systematic critic in Graves; he has frequently used his essays on poetry as vehicles for vituperative and cantankerous attacks on his fellow-poets, and his theories have been, over the years, often wildly inconsistent. Literary historians who have been able to forgive inconsistency in such poet-critics as Sidney, Dryden, Coleridge, and Eliot have not been disposed to disregard it in their evaluations of Graves, and have consequently neglected to mention any of his more positive achievements. The fact is, however, that all of his critical works are filled with common-sense, if splenetic, commentaries on individual poets and their poems; that he was, in *On English Poetry* and *Poetic Unreason,* one of the first to apply Freudian theories to the criticism of poetry; that his analysis of a Shakespeare sonnet in *A Survey of Modernist Poetry* suggested to William Empson the method that he was to employ three years later in *Seven Types of Ambiguity*; and that, with *The White Goddess,* he has given a great amount of inspiration and ammunition to the currently fashionable school of myth or "archetypal" criticism (though Graves has always been careful to dissociate his anthropological theories from any form of Jungian psychology).

Despite the fact that Graves has been a pioneer in almost all of the major twentieth-century critical movements, his criticism is perhaps most valuable as an indicator both of the progress of his ideas about the function of poetry and criticism, and of the standards by which he composed the poems of each of his four periods. It is for these reasons that a study of Graves's critical work is a necessary element in any thorough appraisal of his poetic career.

Graves's reputation today, then, is not at all what it should be.

If it knows of him at all, the general public regards him as a writer of ingenious, if occasionally dry, historical novels; as a skillful, if unorthodox, translator of classical and Biblical texts; and as the author of improbable, if highly interesting, speculations on prehistoric religious systems. Although his poetry is well known in England, it is (except among specialists, and a small corps of lay enthusiasts) largely ignored in the United States—partly because of Graves's attitude toward the public ("For people in general I write prose, and am content that they should be unaware that I do anything else. To write poems for other than poets is wasteful"[8]), and partly because of neglect or misunderstanding on the part of critics of contemporary poetry. About Graves's attitude we can, of course, do nothing; but there is much that we can do to rectify the latter condition.

Yet to remove the obstacles that critics have placed between Graves and posterity is a task which is, if worthwhile, essentially negative: it is one thing to say what he is not, and quite another to say what he *is*. The aim of this work, therefore, will be to provide the reader with a detailed and systematic assessment of the poetry of Robert Graves, organized about the four major periods of his career. The chief focus, of course, is on the poems themselves. Because Graves is still very much in the habit of editing his canon, I have not followed the usual practice of drawing references to individual poems from a single "standard" text, and have instead quoted from the poems either as they have appeared in their original published versions, or (since there is much to be learned about a poet's creative process, his consciousness of his own defects, and his aims from observing the nature of his emendations) as they have appeared in subsequent editions. *Collected Poems, 1961,* is Graves's most recent presentation of his canon, and it is, of course, from this work that I have drawn any quotations intended to illustrate my arguments about his present stature as a poet.

Where to do so would contribute to a fuller understanding of a poem, I have devoted some space to discussing the many forces,

8. Foreword to *Poems, 1938-1945.*

literary, historical, and personal, that have helped shape Graves's career. His criticism, too, has been used as a commentary on the poems. And, finally, because Graves is essentially a subjective poet, concerned primarily with recording his personal responses to his own experiences (either real or imagined), I have attempted to include such elements of his biography as are necessary to allow complete explications of the poems.

# Part One:

## The Georgian and Anodynic Period

# 1

# Juvenilia and the War

Robert Graves began writing verse prolifically in 1910 when, as a rather unpopular "new-bug" at Charterhouse, he discovered that students interested in poetry were invariably left to their own devices by wary upperclassmen. This self-protective measure was not, however, his first attempt at poetic composition: in the foreword to his *Collected Poems, 1938*[1] he tells us that by 1909 (when he was thirteen) he had already begun a series of "difficult technical experiments in prosody and phrasing," occasioned chiefly by an early exposure to the complicated Welsh *englyn,* and by an attempt to render the poems of Catullus into English.

Whether fortunately or not, most of Graves's earliest poems have not survived; but we are told, in the same foreword, that for the most part he wrote "in a romantic vein, of wizards, monsters, ghosts, and outlandish events and scenes"—as was perhaps only natural for a boy whose only exposure to any books other than the standard schoolboy texts had been Lady Charlotte Guest's translation of the *Mabinogion,* and the collection of Celtic folklore and poetry in the library of his father, Alfred Perceval Graves, then a well-known Irish poet and song-writer of decidedly traditional, if somewhat playful, tastes.

1. P. xv.

The boy had, accordingly, never heard of "people like Shaw, Samuel Butler, Rupert Brooke, Wells, Flecker, or Masefield"[2] when he went to Charterhouse.   Once there, however, he was introduced to modern literature by George Mallory (the man who wished to climb Mount Everest "because it is there"), then a young master at the school.   Mallory also made the young poet's work known to Edward Marsh, the influential editor of *Georgian Poetry;* and Marsh liked Graves's poems, although, as he pointed out, "they were written in the poetic diction of fifty years ago and . . . many readers would be prejudiced against work written in 1913 according to the fashion of 1863" (*Good-bye to All That,* p. 80).

Graves included eleven of his later Charterhouse poems in his first published volume of verse, *Over the Brazier* (London, 1916);[3] and almost all of them show the quaintness, the whimsicality, and the somewhat uninspired slickness and metrical conformity that marked so much Georgian poetry.   We find in them the familiar homely and nostalgic paeans to the English countryside; such sturdily Anglo-Saxon virtues as love of comradeship, animals, and strong ale; and that fondness for "cute" words and phrases that characterized what Roy Campbell has called "the 'Merrie England' school of poetry."[4]   Perhaps the most typical example of Graves's style at this time is "Jolly Yellow Moon" (*Over the Brazier,* p. 11):

> Oh, now has faded from the West
> A sunset red as wine,
> And beast and bird are hushed to rest
> And the jolly yellow moon doth shine.

2. *Good-bye to All That* (London: J. Cape, 1929), p. 80. Revised and republished in 1957 by Doubleday Anchor Books of New York.   Unless otherwise noted, all subsequent references will be to the edition of 1929.

3. Published by The Poetry Bookshop.   Second impression, 1917; reprinted, revised, and with a new preface, 1920.   References are to the edition of 1916.

4. "Contemporary Poetry," *Scrutinies, By Various Writers* (London, 1928), pp. 161-80.

Come comrades, roam we round the mead
    Where couch the sleeping kine;
The breath of night blows soft indeed,
    And the jolly yellow moon doth shine.

And step we slowly, friend with friend,
    Let arm in arm entwine,
And voice with voice together blend,
    For the jolly yellow moon doth shine.

Whether we loudly sing or soft,
    The tune goes wondrous fine;
Our chorus sure will float aloft
    Where the jolly yellow moon doth shine.

In deference to the poet Graves was to become, one ought not to dwell too long on these earliest efforts, with their arm-entwined friends, moonlit ghosts, storm-sprites, dying knights, little furry clouds, and fairy pipers; but there are three of the Charterhouse poems which, since they are indicative of the directions his later poetry was to take, should be noted. In "Oh and Oh!" (p. 17), for instance, there is a hint of tension caused by a simultaneously-occurring attraction and aversion to sensual love: the country poet wanders to the city, where

Down dirty streets in stench and smoke
The pale townsfolk
Crawl and kiss and cuddle,
In doorways hug and huddle;
Loutish he
And sluttish she
In loathsome love together press
And unbelievable ugliness.

What at first appears here to be little more than an expression of upper-class schoolboy fastidiousness is really the first of a long series of poems in which Graves struggles with a strong sense of revulsion from physical love, and is also the forerunner of several ascetic and stoical attacks on "pale townsfolk."

In "Free Verse" (pp. 14-15),[5] Graves displays for the first time his indebtedness to the goliardic verse of John Skelton, whose lack of reverence for poetic tradition and whose quick verbal facility he has always admired:

> I now delight
> In spite
> Of the right
> Of classic tradition
> In writing
> And reciting
> Straight ahead
> Without let or omission
> Just any little rhyme
> In any little time
> That runs in my head.

The third significant poem from Graves's Charterhouse phase, and the only one except the retitled "Free Verse" to escape suppression in 1926—the year in which Graves expunged from his canon all poems which did not point directly toward his poetic position at that time—is "In the Wilderness" (p. 16).  It has, however, little in common with any of his 1926 work, and he was to call it in 1929 "a silly, quaint poem" (*Good-bye to All That*, p. 33); but it was by far the most popular of his early poems,[6] and one on which his early critics seemed to look with favor.[7] We may suppose, therefore, that in retaining "In the Wilderness" with only minor revisions, Graves was making one of his rare concessions to popular and critical opinion.  The poem is a straightforward and sentimentally romantic piece of description about Christ during his forty days' trial in the desert, and there is nothing about its easy dactyls and its mildly irregular rhyme-

5. Retitled "In Spite" in *Poems, 1914-1926*.
6. He notes in *Good-bye to All That* (p. 33) that "In the Wilderness" had by 1929 already appeared in at least seventy anthologies.
7. S. P. B. Mais, in *Books and Their Writers* (New York, 1920), p. 102, called it Graves's "most beautiful piece of work."

scheme to suggest the complexity of thought and expression which
were shortly to come:

> Christ of his gentleness
> Thirsting and hungering
> Walked in the wilderness;
> Soft words of grace He spoke
> Unto lost desert-folk
> That listened wondering.
> He heard the bitterns call
> From ruined palace wall
> Answered them brotherly.
> He held communion
> With the she-pelican
> Of lonely piety.
> Basilisk, cockatrice,
> Flocked to His homilies
> With mail of dread device,
> With monstrous barbéd stings,
> With eager dragon-eyes;
> Great rats on leather wings
> And poor blind broken things,
> Foul in their miseries.
> And ever with Him went,
> Of all His wanderings
> Comrade, with ragged coat,
> Gaunt ribs—poor innocent—
> Bleeding foot, burning throat,
> The guileless old scape-goat;
> For forty nights and days
> Followed in Jesus' ways,
> Sure guard behind Him kept,
> Tears like a lover wept.

There is much here that is derivative: J. M. Cohen has pointed
out that Christina Rossetti's "Goblin Market" is a distant model;[8]

8. *Robert Graves,* Writers and Critics Series, No. 3 (Edinburgh, 1960), p. 11.

and the echo in line eighteen of Collins' "Ode to Evening" grows sharper for us when we realize that in *Poems, 1914-1926,* Graves revised the line to read "Great bats on leathern wing." Moreover, we may relate the basilisk and cockatrice of line thirteen to the characteristic fondness of the less realistically-oriented Georgian poets for exotic and archaic beasts as dressing for their fantasies and nursery rhymes. The poem was written when Graves was barely nineteen, at a time when his knowledge of the "new" poets was as yet scanty, and when he still felt most strongly the influence of the late Victorians whose works stood on his father's library shelves, and of the fanciful early poems of Yeats.[9] Scholars have speculated on Graves's immediate source for the poem (Cohen, for instance, says that the poem "perhaps drew its incident from some apocryphal Bible story"[10]); but Graves has himself stated that "The subject was suggested by a reproduction, in a Christmas supplement, of Holman Hunt's 'Scapegoat.' "[11]

The young Graves had by now begun to look askance at the formal religion which had been an integral part of his upbringing (his paternal grandfather had been the Anglican Bishop of Limerick); but he was still strongly attracted to the character of Jesus ("The last thing that is discarded by Protestants when they reject religion altogether is a vision of Christ as the perfect man"[12]). In "In the Wilderness," accordingly, we see him sentimentally depicting the love which all creatures, real and mythical, felt for Christ during the forty days and nights of his lonely trial.

There is something more, however, that one should note about the poem; for this is the first instance in his poetry of a practice which was to remain with Graves throughout his career: the continual subordination of historical to poetic truth. Christ was, throughout his vigil, alone; and there is nothing, either Canonical

9. ". . . I had been attracted at the age of sixteen by the soft music of Yeats's *Countess Cathleen* and *Wanderings of Oisin.* . . ." *The Crowning Privilege* (London: Cassell, 1955), p. 134.

10. *Robert Graves,* p. 12.

11. *A Pamphlet Against Anthologies,* with Laura Riding (New York: Doubleday, 1928), p. 92.

12. *Good-bye to All That,* p. 33.

or Apocryphal, in Christian literature to suggest otherwise. But Graves knew from his reading of the Old Testament (specifically, of Leviticus 16: 21-22) that it was the duty of certain Levite attendants to cast a scape-goat into the wilderness, after having burdened it with all the iniquities of the children of Israel; and he was able to draw an analogy between the sacrificial function of the scape-goat and the vicarious atonement of Jesus, who also took upon himself the guilt of others. It was then only a slight imaginative extension for Graves to picture the two together in the wildnerness, and to illustrate that even the scape-goat, officially the representative of all human sin, joins with the rest of the animal world in its love of Christ. Thus, while the treatment of Biblical material is unhistorical, the internal logic of the poem is valid; and "In the Wilderness" stands as the earliest example of a method which was to typify a great deal of Graves's later work, and which was to cause no little annoyance to the more literal-minded of his readers.

Immediately upon his graduation from Charterhouse in 1914 Graves, still nineteen, enlisted in the Royal Welch Fusiliers. Some months passed before he entered the trenches as a subaltern, and the revulsion in literature against the Rupert Brooke-ish poetry of gallantry and patriotism had by then already taken place. There were few illusions left now about the horrors of modern warfare, and Graves's first war poems, as published in *Over the Brazier* and *Fairies and Fusiliers* (London: Heinemann, 1917) show a curious and somehow pathetic juxtaposition of nostalgic Georgian felicities with starkly realistic descriptions of life and death in the trenches.

Graves did not wait for first-hand experience before becoming a war-poet. One of his most popular pieces, "It's a Queer Time" (*Over the Brazier*, p. 30), was actually written at a depôt in England long before he embarked for the Front. It is a rather inconsequential poem, but still a good example of the way in which Graves came to mix near-realism and absolute romanticism in his verse.

One morning you'll be crouching at your gun
Traversing, mowing heaps down half in fun:
The next, you choke and clutch at your right breast
No time to think—leave all—and off you go . . .
To Treasure Island where the Spice winds blow,
To lovely groves of mango, quince and lime—
Breathe no goodbye, but ho, for the Red West!
        It's a queer time.

We are to infer here, certainly, that the soldier has been killed ("gone West"); and the treatment of death as a passage to an exotic never-never land may be somewhat ironic. But the total effect of the poem is one of almost childlike flamboyance: it is only too obvious that the poet is more schoolboy than soldier.

A few months of actual exposure to modern warfare did much to dispel Lieutenant Graves's carefree attitude toward death. His poems continued to show a mixture of moods, but the romantic mood tended increasingly to become escapist. An example of this development is "Limbo" (*Over the Brazier*, p. 23), one of the short pieces Graves wrote in the weeks before the campaign against La Bassée in August, 1915:

After a week spent under raining skies,
        In horror, mud, and sleeplessness, a week
Of bursting shells, of blood and hideous cries
        And the ever-watchful sniper: where the reek
Of death offends the living . . .
When rats run, big as kittens: to and fro
        They dart, and scuffle with their horrid fare,
And then one night relief comes, and we go
        Miles back into the sunny cornland where
Babies like tickling, and where tall white horses
Draw the plow leisurely in quiet courses.

Comparing rats with kittens is, perhaps, an unapt conceit, and describing the rats' fare as "horrid" is, one may feel, an unsubtle way of directing the reader's emotional responses to the poem; but

what makes "Limbo" an effective work is the sharp contrast between the mud, rain, and horror of the trenches and the bucolic
tranquillities to which the soldier and his comrades withdraw.
In this poem, as in most of Graves's early war pieces, escape from
the Front is invariably to the French countryside, or to "the quiet
of an English wood" ("1915," p. 31), or to a cosy inn or farm-
house, or to

> . . . a cottage in the hills,
> North Wales, a cottage full of books,
> Pictures and brass and cosy nooks
> And comfortable broad window-sills,
> Flowers in the garden, walls all white . . .
>
> *(Over the Brazier, p. 32)*

There is no denying the essential banality of these poems, but
they are nonetheless touching reminders of the pathetically childlike innocence of Graves's generation, which was thrust rudely
from school directly into the appalling brutality of the nastiest
war man has yet fought. Graves, like so many of his time and
class in England, had no time for growing up: he was little more
than a boy when he went into combat, and his responses to war
could not help being boyish. This does not, of course, excuse the
superficiality of much of his war poetry—Wilfred Owen, a member
of the same class and generation, wrote first-rate war poems—but
it does at least account for his failing to do much more with his
poems than use them as a means for imaginative escape.

Late in 1915, as Graves was preparing *Over the Brazier* for
publication, he became acquainted with a young fellow-officer
named Siegfried Sassoon. Already a poet himself, Sassoon, after
reading the poems in Graves's volume, told Graves that "they were
too realistic and that war should not be written about in a
realistic way" (*Good-bye to All That*, p. 224). Except for a few
isolated instances, there was in fact little in Graves's early war
poems to match the vivid rawness of a Wilfred Owen; but Sassoon
had not at the time of his criticism of Graves been long in the
trenches. By the end of the next year he was himself composing

poems which often outstripped Graves's in their graphic and
unromantic portrayals of the sensations of war.  His poem
"Haunted," for example, conveys far more of a sense of emotional
commitment to the present than any of Graves's do:

> Headlong he charges down the wood, and falls
> With roaring brain—agony—the snapt spark—
> And blots of green and purple in his eyes.
> Then the slow fingers groping on his neck,
> And at his heart the strangling clasp of death.[13]

When Graves does permit his imagination to work on the
world about him, as happens occasionally in the later war poems
of *Fairies and Fusiliers,* he is, though undoubtedly sincere, poetically unconvincing.  In "A Dead Boche" (p. 45), he makes an
undeniably forceful protest against the horrors of violent death:

> . . . Today I found in Mametz Wood
> A certain cure for lust of blood:
> Where, propped against a shattered trunk,
>     In a great mess of things unclean,
> Sat a dead Boche; he scowled and stunk
>     With clothes and face a sodden green,
> Big-bellied, spectacled, crop-haired,
> Dribbling black blood from nose and beard.

The description is terse and precise, and we are properly shocked
by it, but the poem is still not a good one, for a number of reasons.
For one thing, the sole emotion expressed by the poet and consequently aroused in the reader is one of disgust: the dead soldier
is seen not as a person, but merely as an object-lesson in the
filthiness of war's leavings.  We are invited not to feel pity for
him, not to see, that is, behind the horrid details in the foreground, but only to be repelled by the extreme ugliness of the
scene.  There is something fundamentally wrong with a poem
that aims at nothing more than an excitation of loathing, that does
not attempt to go beyond disgust to some sort of sympathetic

13. *Georgian Poetry: 1916-1917,* ed. Edward Marsh (London, 1917), p. 48.

understanding of the object, and "A Dead Boche" fails because
it does not do this.[14]

We can recognize here the same fastidious revulsion from
things grossly physical that marks so much of Graves's poetry
throughout his career. Later, in his love poems to the Goddess
especially, he was to make poetic capital out of his often morbid
fascination with the cruel and gross; but here we can find only the
negative quality, with no tempering sense of love and sympathy.
This is, no less than his happier pieces, a romantic poem; but its
romanticism is of that sort which consists in the deliberate exploitation of the ugly or horrible. There are also, as Fraser has
noted, technical reasons for the failure of "A Dead Boche": there
is the "terribly feeble inversion" of "things unclean," and there is
the greater poetic sin of creating the emotional impact not by the
skillful manipulation of noun and verb, but "in the weakest way,
by piling up adjectives":

> Big-bellied, spectacled, crop-haired,
> Dribbling black blood. . . .

But "A Dead Boche" is, whatever its shortcomings, very nearly
Graves's only attempt at absolute, unflinching verisimilitude in
his war poetry; taken as a whole, his work of the 1915-1918 period
dealing with his experiences in France is strongly governed by the
impulses toward the fanciful and quaint with which his background and early reading had equipped him.

At any rate, it was as a war-poet that Graves first became
known to the public; and, especially after Edward Marsh included
eight of his poems from *Over the Brazier* and *Fairies and Fusiliers*
in *Georgian Poetry: 1916-1917,* his reputation as a talented young
soldier-poet was firmly established. Critics became fond of linking him with Sassoon and Robert Nichols; and of these "three
rhyming musketeers," as Louis Untermeyer rather distressingly

14. Much of my discussion of this poem is drawn from G. S. Fraser, "The
Poetry of Robert Graves," *Vision and Rhetoric: Studies in Modern Poetry* (London,
1959), pp. 135-48. This article is without a doubt the best that has thus far been
done on Graves.

called them,[15] it was generally Graves who was ranked first—and, what is most surprising, for those very qualities in his war poems which modern critics have frowned most upon: his callowness, his refusal to treat his experiences responsibly and feelingly, and his forced and artificial blitheness.  Nichols and Sassoon were, it was felt, too bitter in their descriptions of war; but Graves was not bitter at all: he was "a gay young singer, capable of impish mischief and insouciant fancy.  His poems of the war [were] well made, true and beautiful with a boy's spirit of gallantry."[16] What made Graves popular at this time were not, then, poems like "A Dead Boche" or "Goliath and David," where brave young David is slain, and "spike-helmeted, grey, grim,/Goliath straddles over him" *(Fairies and Fusiliers,* p. 25); but instead such noble sentiments as "When I'm Killed" *(Fairies and Fusiliers,* p. 40):

> So when I'm killed don't mourn for me
> Shot, poor lad, so bold and young,
> Killed and gone—don't mourn for me . . .

and "The Assault Heroic" *(Fairies and Fusiliers,* p. 86):

> But with my spear of Faith,
> Stout as an oaken rafter,
> With my round shield of laughter,
> With my sharp, tongue-like sword
> That speaks a bitter word,
> I stood beneath the wall
> And there defied them all.

Perhaps the public responded to such echoes of Henley's muscular self-reliance because it wanted to be reassured that its heroes still had hearts of stout English oak, and were not to be daunted by the Hun; at any rate, the whimsy and shallow gallantry they found in much of Graves's work at this time had a greater appeal for them than did the more honest disillusionment of his

15. *Modern British and American Poetry* (New York, 1923), p. 359.
16. Marguerite Wilkinson, *New Voices: An Introduction to Contemporary Poetry* (New York, 1927), p. 249.

less typical pieces. It is to Graves's credit that he was little affected by his facile success as a war-poet, and that, unlike the other
soldier-poets who survived beyond the Armistice, he continued to
struggle toward a success that was much more worth having.

The Georgian mode predominates in the poems of *Fairies
and Fusiliers* that are not connected with the war, but there are
signs in several of these pieces of themes and techniques that
were to characterize the mature Graves. In "Finland" (p. 31),
for example, the first stanza is as self-consciously quaint as any of
his earliest work:

> Feet and faces tingle
> In that frore land:
> Legs wobble and go wingle,
> You scarce can stand.

The use of the archaic past participle in line two, the near
nursery-rhyme vocabulary in line three, and the artificial homeliness of "You scarce can stand" exemplify all the worst qualities
of Georgianism that beset the early Graves. But in the second
stanza there is an abrupt shift into the compressed and vivid
imagery that Graves's more advanced contemporaries like Hulme,
Flint, Aldington, and the rest of the Imagists had been writing
since 1909:

> The skies are jewelled all around,
> The ploughshare snaps in the iron ground,
> The Finn with face like paper
> And eyes like a lighted taper
> Hurls his rough rune
> At the wintry moon
> And stamps to mark the tune.

Here are no heaped-up adjectives, no trite and conventional
figures of speech, no false heroics. The rhyming is as easy and
light as ever, but otherwise "Finland" is the product of a more
disciplined poet than Graves had heretofore appeared to be.
Here he is seeking to get what Hulme called "the exact curve" of

the thing to be expressed[17]—to select the precise word and phrase, to choose the most accurate simile possible; and he achieves with "The Finn with face like paper" that element of happy surprise which marks a successful analogy. The severe economy of the stanza does not, however, rob it of its vigor, chiefly because of the force of its verbs: the ploughshare "snaps," and the Finn, cold and exuberant, "hurls" his rough rune and "stamps" his feet in time with the song. "Finland," then, is a kind of poetic curiosity: the first stanza follows one poetic tradition, entirely to excess; and the second stanza follows an opposed tradition, with admirable results.

Such terseness as there is in the second stanza of "Finland" is, unfortunately, rare in *Fairies and Fusiliers*. For the most part there is a tendency to preciosity, as in this cosy passage from "The Cottage" (p. 37):

> Snug inside I sit and rhyme,
> Planning poem, book, or fable,
> At my darling beech-wood table
> Fresh with bluebells from the hill. . . .

or to the old bucolic jocularity, as in "Strong Beer" (p. 65):

> "Tell us, now, how and when
> We may find the bravest men?"
> "A sure test, an easy test:
> Those that drink beer are the best,
> Brown beer strongly brewed,
> English drink and English food. . . ."

or to nursery-rhyme, as in "Double Red Daisies" (p. 58):

> Claire has a tea-rose, but she didn't plant it;
> Ben has an iris, but I don't want it.
> Daisies, double red daisies for me,
> The beautifulest flowers in the garden.

17. T. E. Hulme, "Romanticism and Classicism," *Speculations: Essays on Humanism and the Philosophy of Art*, ed. Herbert Read (London, 1924), pp. 3-24.

Although such trifles as these are plentiful in the work, there are in *Fairies and Fusiliers* several poems which, as J. M. Cohen observes, "might be described as Romantically anti-Romantic,"[18] and which point toward some of the major themes of Graves's maturity. The best of these is "A Boy in Church" (pp. 81-82), which, though Georgian in color, and perhaps over-rich in adjectives, shows Graves handling a greater complexity of ideas and moods than he was normally trying to do at this stage in his career. In the first two stanzas the young boy is impatient with the "tuneful gabble" of the minister's sermon, and directs his attention to the storm-swept field he sees from his window. Then Graves contrasts this first mood with the boy's physical pleasure over the solidity of the church structure:

> The parson's voice runs like a river
>> Over smooth rocks.  I like this church:
> The pews are staid, they never shiver,
>> They never bend or sway or lurch.
> "Prayer," says the kind voice, "is a chain
> That draws down Grace from Heaven again."

In the last two lines of the final stanza, however, a third element—an angry, irrational Nature—is introduced, and the drowsy complacency of the preceding stanzas is suddenly shattered:

> It's pleasant here for dreams and thinking,
>> Lolling and letting reason nod,
> With ugly serious people linking
>> Sad prayers to a forgiving God. . . .
> But a dumb blast sets the trees swaying
> With furious zeal like madmen praying.

Outside the sturdy, dull church, where reason nods, there is a furious world which has nothing to do with the forgiving God of the droning minister and the ugly serious people, and which has nothing to do with reason.  Neither man's reason nor his faith, the poet seems to imply, will give him safety from the outside

18. *Robert Graves*, p. 12.

world of violence and irrationality. At the core of the poem, then, is perhaps an indication that Graves is here beginning to recognize the necessity of acknowledging the real world, with all its fury and unreason, instead of ignoring it in favor of a world of child-like fancy.

This distrust of reason, which was to inform much of Graves's later poetry and criticism, is expressed in two other poems from *Fairies and Fusiliers*: in "Babylon" (pp. 26-27), where Graves makes the typically Romantic assertion that only the child, who is as yet uncorrupted by "Truth and Reason," can be a poet and perceive the mysteries of "Spring and Fairyland"; and in the some-what clumsy "Spoilsport" (pp. 47-48), where the poet's familiar ghost, whom he calls "Critic, son of Conscious Brain," persists in preventing him from enjoying the innocent but illogical pleasures of the senses. The latter poem is an undistinguished one, but it announces the appearance of the destructive critical spirit that has plagued Graves throughout his career.

When, in his foreword to his *Collected Poems, 1938,* Graves outlined the stages of his writing career up to that time, he stated that "The first stage is that of being strongly moved by poetic urgencies but attempting to identify them with the impulses of romance." He could not have been more accurate. From 1910 on he regarded himself as a poet by profession, and never ceased to make his chief interest the craft of poetry. At home and in school before 1913 he read the Rossettis, Swinburne, and the early romantic lyrics and fables of Yeats; after George Mallory intro-duced him to their works, he read Hardy, Masefield, Flecker (and, we must suppose, the lesser Georgians); and he carried with him throughout his years in the trenches small editions of Keats and Blake (*Good-bye to All That,* p. 224). There is nothing in any of his writings to indicate that he knew anything of the anti-romantic movement of Hulme, Pound, and the Imagists. It is hardly surprising, then, that Graves should have identified his "poetic urgencies" with "the impulses of romance."

With few exceptions, the early poems we have examined in this chapter demonstrate Graves's close affinities with the tepid and uninspired brand of poetry practiced in early twentieth-century England by the Georgians. Occasionally we can detect elements of the sprightly iconoclasm he got from John Skelton, and at least once (in "Finland") there is a hint of the hard, concrete poetry of the anti-romantics. And in "A Boy in Church" and "Spoilsport" we can notice his recognition of his analytical, skeptical urges which he was not as yet prepared to accept as compatible with poetry. But for the most part the poems Graves wrote at Charterhouse and in France, while they often provide a foreshadowing of the themes and techniques which were later to dominate his poetry, still suffer from the vagueness, whimsy, and self-conscious quaintness that marked the low point of the romantic movement in England. If Graves's poetry of this period suffers from the inevitable naïveté and enthusiasm of youthfulness, it also is hindered by being attached to a worn-out tradition.

# 2

# Poetry as Therapy

On the night of 20 July, 1916, just before the great Somme offensive, Robert Graves was severely wounded when an eight-inch shell burst three paces behind him. He was taken to a nearby dressing-station, where he lay unconscious for the next twenty-four hours. Believing him dead, his regimental commander wrote a consoling letter to his parents, and noted on the official casualty list that Captain Robert Graves, Royal Welch Fusiliers, had "died of wounds." Four days later Graves was on a hospital train, celebrating his twenty-first birthday.

Once in Harlech, North Wales, for his recuperation, Graves was joined by Siegfried Sassoon, who had been sent home from the Front for suspected lung trouble; and the two spent the rest of the summer and fall getting their respective poems in order. In January, 1917, Graves returned to France, where, still unfit for trench service, he was given command of his battalion's Headquarter Company, and passed his time looking after food rations and sitting on court-martials. A month later, ill with bronchitis, he was sent back to England once again—this time to Oxford, where, after leaving the hospital at Somerville College, he was posted to an instructional school for officer-cadets that had been set up in one of the men's colleges. Thus, while his military duties continued beyond the Armistice, the fighting was over for

Graves, and he had now to begin his readjustment to a more orderly life.

The process was a long and difficult one. Even after he had recovered physically from his wounds, Graves suffered acutely from a number of neurasthenic disorders that had resulted from his long exposure to the horrors of trench warfare:

I was still mentally and nervously organized for war; shells used to come bursting on my bed at midnight . . . strangers in day-time would assume the faces of friends who had been killed . . . I could not use a telephone, I was sick every time I travelled in a train, and if I saw more than two new people in a single day it prevented me from sleeping. . . . Since 1916 the fear of gas had been an obsession; in any unusual smell that I met I smelt gas—even a sudden strong scent of flowers in a garden was enough to set me trembling. . . . The noise of a motor-tyre exploding behind me would send me flat on my face or running for cover.[1]

In July, 1917, during his recuperation at Oxford, Graves learned that Sassoon, who had rejoined the regiment and been decorated for heroism, was staging a one-man rebellion against what he felt to be the selfish manipulation of the war by profit-seekers and politicians. After some string-pulling by Graves, the War Office decided not to press the matter of Sassoon's declaration of revolt against authority as a disciplinary case, but to put him before a medical board. Graves applied for permission to give evidence as a friend of the patient, in the hope that, by having Sassoon declared temporarily insane, he could save his friend from a court-martial and imprisonment. While speaking before the board Graves, who was at least as deserving of commitment as Sassoon, burst into tears three times.

Sassoon was sent, with (ironically enough) Graves as his escort, to a convalescent home for neurasthenics at Craiglockhart, near Edinburgh. There he came under the care of Professor W. H. R. Rivers, the prominent Cambridge neurologist, ethnologist, and psychologist. Rivers, one of Freud's followers, and like most of them a dissenter from some of the Freudian dogma, made the

1. *Good-bye to All That*, pp. 330, 352, 354.

conflict of unconscious personalities one of his special studies.[2] Graves, having met him briefly at Craiglockhart, was very impressed with Rivers' theories, and, under Rivers' guidance, embarked almost immediately on a protracted study of Freudian psychology.[3] His applications of these theories to his own poetry, and later to his criticism (as we shall note in the following chapter) were to color his techniques and ideas strongly.

In January, 1918, Graves, at this time on garrison duty in Wales, married Nancy Nicholson, an eighteen-year-old girl he had met some time before on a furlough in Harlech. After his demobilization, they settled in a Harlech cottage rented from her father (William Nicholson, the painter), where Graves set about writing his next book of poems. The new Mrs. Graves could hardly have been much of a balm for her husband's jangled nerves: she was an ardent feminist, and refused to allow herself to be called "Mrs. Graves" in any circumstances; she was a socialist, and drew Graves into the Constructive Birth Control Society, whose literature they distributed among the Harlech women, much to the mortification of Graves's parents. Worst of all, so far as the Harlech townsfolk were concerned, she refused to dress in anything but a farmer's smock and breeches. But Graves was devoted to Nancy Nicholson, and seems for a time passively to have accepted even her wildest theories, especially those which expressed her belief in the inherent superiority of the female to the male. Indeed, from the time of his marriage to the present, Graves has written poems in praise of feminine superiority; and even *The White Goddess* may be seen as a feministic *tour de force*.

The book of poems that Graves was preparing in Harlech during the first year of his marriage was *Country Sentiment,* to be published the following year in London. He describes it in *Good-bye to All That* (p. 342) as "a book of romantic poems and ballads" that he wrote "to forget about the war"; and in the

2. See his *Instinct and the Unconscious* (Cambridge, England, 1924).
3. On page vii of his introduction to *The Common Asphodel,* Graves states: "As a neurasthenic, I was interested in the newly-expounded Freudian theory: when presented with English reserve and common sense by W. H. R. Rivers, who did not regard sex as the sole impulse in dream-making or assume that dream-symbols are constant, it appealed to me as reasonable."

Author's Note to *Whipperginny* (London, 1923) he says that
the poems in *Country Sentiment* were products of "the desire to
escape from a painful war neurosis into an Arcadia of amatory
fancy." He was seeking at this time, in other words, to create
poems which would have a therapeutic value for him—which
would allow him to exorcize the turbulent and potentially self-
destructive emotions aroused in him by his wartime experiences.
Graves's "anodynic" phase, then, consists for the most part of
deliberately childlike and fanciful poems, by which he hoped to
restore to himself some measure of emotional tranquillity.

Superficially, at least, there are no outright references to the
war in *Country Sentiment* (except for the last ten poems, which
are set apart in a section entitled "Retrospect"); but in several
places the implacable and irrational violence of war lies just beneath the surface. In "Apples and Water" (p. 38), for instance,
we find Graves telling, in smooth ballad stanzas, the story of a
young farm girl who wants to quench the thirst and hunger of a
company of soldiers which is passing along the dusty road by her
cottage. Her mother refuses to let her do this, because she herself
had done the same thing years before, for an earlier group of
soldiers, and had suffered for her kindness:

> "There is no water can supply them
> In western streams that flow,
> There is no fruit can satisfy them
> On orchard trees that grow.
>
> Once in my youth I gave, poor fool,
> A soldier apples and water,
> So may I die before you cool
> Your father's drouth, my daughter."

The implication is that soldiers must suffer in endlessly recurring
wars, and that women who offer to help them must suffer, too.[4]

4. This interpretation would seem to be borne out by Graves's revision of the
poem in *Collected Poems, 1938* (p. 27), where he changes the last two lines of
the fourth stanza to read:
> "Ay daughter, these are not the first
> And there will come yet more."

In "Rocky Acres" (pp. 28-29), the best poem in *Country
Sentiment,* and one of the best that Graves has ever written, there
is none of the light and amatory fancy that he had planned to stress
in this volume.  It deserves to be quoted in full:

> This is a wild land, country of my choice,
>> With harsh craggy mountain, moor ample and bare.
> Seldom in these acres is heard any voice
>> But voice of cold water that runs here and there
>> Through rocks and lank heather growing without care.
> No mice in the heath run nor no birds cry
> For fear of the dark speck that floats in the sky.
>
> He soars and he hovers rocking on his wings,
>> He scans his wide parish with a sharp eye,
> He catches the trembling of small hidden things,
>> He tears them in pieces, dropping from the sky:
>> Tenderness and pity the land will deny,
> Where life is but nourished from water and rock
> A hardy adventure, full of fear and shock.
>
> Time has never journeyed to this lost land,
>> Crakeberries and heather bloom out of date,
> The rocks jut, the streams flow singing on either hand,
>> Careless if the season be early or late.
>> The skies wander overhead, now blue, now slate:
> Winter would be known by his cold cutting snow
> If June did not borrow his armour also.
>
> Yet this is my country beloved by me best,
>> The first land that rose from Chaos and the Flood,
> Nursing no fat valleys for comfort and rest,
>> Trampled by no hard hooves, stained with no blood.
>> Bold immortal country whose hill tops have stood
> Strongholds for the proud gods when on earth they go,
> Terror for fat burghers in far plains below.

Here for the first time we see Graves's true, mature manner
sustained throughout an entire poem.  "Rocky Acres" is a splen-

didly stoical work, austere and rugged in its disdainful rejection
of the easy comforts of the soft valleys and plains inhabited by the
"fat burghers" who surely bear some relationship to Siegfried
Sassoon's politicians and war-profiteers. The rugged landscape
around Harlech, with the knobby, grotesquely-shaped Rhinog
range rising in the distance, relates directly to the poet's state of
mind: it is a harsh and uncompromising refuge out of time, a
place unspoiled by easy luxury on the one hand and by needless
and corrupt violence on the other. It is a craggy but ideal haven
for a man who has done with war, but who rejects the softness
of peace.

The structure and diction of "Rocky Acres" match the poet's
mood as completely as does the landscape. The style is obviously,
for so polished a prosodist as Graves, deliberately awkward. Its
abrupt, staccato rhythms distort the basic rhyme royal form almost beyond recognition, and indicate that Graves was still experimenting with the accentual verse of Skelton, Chaucer, and
other medieval poets. The language is earthy and totally un-
embellished, and corresponds exactly to the austerity of the
setting and the mood.

Best of all in the poem, however, is the visual accuracy that
has, from the second stanza of "Finland" on, always marked
Graves's best poetry. The description of the flight of the buz-
zard (for that is what Graves calls this "dark speck" in his revision
of this poem in *Collected Poems, 1938*), his scrutiny of his "parish"
(the ecclesiastical word recalls the frenzied praying of the wind-
swept trees in "A Boy in Church," as an earlier metaphor giving
to the violence of nature a religious significance), and his tearing
apart of his prey, all testify to the care with which Graves, at his
best, observes the subjects of his poetry.

The elves and fauns of the Georgian phase were now meta-
morphosing, perhaps through the warping alchemy of the war,
into the more grotesque shapes of trolls and ogres; and the playful
goblins who romped through *Over the Brazier* were now becoming, by the same distorting process, either brooding ghosts or the
old gods of long-forgotten religions. Graves has generally seen

more to admire about his earthy, sensual old demigods than about the more aloof and ethereal deities of recent civilizations; and in "Rocky Acres" the harsh Welsh hill country is thought of as a fitting base for the "proud Gods" who come from time to time to terrorize the soft burghers of the valleys. But he is not always so uncompromisingly on the side of the pagan spirits, and in "Outlaws" (pp. 40-41) he sees them as "aged gods of fright and lust," who, their old creeds forgotten and their faiths long since disappeared, are reduced to lurking in the shadows of woods and waiting to ambush unwary humans who stray from the accepted paths:

> Old gods, shrunk to shadows, there
> In the wet woods they lurk,
> Greedy of human stuff to snare
> In webs of murk.

Here the gods are the psychological menaces that threaten to ensnare the mind of the man who wanders into dark places with which the blandness of modern civilization and religion has not equipped him to cope.

This feeling of foreboding that underlies all but the lightest poems of *Country Sentiment* becomes overt in the melodramatic "Ghost Raddled" (p. 51),[5] in which a surly old man, asked to sing a song, offers to tell instead

> Of lust frightful, past belief,
> Lurking unforgotten,
> Unrestrainable endless grief
> From breasts long rotten. . . .

and concludes his outburst by asking:

> A song? What laughter or what song
> Can this house remember?
> Do flowers and butterflies belong
> To a blind December?

5. The title was changed to "The Haunted House" in *Collected Poems, 1938* (p. 3), with "frightful," in the first line of the stanza quoted above, replaced by a less-refined "filthy."

Such poems as these give us a clue to the darkness of Graves's mood at this time; and, even though he tries, in the many simple and apparently light-hearted ballads in *Country Sentiment,* to find "flowers and butterflies" in his "blind December," he does not seem to have been very successful in spelling away the troublesome gods with the old Georgian formulae. Though he wished to write romantic poetry of a happy sort, "with the love-theme," so he later declared, "went the old fear-theme, sharpened rather than blunted by the experiences of peace" (Foreword, *Collected Poems, 1938,* p. xxi). And, while many of the lighter ballads are technically very polished and possess a certain charm (see for example "Allie," on page 33, which Graves has retained unchanged in his canon), *Country Sentiment* is a much better work for the presence in it of the poems that derive their strength from the fear-theme.

Having received a government grant of two hundred pounds a year, Graves set off for Oxford in October, 1919. Using his ill-health as an excuse for not living within the prescribed three-mile radius of his college, Graves rented a cottage on Boar's Hill, five miles out, from John Masefield, who thought well of the younger man's poetry (*Good-bye to All That,* p. 357). For the next six years he studied fitfully for his degree in English Literature, in his spare time helping Nancy manage their rapidly growing family (by 1924, they had four children), managing with indifferent success a general store on Boar's Hill, and spending long hours discussing the intricacies of his profession with the other poets who lived nearby.

Boar's Hill was, in fact, at this time a small colony for poets. There at one time or another during Graves's stay were Edmund Blunden, at this time as neurasthenic as Graves himself; Robert Nichols, one of the erstwhile three rhyming musketeers; Gilbert Murray, the classical scholar; Robert Bridges, the sprightly old Poet Laureate; and, of course, Masefield himself. Besides his immediate neighbors, Graves also became acquainted during his

Oxford years with Vachel Lindsay (whom he liked), Ezra Pound
(whom he did not), W. H. Davies, Walter de la Mare, Peter
Quennell, the three Sitwells, T. S. Eliot, and Thomas Hardy.
Of all these, Graves seems to have been most impressed by Hardy,
with whom he and Nancy once spent a weekend in Dorchester.
He liked most about the old man his aloofness from contemporary
fashions, his lack of respect for professional critics, and his firm
insistence that his novels were trivial compared with his poetry.
(Significantly, all of these were attitudes which Graves was soon
to adopt for himself, about his own novels and poetry.)

Surprisingly, none of these literary figures, not even Hardy,
exerted so strong an influence on the career of Robert Graves as
did a man who wrote no poetry himself—T. E. Lawrence, then
Regius Professor of Religion at All Souls'. Lowell Thomas was
at this time lecturing in the United States on "Lawrence of
Arabia," and Lawrence was finding himself the (perhaps) unwilling object of a great deal of public attention. Naturally self-
effacing and introspective (perhaps), he preferred discussing
modern poetry with Graves to being a public figure; and he and
the young poet would spend hours in literary speculations whenever Graves could evade his duties at home and at Oxford.

In the revised edition of *Good-bye to All That* (p. 298), Graves
implies that the discussions with Lawrence consisted mostly of
his explanations of contemporary poetry to the older man; but
Peter Quennell, in his recent autobiography,[6] indicates that
Graves must have been on the listening end of the conversations
at least part of the time:

At the moment, the influence he [Graves] felt most strongly was
that of Lawrence of Arabia; and Lawrence's opinions, often wildly
erratic, he distributed broadcast to all who listened. There were
only three French poets, he once informed me—Villon, Baudelaire
—he had forgotten the name of the third. Where had he learned
this, I cautiously asked him. Lawrence had said so, he replied. . . .

6. *The Sign of the Fish* (New York, 1960), p. 34. Graves has written to me that
Quennell's anecdote is absolutely without factual basis: "I hate Baudelaire; and
if I accepted T. E.'s criticism, I also criticized his poems."

Moreover, Graves has himself noted Lawrence's influence on him during the time of his preparation of his next group of poems, published in London and New York in 1921 as *The Pier-Glass*: "Lawrence made a number of suggestions for improving these poems, and I adopted most of them" (*Good-bye to All That,* p. 371). Although there is perhaps not yet sufficient evidence to warrant any definite conclusions on this score, it seems safe to assume that Graves, who has usually been thought of as most unwilling to listen to anyone's advice about his poetry (except, perhaps, for that of Laura Riding), was moved to accept Lawrence's "suggestions" for his poems through compounded feelings of gratefulness and hero-worship: gratefulness, because Lawrence gave Graves in 1921 four chapters of *Seven Pillars of Wisdom* to sell for serial publication in the United States, thus rescuing him from bankruptcy proceedings;[7] and hero-worship, because of Lawrence's almost legendary wartime experiences.

Graves's war neurosis continued through the Oxford years, but he came by 1920 to realize that the fanciful mood that had prevailed in *Country Sentiment* was not efficacious in quieting his emotional disturbances. In *The Pier-Glass,* accordingly, he continued to write in the sombre, haunted vein of "Rocky Acres," "Outlaws," and "Ghost Raddled."

His predominant mood in *The Pier-Glass* is, as he has said, more "aggressive and disciplinary" than in many of his earlier works;[8] and while he is in many of these poems sardonic and scornful, he is almost always quite seriously concerned with finding a cure for the sickness from which both he and his time were suffering. Several of the poems depict the struggles of men and women who are seeking to relieve their minds of painful memories; and we may be justified in assuming that such men and women are *personae* for the poet.

7. See Graves, *Lawrence and the Arabs* (London, 1927), p. 153; and *Good-bye to All That,* p. 383. *Lawrence and the Arabs* is, incidentally, a very hero-worshipping sort of biography, and it seems to have caused Lawrence no little embarrassment. Cf. *The Letters of T. E. Lawrence,* ed. David Garnett (New York, 1939), pp. 352, 533, 539.

8. *Whipperginny,* Foreword, p. v.

In the title poem (pp. 14-16), for instance, which is inscribed
"To T. E. Lawrence, who helped me with it," the tortured mind
of a woman gradually relieves itself of the repressed memory of
a crime. Ghostlike, but still living, she haunts a deserted manor
that once, long ago, had been the scene of some act of bloody
violence in which she had been involved. "Drawn by a thread of
time-sunk memory," she returns on a gray and gloomy day to the
room in which the crime had taken place, and is frightened by its
eerie lifelessness:

> Empty, unless for a huge bed of state
> Shrouded with rusty curtains drooped awry
> (A puppet theatre where malignant fancy
> Peoples the wings with fear). At my right hand
> A ravelled bell-pull hangs in readiness
> To summon me from attic glooms above
> Service of elder ghosts; here at my left
> A sullen pier-glass cracked from side to side
> Scorns to present the face as do new mirrors
> With a lying flush, but shows it melancholy
> And pale, as faces grow that look in mirrors.
>
> Is there no life, nothing but the thin shadow
> And blank foreboding, never a wainscote rat
> Rasping a crust? Or at the window pane
> No fly, no bluebottle, no starveling spider?

Once again, as in "Rocky Acres," we see Graves relating the
setting of a poem to the state of mind of its central character: the
lifelessness of the chamber is doubly terrifying to the woman because it mirrors so completely her own inner deadness, caused
by the poison of her guilt. We notice here too, as in the earlier
poem, Graves's admirable dependence upon concrete detail to
create his effect: our attention is focussed successively upon the
canopied bed, the bell-pull, the mirror itself and the pallid woman
who gazes into it; and finally upon the rats, flies, and spiders who
ought to be there, but who are not. (The air of decay and foreboding in this passage, created by meticulous attention to detail,

evokes a comparison with Robert Frost, of whose work Graves was shortly to be an ardent supporter.)

The woman implores the pier-glass to give her a sign that somewhere "there still abides/ Remote, beyond this island mystery . . . True life, natural breath; not this phantasma." Her plea is granted; she hears the busy hum of a swarm of bees who have been pent up in the space between the glass and the wall. Thoughts of their judicious order and regularity cause the woman to cease her "labyrinthine wandering," and she comes at last to face the action which has lain at the roots of her neurosis:

> . . . This new mood
> Of judgment orders me to my present duty,
> To face again a problem strongly solved
> In life gone by, but now again proposed
> Out of due time for fresh deliberation.

She decides that her action was just: it was better to have killed than to have forgiven; and the bees support her harsh decision: " 'Kill, strike, again, again,' the bees in chorus hum."

In *Collected Poems, 1938* (p. 27), this somewhat blood-thirsty resolution is deleted, and the woman is left pleading in vain before the mirror. Such a revision is aesthetically justifiable on the grounds that the unity of effect is shattered by the woman's final melodramatic outburst ("Kill, strike the blow again, spite what shall come"), and intellectually justifiable because the droning of the bees is hard to accept as a feasible motivation for the woman's return to life and sanity. But the 1920 ending of "The Pier-Glass" was probably psychologically necessary to Graves at this time, when he was seeking to find through his poetry a way out of his own inner turmoil. By 1938 the necessity was gone, and Graves could treat the problem more objectively.

In "Down" (pp. 46-48), one of the most forceful—and most cryptic—poems in the volume, Graves describes the nightmarish agonies of a sick man who tries to prevent his mind from toppling into the black depths of madness—or death—by recalling a childhood experience:

Oh, to be a child once more, sprawling at ease,
On warm turf of a ruined castle court.
Once he had dropped a stone between flat slabs
That mask the ancient wall, mysteriously
Plunging his mind down with it.  Hear it go
Rattling and rocketing down in secret void.
        . . . he for a while
Lay without spirit; until that floated back
From the deep waters.

As a child he had been able to recall his spirit from the depth of
the subconscious; but now, because of some nameless sin, he is not
able to escape, to repossess his soul once it has sunk to the bottom
of the abyss; and he feels himself slipping, "Funereally with weep-
ing, down, drowned, lost!"  Salvation is not, then, to be gained by
an attempted escape to the simplicity of childhood.  If life is to be
endured, Graves seems to be telling himself, it must be endured
on its own terms.

The aggressive mood of *The Pier-Glass* is in several instances
directed at the blind, implacable God who, ignoring the suffering
of His creatures, condemns them unjustly for crimes of which they
are innocent.  Graves's particular target in "Reproach" (p. 20) is
Original Sin:

Your grieving moonlight face looks down
    Through the forest of my fears,
Crowned with a spiny bramble-crown,
    Dew-dropped with evening tears.

Why do you spell "untrue, unkind,"
    Reproachful eyes plaguing my sleep?
I am not guilty in my mind
    Of aught would make you weep.

Untrue? but how, what broken oath?
    Unkind?  I know not even your name.
Unkind, untrue, you charge me both,
    Scalding my heart with shame.

The black trees shudder, dropping snow,
The stars tumble and spin.
Speak, speak, or how may a child know
His ancestral sin?

The poet's growing cynicism during the postwar years had destroyed the "vision of Christ as the perfect man"[9] that had comforted him at Charterhouse in 1913; and his continuing poetic identification with the innocence of childhood here prompts him to question the mercy and justice of a God who would deny that innocence.

Graves's increasingly rebellious attitude toward his religion is reflected more violently and dramatically in "Raising the Stone" (p. 30), a poem which prefigures the fascination with the older, crueller forms of worship which were later to play such an important part in his poetry. Here, members of some savage prehistoric cult strain frenziedly on a moonlit heath to raise a huge stone to the top of a sacred mound. With "set jaw and hate-maddened eye" they scream with joy "for sacrifice cleansing us all" as the vast stone "lifts, turns, topples, in its fall spreads death." They finally succeed:

. . . Erect in earth we plant
The interpreter of our dumb furious call,
Outraging Heaven, pointing
"I want, I want."

The superficial stimulus for the writing of "Raising the Stone" was probably a visit to Stonehenge that Graves and Nancy had made during a vacation from Oxford; but Graves's own anger at what he felt to be God's injustice is undoubtedly the real motivation for the poem.

There is, despite the undeniably pessimistic tone of most of *The Pier-Glass,* an occasional suggestion that the poet will survive. One instance of this is "Return" (p. 53), in which the poet, having suffered a seven-year exile from his homeland to a

9. Cf. Chapter One, p. 8.

> . . . sterile ground for all time curst
> With famine's itch and flame of thirst,
> The blank sky's counterpart,

returns, threatening to transfer his punishment to an alter ego of
"cold, malicious brain and most uncharitable, cold heart." The
exiled poet relents, however, once he has regained his flowering
and peaceful homeland, and does not call down his curse on his
enemy's head:

> Yet no, I ask a wider peace
> Than peace your heart could comprehend,
> More ample then my own release;
> Go, be you loosed from your right fate,
> Go with forgiveness and no hate;
> Here let the story end.[10]

There is hope, then, that the poet will be able to escape the curse
of spiritual barrenness laid on him by his intellect, and be restored
to "this green place," the proper, fruitful home of his spirit.

Fear of love, and the consequences of unrequited love, are
important themes in *The Pier-Glass*. In "Morning Phoenix"
(p. 28), the poet feels himself being scorched and charred by the
fierce flames of the sun, his love, and longs for

> Caves . . . and cold rocks,
>     Minnow-peopled country brooks,
> Blundering gales of Equinox,
>     Sunless valley-nooks.

He fears that his love is so intense that it will consume him
totally, and wishes that it would slacken from time to time so
that he might restore

10. By 1938, Graves was no longer so charitable to the cold intellect that had
made his spirit its scapegoat. The revised version of the poem in *Collected Poems,
1938* (p. 61), concludes:

> Be off, elude the curse, disgrace
> Some other green and happy place—
> This world of fools is wide.

> Calcined heart and shrivelled skin,
> A morning phoenix with proud roar
> Kindled new within.

Yet even while a strong love is to be feared, the poet should desire it, for it enhances his powers of vision—especially when the love is a hopeless one. We see this notion expressed in "Lost Love" (p. 35):

> His eyes are quickened so with grief,
> He can watch a grass or leaf
> Every instant grow; he can
> Clearly through a flint wall see,
> Or watch the startled spirit flee
> From the throat of a dead man.
> Across two counties he can hear . .
> . . . noise so slight it would surpass
> Credence:—drinking sound of grass,
> Worm talk, clashing jaws of moth
> Chumbling holes in cloth. . . .

Graves felt at this stage in his career that a degree of neurotic tension, whether caused by lost love, as in the poem above, or by guilt, as in "The Pier-Glass" and "Down," might well be essential to the writing of good poetry. In *Good-bye to All That* (p. 381) he recalls that

Somehow I thought that the power of writing poetry, which was more important to me than anything else I did, would disappear if I allowed myself to get cured; my *Pier-Glass* haunting would end and I would become merely a dull easy writer. It seemed less important to me to be well than to be a good poet.

He recognized that the troubled, dark poems in *The Pier-Glass* were far better than such expressions of easy feeling as "The Patchwork Bonnet" (p. 42) and "The Treasure Box" (pp. 31-32), which seemed to partake more of the lighter mood of *Country Sentiment* than that of the later volume; but he was at the same time afraid that the very emotional resolution he was trying to effect by the incorporation of his neuroses into his more serious poems might destroy his talent.  As the result of this apparently irreconcilable conflict in motivation, Graves came to feel, as we shall see in Part II, that he must no longer continue to put so much of himself into his poems; that he must now strive for a poetry of detachment rather than of emotional intensity.  (Eliot had, it is true, made his plea for impersonality in poetry only a year before, in *The Sacred Wood*; yet, while Graves probably did read Eliot's work, it seems likely that Graves made his decision for objectivity independently, without any appreciable influence by Eliot, for the reasons noted above—and because Graves was not in any case likely to be influenced by what Eliot said about things.)[11]

This rejection of subjectivity may or may not have helped Graves as a man; but there is little doubt that it hurt him for some time as a poet.  He was then, as he is now, essentially a romantic poet whose themes are intensely personal, stemming as they do from his own sense of complex maladjustment between the mind and the body, between the intellect and the emotions, between idealistic and sensual love, between the need for tension and fear and the longing for peace and stability.  We can see him beginning to recognize these themes and attempting to come to grips with them in the best poems of *Country Sentiment* and *The Pier-Glass;* and we shall notice shortly how the quality of his work falls off when he turns from them to the more abstract metaphysical and psychological speculations of the second period of his career as a poet.

11. Graves writes me that he has yet to read Eliot's criticism.

3

# On English Poetry:
## The First Criticism

It should come as a surprise to no one after an examination of Robert Graves's early poetry to learn that he began his career as a critic with a work that is thoroughly romantic in its concerns. There is in *On English Poetry: Being an Irregular Approach to the Psychology of This Art* (London: Heinemann, 1922) little, in fact, that had not been said in the first half of the nineteenth century by Wordsworth, Coleridge, Shelley, Hazlitt, and Poe. There is almost no system or organization in *On English Poetry*, which is really only a series of notebook reflections put together, as Martin Seymour-Smith has pointed out, "more with a view to clarifying its author's own difficulties as a practising poet than with the intention of putting forward a new theory of poetry";[1] but the student of criticism will have little difficulty in recognizing the book's close alignment with the romantic tradition. *On English Poetry* is more, however, than a mere resumé of oft-expressed romantic tenets: it represents one of the earliest attempts in this century to explain those romantic tenets in terms of

1. *Robert Graves*, Writers and Their Work Series, No. 78 (London, 1956), p. 12.

Freudian concepts—to apply modern psychological theories to the criticism of literature in general, and to an investigation of the creative process in particular. Since his first meeting with W. H. R. Rivers at Craiglockart in 1917,[2] Graves had been trying to find a way to explain the composition and function of poetry by the use of Freudian theories; and in *On English Poetry* he makes his theme the crucial importance to poetry of the conflict between what Rivers had called the poet's sub-personalities.

Here Graves gives for the first time his definition of poetry, controlled and uncontrolled, distinguishing classic from romantic, fake from real. The best poetry is the product of a complicated process involving a primary synthetic action of the subconscious (which is the seat of the imagination) and a secondary analytic action of the conscious intellect (the seat of reason).

There are two meanings of Poetry as the poet himself has come to use the word:—first, Poetry, the unforeseen fusion in his mind of apparently contradictory emotional ideas; and second, Poetry, the more-or-less deliberate attempt, with the help of a rhythmic mesmerism, to impose an illusion of actual experience on the minds of others. In its first and peculiar sense it is the surprise that comes after thoughtlessly rubbing a mental Aladdin's lamp, and I would suggest that every poem worthy of the name has its central idea, its nucleus, formed by this spontaneous process; later it becomes the duty of the poet as craftsman to present this nucleus in the most effective way possible, by practising poetry more consciously as an art. He creates in passion, then by a reverse process of analyzing, he tests the implied suggestions and corrects them on common-sense principles so as to make them apply universally. (*On English Poetry*, p. 1)

The mind of the true poet is disturbed by conflicting issues which he has been unable to reconcile logically; he slides into a sort of trance, writes his initial draft, then awakens, and applies to his inspired but disorganized words some logical pattern which will render them intelligible to the readers of the poem—who will themselves then benefit from the poet's attempted reconciliation

2. Cf. Chapter Two, p. 21.

of his own subconscious difficulties. Bad poetry is simply the work of a man who solves his emotional problems to his own satisfaction but not to anybody else's. Fake poetry is written when an uninspired poet, finding himself unable to go into the required poetic trance, borrows the dreams and the ideas of true poets, then applies this stolen inspiration to whatever formal pattern is currently fashionable. No poet can present suffering or pleasure beyond his own experience. The attempt to do this is one of the chief symptoms of the fake poet; ignorance forces him "to draw on the experience of a real poet who actually has been through the emotional crises which he himself wants to restate" (p. 97). The fake poet, while often superficially more skillful, is more to be condemned than the bad poet, who is likely to have "suffered and felt joy as deeply as the poet reckoned first class, but who has not somehow been given the power of translating experience into images or emblems, or of melting words in the furnace of his mind and making them flow into the channels prepared to take them" (p. 98). Unfortunately, the true, good poet frequently weakens his imaginative power by his own ability to resolve the emotional disturbances which have provided him with his inspiration (cf. Chapter Two above, p. 36). He progresses to a calmer state of meditation on philosophic paradox; and poetry, which is by Graves's definition sensuous and passionate, is no proper vehicle of expression for this state. "Impersonal concepts can perhaps be expressed in intellectual music, but in poetry the musical rhythm and word-texture are linked with a sensuous imagery too gross for the plane of philosophic thought" (p. 36).

How does the poem come about through the poet's grappling with his emotional disturbances? The process, for Graves, is apparently somewhat akin to Eliot's conception of the poet's sensibility as "constantly amalgamating disparate experience,"[3] and then embodying this fusion in the poem; but Graves sees the conflict as a much rowdier event than does Eliot:

The poet is consciously or unconsciously always either taking in or giving out; he hears, observes, weighs, guesses, condenses,

3. "The Metaphysical Poets," *Selected Essays* (London, 1953), p. 287.

idealizes, and the new ideas troop quietly into his mind until suddenly every now and then two of them violently quarrel and
drag into the fight a group of other ideas that have been loitering
about at the back of his mind for years; there is great excitement,
noise and bloodshed, with finally a reconciliation and drinks all
round.   The poet writes a tactful police report on the affair and
there is the poem.   (p. 26)

Once the police report on this mental pub brawl is written, the
conflict is—for a time, at least—resolved, and the urge to write
poetry subsides.

The manner in which the record in poetry of the poet's
struggles acts to relieve the emotional tension of the reader is
explained by Graves in a much less frivolous manner:

Poetry as the Greeks knew . . . is a form of psychotherapy.   Being
the transformation into dream symbolism of some disturbing
emotional crisis in the poet's mind (whether dominated by delight or pain) poetry has the power of homeopathically healing
other men's minds similarly troubled, by presenting them under
the spell of hypnosis with an allegorical solution of the trouble.
Once the allegory is recognized by the reader's unconscious mind
as applicable the affective power of his own emotional crisis is
diminished.   (p. 85)

As a romantic poet, however, Graves's primary concern is
with the poet, not the audience for poetry.   The internal conflicting forces he speaks of are, he implies, what were for Rivers
the poet's sub-personalities; they are the components of character
that are created by heredity, environment, and experience:

. . . a poet is born not made . . . a man is not a poet unless there is
some peculiar event in his family history to account for him. . . .
the poet, like his poetry, is himself the result of the fusion of incongruous forces.   Marriages between people of conflicting philosophies of life, widely separated nationalities or (most important) different emotional processes, are likely either to result
in children hopelessly struggling with inhibitions or to develop
in them a central authority of great resource and most quick
witted at compromise.   (p. 33)

As he no doubt had in mind here, Graves was himself the product of an unusual marriage, and he has dwelt at length on the split in his own personality caused by the sharp divergence in character, philosophy, and nationality of his parents (*Good-bye to All That,* Chaps. I-V). He has some respect, but little real fondness for his father's family: the Graveses of Limerick were "thin-nosed and inclined to petulance"; there was a coldness in them which was "anti-sentimental to the point of insolence." They were good at games and puzzles, but apt to be querulous and talkative. When Graves speaks of his father, he is condescending: "I am glad in a way that my father was a poet. This at least saved me from any false reverence of poets. . . . He never once tried to teach me how to write, or showed any understanding of my serious work" (*Good-bye to All That,* p. 23). On his mother's side Graves was descended from the German Von Rankes, who were high-principled, easy, generous, and serious. He associates all that is spontaneous and emotional in his nature with this side, and mentions in his autobiography how much more he owes, as a writer, to his mother than to his father. Graves feels that his own personality, then, is split between the cold, analytical qualities of the Graveses and the warm, intuitive faculties of the Von Rankes; and it is doubtless this inherent divergence between his two sub-personalities that he has in mind when he says in *On English Poetry* that an unusual family background is a prerequisite of a good poet. His criticism, we realize, is no less personal than his early poetry.

It is difficult, incidentally, to speculate with any authority on the influence that a man's antecedents have on his temperament, but it seems also quite possible that Graves's heritage as an Anglo-Irishman has been just as important in determining the course of his career as poet and critic as has the conflict in him between Graves the poet and Graves the soldier. For concern with chastity and moral rectitude—as well as for sexual self-consciousness—there is no one to match the Irish Protestant; and Graves could hardly have avoided absorbing some of this concern. Graves's father, moreover, was a witty man with a good deal of facile charm—which may go a long way toward explaining Graves's lifelong distrust of too much smoothness, too much bland wit, too much charm.[4] Accordingly, it is possible for us to see how Graves could come to be simultaneously attracted and repelled by sensuality, by lust; and to understand how he should, though obviously a witty, urbane man, choose deliberately to affect a roughness and irascibility in his writing.    One cannot help absorbing the stronger prejudices of his progenitors; but one must not be like his father.

Graves also gives in this work for the first time his definitions of the romantic and classical conceptions of poetry, the two classes into which he feels all poetry may be separated.    Classical poetry is "characteristic" and romantic poetry is "metamorphic"; that is, though they are both expressions of a mental conflict, in classical poetry this conflict is expressed within the confines of waking probability and logic, in terms of the typical interaction of typical minds; in romantic poetry the conflict is expressed in the "illogical but vivid method of dream-changings" (p. 74).    The founder of the classical doctrine is Aristotle, who tried "to weed poetry of all the symbolic extravagances and impossibilities of the dream state in which it seems to have originated, and to confine it within rational and educative limits" (p. 73).    Because of his influence, classical poetry stresses the importance of the set verse-forms and the traditional construction of drama.    It is social rather than personal.    It is uninspired, relying for its imaginative quality on its borrowing of "shreds of metamorphic diction and legend" (p. 74) from earlier efforts by romantic poets.    Thus classical poets are fake poets and romantic poets are true poets, who have made their poems out of their own inner struggles, and who have written out of inspiration, without initial regard for form or logic. Any poetry which is not of this unconscious type, Graves labels as "didactic" or "careeristic"; he scorns any poem which has been composed with a conscious, predetermined aim and form.

Graves does not, however, advocate anything like the undisciplined freedom of *vers libre* as the proper vehicle for true poetry,

4. As an interesting example of Alfred Perceval Graves's skill, see his autobiography, *To Return to All That* (London, 1930), which is in part a genial chastisement of his son for having written *Good-bye to All That*.

as we might have expected him to do. *Vers libre* seems to him only "Prose Poetry, broken up in convenient lengths" (p. 45); and he agrees with Hardy, whom he quotes as having denied that there was any such thing as *vers libre*—that "if it was *vers* it couldn't be truly *libre* and if it was truly *libre* it couldn't possibly come under the heading of *vers*" (p. 48). When the poet, after his poem emerges from the hidden thought processes that gave it birth, reviews it with the conscious part of his mind, he must not see his task as one of rules or precedents, it is true; but neither can he allow his thought to remain in its original formless, incoherent state. He must temper his inspiration, not with blind reliance on tradition or manner, but with common sense. The dream-quality, the irrationality of his poem, must remain if the poem is to arouse the imaginations of its readers; but the poem must be rendered intelligible, and some degree, at least, of metre and rhythm is necessary for this.

Although the speculations about the psychological origins of art and the defenses of romantic poetry are generally perceptive and refreshing, the most instructive passages in *On English Poetry* (and certainly the most important to a study primarily concerned with Graves's poetry) are those in which Graves illustrates his theories about the creative process with examples taken from his own work. He gives here several instances of the manner in which he takes his poems from the initial rough versions through revision after revision until they acquire the finality and polish we associate with a Graves poem.

In Chaper XLIV he traces this conscious part of the creative process through a series of revisions he made on "Cynics and Romantics," a poem which was never published. In the first draft he wrote his beginning stanza as follows:

> In club or messroom let them sit,
> Let them indulge salacious wit
> On love's romance, but not with hearts
> Accustomed to those healthier parts
> Of grim self-mockery. . . .

But it was too soon in the poem, he felt, for the jerkiness of
"Let them indulge"; and "Indulge salacious" was too hard to say.
The second draft, therefore, read:

> In club or messroom let them sit
> Indulging controversial wit
> On love's romance, but not with hearts
> Accustomed. . . .

But this did not seem right, because he now had the first two
lines beginning with "In," which worried the eye. And "sit,
indulging" put two short "i's" close together. "Controversial"
was bad, too: it made the men sound as if they were angry, but
they were too blasé for that. "Love's romance" was wrong because it was "cheap for the poet's ideal." In the third draft, therefore, the stanza was altered to

> In club or messroom let them sit
> At skirmish of salacious wit
> Laughing at love, yet not with hearts
> Accustomed. . . .

"Skirmish" was good because it suggested the profession of the
men; but now there were three S's—"sit," "skirmish," and "salacious." And there were two "at's" too close together. Hence
the fourth version:

> In club or messroom let them sit
> With skirmish of destructive wit
> Laughing at love, yet not with hearts
> Accustomed. . . .

Now there were two "withs" which did not quite correspond;
and there were the two short "i's" next to each other again. The
first "at" must be put back, and "laughing at" changed to "deriding."

> In club or messroom let them sit
> At skirmish of destructive wit
> Deriding love, yet not with hearts
> Accustomed. . . .

This was better; but now there were "*destructive*" and "*deriding*" too close together. "Ingenious" would be a better word: it had a long vowel, and suggested that it really was a witty performance. "Accorded" was better than "accustomed": it was more accurate and sounded better somehow. Thus the sixth and final draft read:

> In club or messroom let them sit
> At skirmish of ingenious wit
> Deriding love, yet not with hearts
> Accorded. . . .

This may seem somewhat overdone, but it is probably fairly typical of the extreme painstakingness of a poet who has too often been taken by critics as a writer of too-easy verses. One is strongly inclined to believe Graves when he says in *Good-bye to All That* (pp. 388-89) that "My poetry writing has always been a painful process of continual corrections and corrections on top of corrections. I have never written a poem in less than three drafts. . . . The average at this time [1921] was eight; it is now [1929] six or seven." His record number of revisions, he tells us in the same place, was thirty-five, with a very light and facile-seeming piece in *The Pier-Glass* called "The Troll's Nosegay." We cannot help but marvel at the immense time and labor expended on the secondary phase of correction by this Romantic poet who insists in his criticism that poetry must be primarily the product of unconscious inspiration, and only secondarily the product of conscious craftsmanship.

As Graves himself admits in his autobiography (p. 388), *On English Poetry* is an uneven work, in many places "scrappy, not properly considered and obviously written out of reach of a proper reference-library." There is much in it that is trivial, brash, and flippant, and Graves seems often to sacrifice consistency and accuracy for the sake of cleverness. He is frequently self-contradictory. For instance, though he turns immediately to close semantic analysis when confronted with an individual poem to be criticized, he says at one point that "The analytic spirit has been, I believe, responsible both for the present coma of religion among

our educated classes and for the disrespect into which poetry and
fine arts have fallen" (p. 88). Again, after dividing all of English
poetry into his romantic and classical categories, and demon-
strating the manner in which they follow one another in a cyclic
pattern, he remarks: "The history of English poetry is a subject
I hope I shall never have to undertake, especially as I have grave
doubts if there really is such a thing. Poets appear spasmodically,
write their best poetry at uncertain intervals, and owe nothing
worth mentioning to any school or convention" (p. 86). And
finally, although his central thesis in *On English Poetry* is a defense for the criticism of poetry by the use of psychoanalytical
apparatus, we find him concluding an attack on psychological
criticism with what many would feel a very apt prophecy: "The
study of poetry will soon pass from the hands of Grammarians,
Prosodists, historical research men, and such-like, into those of
the psychologists. And what a mess they'll make of it; to be
sure!" (p. 103).

Yet, despite all Graves's lapses in technique and logic, and
despite his often startling lack of originality as a critical theorist
(at one point he proceeds with naïve satisfaction to condemn a new
poetic evil, which he names the "heresy of the Didactic"), there
are two positive qualities of *On English Poetry*: its use of modi-
fied Freudianism to explore the psychological processes involved
in the composition of poetry, which makes the book valuable to
the historian of criticism; and the presence in it of the careful
descriptions of Graves's own writing techniques, which makes it
an extremely useful commentary for the student of his poetry.
If Graves emerges from *On English Poetry* as a romanticist in
theory, he has also here revealed himself as a classicist in practice,
in that he is at least as concerned with the manner as with the
matter of his poetry.

# Part Two

## The Poetry of Detachment

# 4

# Avoidance of Intensity

In June, 1921, soon after the publication of *The Pier-Glass,*
Graves, having failed to sit for his degree, moved himself and his
rapidly growing family from the Boar's Hill cottage to another
in Islip, a farming village six miles from Oxford.  As he tells
us in *Good-bye to All That* (p. 394), his brief success as a poet,
occasioned chiefly by the inclusion of his work in Edward Marsh's
*Georgian Poetry* series, seemed over: *Country Sentiment* had
hardly been noticed by the public or the critics, and *The Pier-
Glass* had done no better.  Largely because John Masefield,
Robert Nichols, and Siegfried Sassoon had lectured in America
on the English war-poets, there had been enough interest in
Graves on this side of the Atlantic to prompt Alfred Knopf to
publish these two volumes, along with *Fairies and Fusiliers* and
*On English Poetry*; but Graves's American publications met with
no more success than did his English ones.

Up to this time, as we have seen in the preceding chapter,
Graves had been very much concerned with the effect of his poetry
on his readers.  As he says in his autobiography (p. 394), "I expected success. . . .  I still believed that it was possible to write
poetry that was true poetry and yet could reach, say, a three or
four thousand-copy sale."  His poems had, he felt, been offering
his readers a panacea for their own psychological ailments; but his

erstwhile patients had spurned his cure. This rejection did not discourage him from writing poetry—nothing could do that; but it did greatly alter his attitude toward his work:

I published a volume of poems every year between 1920 and 1925; after *The Pier-Glass* . . . I made no attempt to write for the reading public, and no longer regarded my work as being of public utility. I did not even flatter myself that I was conferring benefits on posterity; there was no reason to suppose that posterity would be more appreciative than my contemporaries. I only wrote when and because there was a poem pressing to be written. Though I assumed a reader of intelligence and sensibility, and considered his possible reactions to what I wrote, I no longer identified him with contemporary readers or critics of poetry. He was no more real a person than the conventional figure put in the foreground of an architectural design to indicate the size of the building. (*Good-bye to All That,* pp. 401-2)

This change in attitude, caused thus partly by his failure as a public poet, was also a product of Graves's fear that, by writing poems in which he himself was intensely involved, he might effect a cure for his own neuroses, and thus destroy his imaginative power (cf. Chapter Two, p. 36; and *Good-bye to All That,* p. 381). He believed that it had become necessary to his survival as a poet for him to alter his subject-matter radically.

This shift took place midway through his next book of poems, *Whipperginny,* published by Heinemann in 1923. In his Author's Note to this volume Graves explains that the first group of poems included is a continuation of the "aggressive and disciplinary" mood of *The Pier-Glass,* but that "in most of the later pieces will be found evidences of greater detachment in the poet and the appearance of a new series of problems in religion, psychology, and philosophy, no less exacting than their predecessors, but, it may be said, of less emotional intensity." His new scorn for the public suggests itself in his conclusion to the Note: "To those who demand unceasing emotional stress in poetry at whatever cost to the poet—I was one of these myself until recently —I have no apology to offer; but only this proverb from the

Chinese, that *the petulant protests of all the lords and ladies of the Imperial Court will weigh little with the whale when, recovering from his painful excretory condition, he need no longer supply the Guild of Honorable Perfumers with their accustomed weight of ambergris.*"

Although the alteration in approach becomes most sharply defined at a point two-thirds of the way through *Whipperginny*, it is apparent at the very outset of the work that Graves intends no longer to throw himself so wholeheartedly into his poetry. The title poem (p. 1), which explains that Whipperginny, in addition to being an old nick-name for Purgatory, is an obsolete card game, announces that his poems now are to serve as a sort of buffer between himself and his problems, internal and otherwise.

> To cards we have recourse
> When Time with cruelty runs,
> To courtly Bridge for stress of love,
> To Nap for noise of guns.
>
> Our fairy earth we tread,
> No present problems vex
> Where man's four humours fade to suits,
> With red and black for sex.
>
> Where phantom gains accrue
> By tricks instead of cash,
> Where pasteboard federacies of Powers
> In battles-royal clash.
>
> Then read the antique word
> That hangs above this page
> As type of mirth-abstracted joy,
> Calm terror, noiseless rage,
>
> A realm of ideal thought,
> Obscured by veils of Time,
> Cipher remote enough to stand
> A namesake for my rhyme,

A game to play apart
    When all but crushed with care;
Let right and left, your jealous hands,
    The lists of love prepare.

The old traumata, the wartime spectres that he had sought to
exorcise in the dark poems of *The Pier-Glass,* then, are still with
him; and it would seem from "Whipperginny" that, instead of
being "aggressive and disciplinary," he intends once again to seek
escape from them into the same "Arcadia of amatory fancy"
(*Whipperginny,* Author's Note, p. v) that he had repeatedly
invoked in *Fairies and Fusiliers* and *Country Sentiment,* by
writing poems of "mirth-abstracted joy, calm terror, noiseless
rage."

  Several of the early poems in *Whipperginny* would appear
to bear out this suspicion.  There are a few of these that are,
while without much weight or extent of subject or movement,
evidence that Graves still felt most at home in the composition
of simple, even childlike, lyrics.  "Henry and Mary" (p. 34), for
instance, which has escaped excision from the canon, is pure
nursery-rhyme:

Henry was a worthy king,
    Mary was his queen,
He gave to her a snowdrop,
    Upon a stalk of green.

Then all for his kindness
    And all for his care
She gave him a new-laid egg
    In the garden there.

Love, can you sing?
                I cannot sing.
Or story-tell?
                Not one I know.
Then let us play at king and queen,
As down the garden lawns we go.

And in "An English Wood" (p. 35), also retained in recent collections of his verse, Graves returns to the frank monsters he had
introduced into his early fanciful poems—rocs, gryphons, and
harpies—if only to say, somewhat regretfully, that such beasts do
not exist in English forests, where only "calm elementals brood"
over the static tranquillity of soft lawns, grave old trees, and
small pathways that "idly tend/ Towards no uncertain end."

But if we concentrate only on such pretty, unworried pieces
as these, we fail to see that Graves's internal struggle was continuing unabated during the early stages, at least, of *Whipperginny*, and that it was leading him toward extremes of pessimism
and doubt. In "Children of Darkness" (p. 14), which Geoffrey
Bullough has called a poem of "sick horror,"[1] Graves's theme is
guilt—the guilt which parents feel during the day for their actions
in "the lusty dark"; and in a skillful construction of opposition
between the children and the parents who conceive them, between
the womb and the world, the poem's burden becomes that,
paradoxically, dark is the time of innocence and faith, and light
the time of guilt and doubt.

> We spurred our parents to the kiss,
> Though doubtfully they shrank from this—
> Day had no courage to review
> What lusty dark alone might do—
> Then were we joined from their caress
> In heat of midnight, one from two.

The children, once conceived, are full of certitude, know no
discontent, and hurry eagerly to be born, so that they might enjoy
the light. But the light will destroy the peace they have felt:

> Was Day prime error, that regret
> For darkness roars unstifled yet?
> That in this freedom by faith won,
> Only acts of doubt are done?
> That unveiled eyes with tears are wet,
> They loathe to gaze upon the sun?

1. *The Trend of Modern Poetry* (London, 1949), p. 77.

In "Old Wives' Tales" (pp. 21-22),[2] Graves states that the
mermaids, dragons, and the "hornéd fiend of Hell" that he had
learned of in his childhood are nonetheless real for existing as
such only in fairy-stories: they are in reality the outward manifestations of inner fears, and are the more frightening for being
so. Now grown, he has met the mermaids, and has found that
they "have neither tail nor fin"; he knows the dragons, and has
seen that they

> have no darting tongues,
> Teeth saw-edged nor rattling scales,
> No fire issues from their lungs,
> Poison has not slimed their tails.

They are instead

> creatures of dark air,
> Unsubstantiated tossing forms,
> Thunderclaps of man's despair
> In mid-whirl of mental storms.

The mermaids are man's lust, the dragons his despair; and the
true fiend is not Satan, but he whom men call "God," the being
who stands in reality for worldly desires, for what men falsely
worship as good. And these monsters will prevail:

> Mermaids will not be denied
> Of our last enduring shame,
> The dragon flaunts his unpierced hide,
> The fiend makes laughter with God's name.[3]

Certainly there is little accord between this nightmarish poem and
the poet's escapist aims as stated in "Whipperginny": Graves is
still joined in battle with his fears.

In one of the last poems of the first section, however, there is
a suggestion that he might win this battle: "The Rock Below"

2. Retained, with much revision, in the canon as "Mermaid, Dragon, Fiend."
Both Seymour-Smith and Cohen incorrectly assign this poem to *The Pier-Glass.*

3. In his 1938 version of this poem, Graves makes his point somewhat clearer
by altering the last line to read: "The true fiend governs in God's name."

(p. 40) is the symbolic record of his struggle to conquer his neuroses and still survive as a poet, and it shows him as ultimately victorious. Here, the poet's land is at first seen to be overgrown with weeds. A "muttering from the earth" tells him to clear the ground and "Search what hides below." This he does, only to discover that under the weeds lies a network of thorn-stocks, "Grappled in the ground." He wrenches these out as well, and sets a rose-bush in their place. But the bush soon begins to wither, for its roots are impeded by a rock which lies beneath it. Angrily the poet tears out the rose-bush and sees it die. Then he attacks the rock itself, and succeeds in breaking it.

> Now from the deep and frightful pit
> Shoots forth the spiring phoenix-tree
> Long despaired in this bleak land,
> Holds the air with boughs, with bland
> Fragrance welcome to the bee,
> With fruits of immortality.

While clearing the upper layer of conflict from the mind may for a time permit the production of pleasant poetry, there is a greater disturbance far beneath the surface that will eventually destroy the poet's talent, unless it too can be removed. If it is, then the poet's true art will blossom forth, giving beauty to its beholders and immortality to the poet.

Like most of the more romantic, subjective pieces in *Whipperginny*, "The Rock Below" was deleted from Graves's canon during the Twenties, as being inconsistent with what he felt to be his natural line of development: the trend away from emotional intensity, and toward a detached, analytic treatment of "problems in religion, psychology, and philosophy." The poems of *Whipperginny* that survived, for a time at least, were those that seemed to belong to this new mode: poems which were of the head, not the heart; poems which were "cerebral and Metaphysical, not so much by [their] abstraction and wit, as by [their] preoccupation with psychological problems, the relativity of knowledge, the problems of identity, discontinuity of experience, dissociation of

sensibility."[4]   The subjective conflict remained, but Graves now
sought to avoid it by concentrating in his poetry not on emotion
but on intellectual speculation.   Now began his period of what
Edwin Muir has called "busy, temporizing, hypothetical verse,
verse which seems to say, 'This may be true, or it may not' ";[5] and
of what J. M. Cohen terms Graves's "new poetry of ironic hypothesis—Consider this case or this."[6]   Whatever name we assign
it, the phase of his career that begins in *Whipperginny* and runs
through 1927 (and that, indeed, carries over in some respects to
this day) is marked by Graves's almost absolute noncommitment
to humanity, to love, to religion—in short, to anything the espousal
of which might put him in a vulnerable position.   He assumes a
*persona* that will allow him to be witty and cynical about things
which he is temperamentally inclined to take very seriously.   He
seems to be making a conscious rejection of any material, attitude,
or technique that might be broadly termed "romantic."   In a
tone that often resembles the matter-of-fact flatness of Robert
Frost in the *North of Boston* poems, Graves continually insists on
excluding from a number of potentially moving and dramatic
situations any emotion and any action which might tend to brand
him as a subjective writer.

   This enforced dryness is highly effective in "The Lord Chamberlain Tells of a Famous Meeting" (pp. 44-47), a long narrative
poem in which the inactivity of the principals sets up a tension
which is skillfully maintained throughout.   The Lord Chamberlain's story concerns two powerful princes, rulers of Eastern and
Western kingdoms respectively, who accidentally meet, while
disguised, in the messroom of a Middle Kingdom's army camp,
where they have both come as spies.   When the two rulers, recognizing but not acknowledging one another's identity, sit down to
play cards, the reader prepares himself for any number of winks,
innuendoes, veiled threats, and perhaps for a conclusion of swash-
buckling violence.   But Graves, or rather the Lord Chamberlain,
will not allow this:

4. Bullough, *The Trend of Modern Poetry*, p. 76.
5. *Transition: Essays on Contemporary Literature* (New York, 1926), p. 175.
6. *Robert Graves*, Writers and Critics, No. 3 (Edinburgh, 1960), p. 33.

> They played together there
> For half an hour or more; then went their ways.

The whole point is that nothing at all happens; and Graves keeps this undramatic drama from becoming tedious by building the poem about a series of negations by the Lord Chamberlain, who tells us never to believe "such credulous annalists" as those who have suggested that the two princes communicated in some sly way through card tricks; and never to believe "approved biographers" who have shown that the two "spoke" to one another by deftly switching from one game to another:

> It's said, spectators of this play grew dazed,
> They turned away, thinking the gamesters drunk.
> But I, who sat there watching, keeping score,
> Say they observed the rules of but one game
> The whole bout, playing neither well nor ill
> But slowly, with their thoughts in other channels,
> Serene and passionless like wooden men.

Neither was there any witty talk between the princes, nor treaties signed in blood beneath the table, nor divine interference, as the allegorical painters would have it—and so on, until the poem's memorable conclusion:

> One thing is true, that of all sights I have seen
> In any quarter of this world of men,
> By night, by day, in court, field, tavern or barn,
> That was the noblest, East encountering West,
> Their silent understanding and restraint,
> Meeting and parting like the kings they were
> With plain indifference to all circumstance;
> Saying no good-bye, no handclasp and no tears,
> But letting speech between them fade away
> In casual murmurs and half compliments,
> East sauntering out for fresh intelligence,
> And West shuffling away, not looking back,
> Though each knew well that this chance meeting stood
> For turning movement of world history.
> And I?  I trembled, knowing these things must be.

There were no romantic gestures, no flamboyant displays of emotion—there was nothing but a noble exercise of restraint (a quality
for which Graves by now felt increasing respect) in the face of a
potentially explosive situation.  The poet has avoided melodrama
at one extreme, and boredom from such absolute passivity at the
other, by exploding the romantic hypotheses of the annalists,
biographers and painters on the one hand, and by including those
same hypotheses on the other.  The poem is thus a form of romantic anti-romanticism, an instance of poetically having one's
cake and eating it too.

In "An Idyll of Old Age" (pp. 42-43), a recasting of the Baucis
and Philemon myth, Graves pokes a little flippant fun at constancy, old age, and the gods' lack of a sense of humor.  Zeus and
Hermes, having descended to earth and presented themselves as
guests at the poor cottage of the humble couple, overhear their
hosts' conversation at night, after retiring.  They are at first
amazed to hear Baucis and Philemon both express a desire to take
on new lovers, and then are appalled to discover how sweetly they
give one another permission to do so.  But Hermes, totally
lacking in humor, considers that the couples' love for one another
is so strong that they could not bear to be untrue to one another;
that what they have overheard must have been only a pair of
most generous gestures.  Hermes is partly right, for these are
gestures, if not necessarily noble ones; for infidelity is forbidden
the couple not by their love, but by their age:

> Baucis, kind soul, was palsied, withered, and bent,
> Philemon, too, was ten years impotent.

In "Richard Roe and John Doe" (p. 15), one of the few poems
in *Whipperginny* to be retained in recent collections of his poetry,
Graves's cynicism is not quite so crude as in "An Idyll of Old
Age."  Richard Roe, cuckolded by John Doe, wishes himself, in
a series of brief fantasies, Solomon, Job, and Alexander, that he
might have the "cunning, patience, power to overthrow/ His
tyrant"; but more than all these he would prefer to be one man—
John Doe.

While this sort of light verse is at this stage in his career the usual vehicle for Graves's misanthropic scorn, there are several poems in *Whipperginny* in which his skepticism is directed at more serious targets. Typical of these is "To Any Saint" (p. 70), a brief commentary on the nature of martyrdom. The victory over his persecutors that the saint achieves through suffering teaches not love, but "a newer sort of hate" to his followers, who see that such passive resistance is a most effective way of plaguing their enemies—that martyrdom, "this baffling stroke of naked pride," is

> not less violent, not less keen
> And barbéd more than murder's blade!

Graves had now begun to feel that Christianity, as an organized religion, was corrupt—that the followers of Christ had, in erecting a complex and rigid theology around the basically simple teachings of Christ, destroyed the purity and innocence of those teachings. As he had attacked the perverters of the spirit of martyrdom in "To Any Saint," in "A Manifestation in the Temple" (pp. 68-69) he mocks the priests who have set themselves and their idols up between men and their God. Here a humble man, drawn by his instinctive love of God to a religious ceremony in a temple, finds that the priests are not preaching the faith, but are instead bilking the worshippers, by the concoction of false miracles, into

> Prompt sacrifice, and a care for priestly needs . . .
> A generous measure for wine, for oil, for cloth,
> A holding fast to the law that the stones ordain,

and abject obedience to their own, not Christ's, decrees. The peasant rebels against this corruption, and cries out against the priests:

> Out, meddlesome imps, whatever Powers you be,
> Break not true prayer between my God and me.

If, as J. M. Cohen claims, "The one consistent note in *Whip-perginny* is a lament for the loss of pure emotion,"[7] these last two

7. *Ibid.*, p. 37.

poems could be offered in partial support of such a claim, for both
are in a sense laments for the loss of a pure religious emotion. In
"Song of Contrariety" (p. 5), moreover, the same theme, now
secularized to apply to sexual love, obtains. Whereas in Graves's
earlier volumes love was usually conceived of as a relatively
simple experience that was capable of assuaging grief or fear, now
it has become an ephemeral, paradoxical emotion that intensifies,
rather than alleviates, despair. Here, where

> Far away is close at hand,
> Close joined is far away,

prospective union with the loved one seems to promise relief
from "dream-despair." But, the union once obtained, joy rapidly
gives way to an even greater despair:

> Is the presence empty air,
> Is the spectre clay,
> That love, lent substance by despair,
> Wanes, and leaves you lonely there
> On the bridal day?

For the most part, then, the poems of *Whipperginny* bespeak
a sense of disillusionment on the part of the poet—nothing is as it
seems, no values are fixed; and the only solution is an ironic aloofness to life, the maintenance of a cynical and uncommitted
restraint.

Graves's new detachment proved no more saleable than his
earlier involvement: "As a result of this greater strictness in
writing I was soon accused of trying to get publicity and increase
my sales by a wilful clowning modernism" (*Good-bye to All That,*
p. 402). His continued failure to find an audience solidified his
intentions to go his poetic course alone, to write for himself and
to himself—although he was still willing to be read by the select
few who shared his interest in the poetic treatment of his religious,
psychological, and philosophical problems.

One of these admirers was John Crowe Ransom, whose own

poetry Graves has always respected.[8]  Ransom's 1919 collection of
verse, *Poems about God*, had caught Graves's attention; believing
that he had discovered another poet who shared his increasingly
esoteric interests, he began an occasional correspondence with the
American.  And when, in 1923, Leonard and Virginia Woolf's
Hogarth Press published a limited edition of his *The Feather Bed*,
Graves included in it a dedicatory letter to "John Ransome [*sic*],
the American poet."

This new work, which (he tells Ransom in his dedication)
"was more than a year writing," consists of a long interior mono-
logue sandwiched between a poetic Prologue and Epilogue.  It
is an involved psychological study of a man whose lover has deserted him to enter a nunnery, and Graves fancied that the hereti-
cal opinions expressed in it by the young man might offend any
chance readers of the poem (to Ransom: "It would be as well
. . . not to let the honest burghers of Nashville, Tenn., already
scandalized by your *Poems about God*, see a copy of *The Feather
Bed*").  He need not have worried, for there is not much about
the poem that seems any more extreme than, say, Browning's
"Soliloquy of the Spanish Cloister" and "My Last Duchess"—both
of which, in fact, *The Feather Bed* resembles in several ways.

As Graves tells Ransom, the poem is "the study of a fatigued
mind in a fatigued body . . . under the stress of an abnormal
conflict": the young man has just received his goodbye-letter from
Rachel, his lover; and, bitterly mocking the childlike simplicity
of her writing, prepares to sleep in the drab and dusty room he
has rented in an old inn.  He is angry over Rachel's desertion, but
as he drifts into a troubled doze he is still undecided whether to
maintain his love for her, or "to beat Love down with ridicule."
Once he is asleep, his subconscious mind takes over and presents

8. Graves has written to me that he was instrumental in getting Ransom's
*Grace after Meat* (1924) published in England. He also included in the same letter
some indication that his admiration for Ransom is limited to the American's earlier
work: "Ransom died as a poet around 1930." In the Winter, 1923, issue of *The
Owl*, which he edited with William Nicholson, his father-in-law, Graves included
two of Ramsom's early poems: "An American Addresses Philomela" and "Winter
Remembered."

him with a series of fantasies which define the precise nature of his conflict.

We learn that Rachel, a pious and ingenuous girl, had been frightened by his bullying attitude toward her, and by his blasphemous attacks on what he felt to be her naïve religiosity; and that, believing that she must make a choice between her love for Christ and her love for the young man, she had chosen the former. His awareness of his guilt is revealed by the nature of a number of nightmares which now assail him: after a bizarre parade passes by his bed, led by the somewhat incongruous quartet of Keble, Pusey, Moody, and Sankey, he imagines what convent life will be like for Rachel. Her physical beauty will be rapidly worn away by the ordeals of her novitiate; and her spiritual purity will be corrupted by a snobbish and perverted Mother Superior, who will first ascertain from Burke's *Landed Gentry* that Rachel is "a suitable candidate for the Order of Seven Sorrows," and who will then proceed to gratify herself sexually by the vicarious enjoyment she will get from forcing Rachel to reveal the innermost secrets of her affair with the young man.

The dreamer awakes from time to time, and allows his conscious mind to dwell on what he has just dreamed. Then, in a final outburst of bitterness, he completely rejects both Rachel and the traditional religion she has come to represent; and falls asleep again, hoping that he has successfully resolved his conflict. But his guilt is still with him, and the poem ends with a final outrageous nightmare in which the Mother Superior appears once again:

> Mother Superior
> Secretly with one finger at her lips,
> Re-enters, carefully locks my bedroom door,
> Now she disrobes with fingers trembling so
> They tear the fastenings—naked she steps out
> To practise with her long-past-bearing body
> The wiles of the Earthbound. . . .

The poem is certainly Graves's most sustained and involved psychological study up to this time, and it deserves attention for at least two reasons. First, there is its subtlety of characterization. As in Browning's best dramatic monologues and soliloquies, there can be no conclusive evaluation of the actors: just as we cannot be sure of the degree of guilt—if any—of the Duke's departed spouse, and just as we end by suspecting that there might be more than a grain of justice in the monk's bitter invective against Brother Lawrence, so here we remain undecided about the relative guilt and innocence of Rachel and her lover. Granted that he is a cynic and a bully, might it not also be possible that he has been goaded into his viciousness by Rachel's rigid piety and childish obstinacy? (Here, then, as in several of the later *Whipperginny* poems, there is the refusal to assign absolute values—truth must be seen as relative only.)

Second, there is the very intricate way in which the man's logical argument, broken by the circlings of associative thought in the dreams—all, however, relevant to the emotional disturbance—is continually being caught up again by the drowsy intellect, until the man solves the problem to his conscious satisfaction. Because of Graves's care in working out this scheme, *The Feather Bed* is an impressively ingenious poem, an intellectual exercise that is deftly handled. Unfortunately, however, Graves apparently failed to recognize here that, however frightening nightmares are to the dreamer, they tend to appear somewhat ludicrous when recounted; and the emotional impact of the poem is greatly lessened by the fact that we laugh when we were meant to be appalled at the man's torments. Graves was, of course, apparently more interested at this time in presenting a case study of neurosis than in creating an internally coherent imaginative experience; and, if we care to make allowances for his intentions, then there is much to admire about *The Feather Bed*.

Then, later in 1923, an event occurred which caused the study of metaphysics to replace psychology as Graves's primary extra-literary interest. This was his meeting with Basanta Mallik, a

Bengali intellectual who had been sent by the Maharajah of
Nepal to Oxford for courses in "British political psychology."
Although one of the results of Graves's education "was a strong
prejudice, amounting to contempt, against anyone of non-Euro-
pean race" (*Good-bye to All That*, p. 402), he was immediately
attracted to Mallik and his philosophy, which was

a development of formal metaphysics, but with characteristically
Indian insistence on ethics. He believed in no hierarchy of ultimate values or the possibility of any unifying religion or ideology.
But at the same time he insisted on the necessity of strict self-
discipline in the individual in meeting every possible demand
made upon him from whatever quarter, and he recommended
constant self-watchfulness against either dominating or being
dominated by any other individual. This view of strict personal
morality agreed well with my practice. (*Good-bye to All That*,
pp. 403-4)

Mallik was for some months a constant visitor at the Islip
cottage, and Graves's new fascination with philosophical speculation threatened for a time almost to replace poetry as his vocation.
But in 1924 the Hogarth Press published *Mockbeggar Hall*, a collection of fifteen new poems by Graves as well as his "re-English-
ing" of an "actionless drama for three actors and a moving background" by Mallik. As Graves's poems have always been strongly
colored by whatever his extra-literary concerns have been at the
time of their composition, so these new pieces reflected strongly
his fascination with his new hobby-horse. And, as T. E. Lawrence
wrote Graves after reading *Mockbeggar Hall*, "[It is] not the sort
of book that one would put under one's pillow at night" (*Good-
bye to All That*, p. 402); for several of its poems are as intellectually demanding as any Graves had written.

Mallik's anti-institutional fervor apparently strengthened
Graves's inclinations toward agnosticism, or at least toward the
refusal to allow any system which sought to circumscribe the
concept of deity. The two poems which set the tone of *Mockbeggar Hall*, "Knowledge of God" (p. 58) and "The Rainbow and

the Sceptic" (pp. 77-78), both postulate a God whose ways cannot be fixed by any system, whether theological or philosophical. The theories expressed in them could hardly be called original, but Graves's ingenious presentation, coupled with his obvious and rather naïve enthusiasm, lends to them an air of freshness.

In "Knowledge of God" there is, as Cohen has noted, "an echo of the Pythagorean belief in eternal recurrence,"[9] with perhaps overtones of Eastern theology derived from the poet's conversations with Mallik.

> So far from praising he blasphemes
> Who says that God has been or is,
> Who swears he met with God in dreams
> Or face to face in woods and streams,
> Meshed in their boundaries.

To say that God "has been" or "is," or to assert with assurance that He takes an active part in the endless round of existence, directing the seasons, sporting with the Danäe, fighting with "rebel demons," and generally giving proof of his omnipotence, is wrong-headed: if God is God, then he must be invisible, unknowable, outside of Time and Space:

> The caterpillar years-to-come
> March head-to-tail with years-that-were
> Round and around the cosmic drum,
> To time and space they add their sum
> But how is Godhead there?
>
> Weep, sleep, be merry, vault the gate
> Or down the evening furrow plod,
> Hate and at length withhold your hate,
> Rule, or be ruled by certain fate,
> But cast no net for God.

In "The Rainbow and the Sceptic" a despondent man wanders through a rain-drenched forest, greatly disturbed be-

9. *Robert Graves*, p. 40.

cause of his conviction that God, who he feels ought to govern by
fixed and immutable laws, is in reality a whimsical and quixotic
deity.   The poet cynically takes the rainbow which shines above
the horizon as a symbol for God's decrees—promising, but transi-
tory and unattainable.   But a "spirit of air" suddenly challenges
him, and says that he should instead take the rainbow as a symbol
for hope-through-mutability: all man can know is that laws, like
the rainbow, come and go; he can never hope to judge such
divine manifestations by any time-bound system of cause and
effect.   He must hope only that evidence of mutability in the
universe and its laws argues a God who exists beyond such laws:

> Yet beyond all this, rest content
> In dumbness to revere
> INFINITE God without event,
> Causeless, not there, not here.

> Neither eternal, not time-bound,
> Not certain, nor in change,
> Uncancelled by the cosmic round,
> Nor crushed within its range.

There is a distant echo in "The North Window" (p. 13) of
Graves's early "A Boy in Church," from *Fairies and Fusiliers*.
Once again we are at a service in a country chapel while a storm
rages outside; but here the stained-glass windows, reflecting light
from the glowing lamps during this celebration of All Souls' Eve,
are almost opaque: the congregation cannot see that, outside the
chapel, the damned souls of unbaptized infants, betrayed mothers,
and murderers have risen from their graves and are conducting
their own service in the light that shines through the church
windows.   What these wraiths celebrate, however, amounts to a
Black Mass, because they gaze on the backwards-reflection of the
scene depicted on one of the windows—*The Hour of Doom*, in
which Christ separates the sheep from the goats—and thus the
lesson they learn from the picture is a completely perverted one,

and their worship becomes blasphemy: the Christ *they* worship
is one who sends his sheep to Hell and his goats to Heaven.

> With the scene reversed, and the legend backwards too,
> Displaying in scarlet and gold the Creator who damns,
> Who has thrust on His Left the bleating sheep and the lambs,
> Who has fixed on His Right the goats and kids accurst,
> With *Omega: Alpha* restoring the last as first:
> Then the psalms to God that issue hence or thence
> Ring blasphemy each to the other's Omnipotence.

The lesson to be drawn from "The North Window" is less
easily seen than in the other poems of *Mockbeggar Hall*, perhaps
partly because Graves here allows his imagination to govern his
intellect, and concentrates more on creating a dramatic effect than
on working out the religious and philosophical implications of the
poem. Cohen may be right in proposing that the poem "may al-
legorize the contradictions between conscious and unconscious
mind"[10]; but, when we consider the lessons taught in the other
poems of this volume, it seems more likely that Graves is here
attempting to present a more dramatic illustration of his thesis
that God is infinitely more complex than man can imagine—that
when we believe we are praising Him, our worship may, when seen
from another vantage-point, be blasphemous—whether we are
within or without the church.

The same rather sardonic humor that we noted in several of
the *Whipperginny* poems is also present in *Mockbeggar Hall*.
In the Skeltonics of "Attercop: The All-Wise Spider" (pp. 14-15)
it is used to deride both the pragmatic and the mystical approach
to God: James, a philosopher (presumably William) and Walter,
a poet-scholar (possibly Sir Walter Raleigh, Graves's mentor at
Oxford) are represented as a pair of disputing flies that are
trapped in a net—the world—spun by Attercop, the primordial
Spider-God. The poet, who rejects the views of both the flies,
watches as James, "composed, with spectacles on brow," analyzes
their situation:

10. *Ibid.,* p. 40.

He ponders where the Primal Den can be,
He holds the web to have no finity
And boldly adds, "Attercop has no base
In any sure discoverable place . . .
He's mad or possibly long years deceased;
But this web serves as flooring for us flies.
Who disregards this web binding the skies,
That man himself denies.
The web! Life! Liberty! all else is lies!"

Walter, however, has no use for such abstractions. He sees
Attercop as a tyrant God whose control can be broken by a
natural-magic charm. So, while James reasons and Walter chants,
the giant spider, undisturbed by their buzzing, prepares to devour
them.

Only once in *Mockbeggar Hall* does Graves turn from his
philosophical disquisitions to love-poetry. "Full Moon" (pp. 8-9),
like *Whipperginny*'s "Song of Contrariety," speaks of a love that
is destroyed as it is fulfilled. Here the Moon, the "tyrannous
queen above," jealously casts a frosty spell over the lovers and
the field in which they lie, so that

Forgetful of the feverish task
In hope of which they came
Each image held the other's eyes
And watched a grey distraction rise
To cloud the eager flame.

The Moon, attended by her mermaids (the lustful creatures of
"Old Wives' Tales"), sails between them, and they find that their
love has grown cold. Here, as is increasingly the case in Graves's
love-poems, the sad conclusion to be reached is that love is a
fragile feeling, one which we should not expect to be able to
maintain for long. Here also we may note Graves's lifelong inclination to see love—or passion, at least—as something pathological rather than normal: the couple in the field are not making
love, they are engaged in a "feverish task."

Although "Full Moon" represents a momentary return to Graves's old romantic mood, and although he apparently allowed the same impulse to obscure his argument in "The North Window," the poems in *Mockbeggar Hall* chiefly show that Graves was still determined to pursue the course toward abstraction and generalization that he had set in the later *Whipperginny* poems.

W. H. Auden has recently stated that "No poet has been more concerned than Mr. Graves with poetic integrity, with being true, at all costs, to his real self."[11] In general, this is certainly true, especially of the later Graves. But the impression one receives from the first three volumes of this period of his career is that Graves was now attempting to *avoid* his "real self," or at least to make himself over into a different sort of person, a different sort of poet. By natural instinct a romantic lyricist of highly subjective inclinations, he was seeking, for reasons discussed at the beginning of this chapter, to divorce his poetry from his own emotions, and to develop a style and an attitude that would provide him with a sort of shield against his own conflicts. Adopting a satiric and cynically objective manner, he used his poetry first to illustrate his psychological theories, and then to discourse on the metaphysical tenets he had learned from Basanta Mallik. Occasionally, as in "Children of Darkness," "Old Wives' Tales," and "The Rock Below" from *Whipperginny,* and in "Full Moon" and "The North Window" from *Mockbeggar Hall,* the old impulse crowds through again. But this had become in the main Graves's period of detachment, the time when he consciously set himself to become a poet of ideas, not of emotions.

There is much that we can say for Graves's wit and ingenuity during this second period, and there is no doubt that it was at this time that he began formulating and solidifying the attitudes and beliefs that were later, when more fully assimilated by his consciousness and fused into an organic union with his own highly individual sensibility, to make him the major poet that he has become. But there is no denying that the characteristic poems of this period suffer from Graves's refusal to involve himself in

11. "A Poet of Honor," *The Mid-Century,* No. 28 (July, 1961), pp. 3-9.

them, to make them more than clever arguments for a relativistic and faintly scornful approach to reality. This is not to say, of course, that such disengagement is necessarily a defect in a poet; it is a question of temperament. But Robert Graves was and is by nature a moralist (as we have noted earlier, in some ways almost a Puritan) and a romantic; he is only at his best when his poetry reflects an impassioned commitment to something in which he believes fervently.

# 5

# Psychological and
# Sociological Criticism

The gap between Robert Graves's poetic theory and practice widened in this second period of his career, chiefly because his poetry changed while his criticism remained basically allied to the psychological tenets he had espoused in *On English Poetry*. Graves himself recognized this lack of agreement between theory and practice, and later said of this period that "anything worth preserving that I wrote between 1922 and 1926 was written in spite of, not because of, my . . . theories."[1]  In his poetry he was following—or attempting to follow—the very course that he had warned against in *On English Poetry*—that of the true poet who, having by his own ability resolved the emotional disturbances which had provided him with his inspiration, moves on to a calmer state of meditation on philosophic paradox. But in his criticism Graves was still asserting that the only true poetry was that which provided a symbolic record of the poet's struggle with and resolution of his own emotional problems.

By 1925, Graves's financial situation, never very satisfactory, had worsened; and, with four children to maintain and with

1. Foreword to *Collected Poems, 1938*, p. xxi.

Nancy's health waning, it became apparent that he would have to take a job. Teaching seemed the least objectionable of the pursuits he considered, but he still lacked his degree. Sir Walter Raleigh, Merton Professor of English, allowed Graves to present a B.Litt. thesis, graciously "deeming" that he had taken a B.A. degree. Graves thereupon submitted a critical work which he had just published as *Poetic Unreason and Other Studies* (London: Cecil Palmer, 1925); and, somewhat to his surprise, found it accepted and himself an Oxford graduate in the spring of 1925.

As he states in his Author's Note to this volume, *Poetic Unreason* was an attempt at a "sober development" of the "wayward notes on poetic psychology" he had published three years before as *On English Poetry*. The influence of W. H. R. Rivers is still obvious (the book is dedicated to Dr. Henry Head, a neurologist and a colleague of Dr. Rivers), and once again poetry is held valuable for its therapeutic qualities:

For the poet, the writing of poetry accomplishes a certain end, irrespective of whether the poem ever finds another reader but himself; it enables him to be rid of the conflicts between his sub-personalities. And for the reader, without necessarily any direct detailed regard to the history of the poet, the reading of poetry performs a similar service; it acts for him as a physician of his mental disorders. (*Poetic Unreason*, p. 2)

Although the literary critics of every age assign absolute values of "goodness" or "badness" to poetry only insofar as it does or does not obey the arbitrary rules set by that age, the judgment of poetry should be an entirely individual thing: "bad" poetry may only be defined as "Yours, when I do not understand you and when your work has no help to offer me in my troubles" (p. 24); and the only "good" poetry is that which resolves the inner conflicts of the author and the reader. Thus, Graves is led to a highly relativistic view of poetic creation (which corresponds to the philosophical relativism he had preached in *Mockbeggar Hall* the year before); for what may leave one reader uncured may be powerful medicine to the next. "Badness" or "goodness" are terms applicable only to individuals and moments; "it is not possible to lay down absolute canons of criticism that favor one poem and damn the next" (p. 2).

Although Graves is now not quite so scornful of classical, formal, rational poetry, he feels still that it is the illogical, metamorphic, romantic composition that is most likely to strike at the roots of the subconscious disturbances of its author and its readers, and thus to become a successful creation.

That romantic poetry, by virtue of its irrationality, its dreamworld quality, has been relegated largely to the realm of nursery-rhyme or nonsense-verse, is indicative of the fact that we are in the midst of an Age of Classicism, where logic and order prevail. The classical mode has always sought to suppress the romantic:

Poetry of the kind that we recognize as Romantic or Fantastic or Inspired being, as Coleridge first showed, dependent on associative thought, its symbolism being bound up with a vast number of false premises, a defiance of the ordered spatio-temporal structure which the civilized intellect has built for its habitation—this Poetry when Logic was first achieving pre-eminence under the Greeks, either had to be banned, or had to submit itself to a severe examination and systematization—hence Aristotle's *Poetics*. (p. 117)

So suppressed has the romantic, associative mode become that Freudian psychologists have come to believe it to be a survival of childish impulses, and Jungian psychologists have come to see it as an indication that civilized man retains the particularized memory of a savage state enjoyed by his ancestors. But Graves insists that the romantic mode is not infantile or primitive; that it has a definite place in civilized life; that associative, illogical thought is as modern and as reputable as characteristic, intellectual thought; and that only the analysis of a romantic poem will provide a key to the creative process of true poetry.

In this last point, as throughout *Poetic Unreason*, still following the theories of Rivers, Graves bases his argument on the proposition that the mechanism of the production of poetry is analogous to the production of dreams, and that the analyst of poetry must go about his task in precisely the same manner in which the psychoanalyst goes about his. From Rivers, Graves had learned that before the psychoanalyst can get at the real significance of a dream, he must first separate it from its "secondary elaborations" —the conscious order imposed upon it by the dreamer while in the process of recounting his dream to the psychoanalyst. The same holds true for poetry, Graves feels: before the analyst of a poem can determine its true worth, he must extract its original, unconscious sense from the layers of secondary elaboration the poet has employed to make it "a grammatical entity, a piece of history, a rhyme-scheme, a piece of word music" (p. 101); to make it conform, in other words, to some common-sense standard of form and logic. Classical poetry is that which exists solely for the sake of intellectual concept, embodied in a predetermined form; it is *all* secondary elaboration: it has no kernel of un-reasoned inspiration at its center. Only purely romantic poetry, existing prior to and outside of any logical system, will reward the reader with a glimpse of eternal, universal values.

There is in *Poetic Unreason,* however, evidence of a shift in Graves's theories at this time, in which the distinction between the romantic and classical modes no longer appears so clear-cut. In his chapter on secondary elaboration he uses as an illustration of his theories a comparison of two versions of "The Bedpost," a poem which had first appeared in *Whipperginny* (pp. 2-3), but which he had described in his Author's Note to that volume as "bankrupt stock of 1918." In its first version, the poem had been only a sentimental account of a little girl's amusing herself in bed by imagining that her bedpost was telling her bloodthirsty old legends and ghost-stories. According to Graves in *Poetic Unreason,* the poem, simple as it then was, nevertheless con-tained, in allegorical terms (at the time unrecognized by the poet), the account of an emotional conflict of Graves's: simultaneous love for his own young daughter and fear left over from the horrors of the late war. This unconscious conflict, along with a host of other hidden references, was recognized by Graves when he picked the poem up again three years later. It was, he saw, potentially also a symbolic representation, through the use of Freudian imagery, of the sexual struggle that awaits any young girl. With this discovery in mind, then, Graves revised the poem, retaining the old allegory and, by strengthening the sexual imagery (such as emphasizing the phallic nature of the bedpost itself), adding the new one. His idea now was that his readers might be "hypnotized," their subconscious minds attracted and held, by the repetition and intensification of the Freudian imagery, until the poem became for them not only a nursery-rhyme about a little girl but also a therapeutic device that should cure their own sexual trepidations. Just *how* it was to do this is not clear—like most pseudo-scientists Graves grows vague when he comes to the actual implementation of his theories—but what *is* clear is that the account of the development of "The Bedpost" represents a partial contradiction of his statements throughout the body of *Poetic Unreason* that the only true poetry is that which comes into full being organically and unbidden. For, if this last were the case, then the original version of "The Bedpost," which Graves rejected as being an imperfect and unrealized account of his struggle, would be the "true" poem; and the second version, which he favored as being a more logically worked-out presentation, would be, because of its secondary elaboration on the psychological plane, one step further from being a "true" poem. His Freudian applications tend toward an artificial, manufactured poetry, during the entire composition of which the rational, intellectual aspect of the poet's mind is in control; yet Graves says in this chapter that the creative process is not complete until the poet has written down his inspiration, organized it, and then come back to it again, to view it as a complete poetic experience—after which he is able to reorganize it so as to give it all the psychological significance it must possess if it is to have its desired effect. Somewhere in this confusing process the distinction between classical and romantic is almost totally submerged; and we can understand why Graves should say in his autobiography that "I rewrote [*Poetic Unreason*] in all nine times, and it was unsatisfactory when finished" *(Goodbye to All That*, p. 401). Graves, while remaining more or less true to his position that romantic poetry is the only true poetry, has since rejected most of the arguments of *Poetic Unreason* as wrong-headed and even mischief-making, and has himself written perhaps the best evaluation of the work:

The awkward position into which I had put myself by too close an interest in morbid psychology did not appear clearly until I tried, in *Poetic Unreason,* to elaborate my findings for academic purposes. . . . It remained a tangle of contradictions or difficult evasions of contradictions.[2]

Graves has always been more coherent as a commentator on the literary scene than as a theorist, and *Contemporary Techniques of Poetry: A Political Analogy,* published later in 1925 by the Hogarth Press, gives us a clearer view of him as a very astute, witty, and intuitive analyst of poetic trends. The analogy of the subtitle is between the Conservatives and Left-Wingers of Parliament and the Conservatives and Left-Wingers of poetry— who resemble closely the Classicists and Romanticists of *On English Poetry* and *Poetic Unreason.* The Conservatives are the staunch traditionalists of the Establishment, who believe in a God of Love, and who feel that "the Just, the Good, the Beautiful, though temporarily dimmed, must always have the last word: horror and pain must be under the strictest restraint. Squalor and filth must be kept out of sight."[3] They revere—and emulate —the poetry of Jonson, Milton, Gray, Pope, Landor, the later Tennyson, and Arnold.

The Left-Wingers are the "hooligans and atheists, neurotics and rowdies" whose attitude toward poetry is generally anarchical. Blunt sincerity is their chief characteristic. They dislike the Right and scorn the Center; they even distrust their fellow-revolutionaries, their only point of agreement being that rebellion is necessary. Their most prominent members are Aldous Huxley, Robert Nichols, T. S. Eliot, all three Sitwells, Ford Madox Ford,

2. *The Common Asphodel,* p. viii.
3. *Contemporary Techniques of Poetry,* p. 8. It is perhaps a sign of his own bias that Graves mentions as examples of poetic conservatism only three people, none of whose reputations have survived to the present: Reginald Cripps, Herbert Trench, and someone identified as "R. C. Macfie, an LL.D of Aberdeen."

Siegfried Sassoon, Isaac Rosenberg, Richard Aldington, and Gertrude Stein.

Between these two extremes are the Liberals of poetry, the Georgians, who write "verse of a sweet-flavored, well-mannered, highly-polished kind; free from heroics and rant on the one hand, and from roughness and violence on the other" (p. 10). The top Liberals are John Masefield, Edmund Blunden, Walter de la Mare, and A. E. Housman. Since they are basically non-controversial, Graves has little more to say about the Liberals in this pamphlet.

Outside these three classifications are poets like Thomas Hardy and Robert Frost, "who have not had to cultivate poetic simplicity or strength, because simplicity is their birthright and strength is in their daily habit of life" (p. 11). Their independence and hardiness have allowed them to stand aloof from the quarrels of the poetic factions, and Graves makes it clear that, while his own sympathies lie somewhere left-of-center, he admires the position of Hardy and Frost most of all.

The focus of attention in this brief but illuminating pamphlet is on the areas in which the two extreme factions oppose one another: in their views about diction, metre, rhyme, texture, and structure.

The argument about diction centers in the word *beauty*, concerning which each group makes its own violent claims. The Conservatives have a dualistic rule that all words can be classified as either poetical or non-poetical; the Left-Wing believes that all words and phrases are equally suitable for poetry, with the exception of those particularly recommended by the Conservatives, which they condemn as trite. Where the question of grammatic construction arises, the Conservatives permit certain well-established poetic inversions and distortions, but their freedom is generally restricted. The Left, however, "makes particular play with grammatic colloquialisms, false concords, omission of particles, false catenation, aposiopesis, with little interlarded phrases of French, German, Italian, Chinese, Volapuk, and beche-de-mer" (pp. 15-16).

With metre, the disagreement is over the amount of variation allowed on a conventional pattern, the direction of that variation, the legitimacy of evolving new patterns, the legitimacy of doing without patterns at all. Conservatism stands for "a jealous maintenance of metre in its strictly Victorian usage" (p. 24):

With the Conservative the prosody is always that of the five iambic feet and the caesurae that can have only three legitimate places. . . . The extra syllable at the end is forbidden by many, but by others permitted only as an occasional licence to register emotion or vary monotony. Its frequent use is regarded as decadence. (p. 25)

The Left-Wing may do almost anything to blank verse, and does. Most often, it regards metre as a rhythmic crutch on which words may be hung, believing that the true poet must make a rhythm that will please our ears for its own sake.

The Conservatives are of two minds about rhyme: some, following Spenser, Milton, and Campion, believe it must be eschewed; the majority, however, favor it. On the Left, rhyme is seen either as a silly ornament or as a device with which many liberties may profitably be taken.

Texture, which Graves acutely defines as "the relationship of vowels and consonants regarded as mere sounds" (p. 5), is regarded by the Conservatives as a means of achieving euphony, and, within the strict forms favored, variety. The Left either scorns all thought of texture as being "another of those heavy chains clamped on the naked limbs of poetry" (p. 30), or uses its knowledge of the art to supplement its ends, as Eliot does in the second line of this passage from *The Waste Land,* making a "realistic snuffle":

> Madame Sosostris, famous clairvoyante,
> Had a bad cold, nevertheless
> Was known to be the wisest woman in Europe,

and even leaving "an interval in the blank verse line for the nose to be blown" (p. 30).

As for structure, the problem is about what conventional

connections must be maintained between the individual ideas, or between the groups of ideas that make up a poem; about whether the connections should be predetermined, and whether any connection is desirable at all. The Conservatives believe that there are certain definite, prepared moulds into which any feelings or thoughts can and must be poured; the Left-Wing "will expect a poem to have any growth it pleases, provided that it is organic growth" (p. 41). As examples of this, Graves cites *The Waste Land,* the *Spoon River Anthology,* and Edith Sitwell's *Sleeping Beauty.*

Graves is posing here as the disinterested historian who is attempting merely to point out that a conflict in poetic standards exists, and to outline the areas in which the battle is being fought. But it is obvious at once that, while he has some misgivings about the excesses of the Radicals, he nevertheless is in favor of any movement which will root English poetry out of what he considers a slough of spiritless traditionalism. He deplores, for instance, the utter chaos of Gertrude Stein's poems; but he insists that he has great respect for the sincerity, the depth, and the "mental strength and activity" of her work. But in *Contemporary Techniques of Poetry* Graves's personal prejudices, usually an integral part of his criticism, are kept for the most part in the background, and his very acute discussions of the technical aspects of modern poetry make the pamphlet a useful one, particularly for the student of recent literary movements. Perhaps most important of all, however, to the student of Robert Graves is the evidence this work provides that, if Graves preferred to remain faithful to nursery-rhymes, ballads, and Skelton as his favorite models, this was not because of any ignorance of what prosodic experiments were being made around him. He was very much aware that many of his contemporaries were becoming famous— or at least notorious—through their experiments and innovations in metre and poetic organization; yet he continued to employ traditional forms in his own poetry, and to strive for originality only in his attitude toward his subject-matter. While theatricality has too often marred his criticism, he was striving at this time, as we have seen, to keep his poetry free from it.

In 1926, shortly before he left England for Egypt, Graves was prompted by the publication of two recent works which questioned the usefulness of poetry to modern society to write a short defense of that art. The two studies were Robert C. Trevelyan's *Thamyris; Or, Is There a Future for Poetry?* (New York, 1925), and J. B. S. Haldane's *Daedalus; Or, Science and the Future* (London, 1924). Graves's defense, published once again by the Hogarth Press, was entitled *Another Future of Poetry*, and consisted of a step-by-step refutation of the arguments of Trevelyan and Haldane, followed by "an independent forecast" of the function of poetry in the twentieth century.

Trevelyan's thesis was that poetry had lost its force and usefulness progressively as "it ceased to be chanted or sung, and began a new life as the spoken, written, or printed line" (*Another Future of Poetry*, p. 5). Poetry, Trevelyan felt, had become weakened when it ceased to be sung; that is, when it began to appeal more to the eye than to the ear. Graves's rebuttal to this was that "poetry read silently and poetry spoken aloud are divergent arts" (p. 7); that the authors of each kind have entirely different aims and techniques, and that their compositions must be evaluated by their own standards. Oral poetry, such as that practiced in ancient times by the Anglo-Saxons, and more recently by such upholders of the bardic tradition as Vachel Lindsay, must be of simple content, and must be addressed primarily to the "outward ear," which

has a far shorter memory than the conjunction of eye and inner ear. It readily forgets end-rhymes separated by more than three intervening lines, unusual words recurring at a longish interval, and structural signposts of various kinds; but it has a far greater sensitivity to the variation of vowel and consonant, to internal rhyme, and to awkward concurrence of consonants.  (p. 7)

Most modern poetry, on the other hand, strives for a "highly concentrated content" which appeals to the "inward eye," and which is "impossible to hear with enjoyment until it has been read and thoroughly digested by the eye" (p. 8). Moreover, modern poets have begun experimenting with a number of typographical and organizational tricks which, by appealing initially to the "outward eye," seek to reach and direct the "inward ear." Graves feels that these two kinds of poetry need not be so mutually exclusive, and that poets of the future "will be concerned for a start with the problem of how the outward ear, which carries with it the inward eye, and the outward eye, which carries with it the inward ear, may be satisfied by the same poem equally" (p. 9). This problem, he maintains, is "partly of word-mechanics and partly of psychology," and will involve a study not only of the senses of sight and hearing, but also of the "subsidiary senses"— smell, touch, taste—which, while they are not the "direct means by which we take in poetry, as inward senses they are the most important vehicles of thought, and must be used to give completeness to the poetic life" (p. 11). Graves believes, then, that Trevelyan is wrong in asserting that the ascendance of visual poetry necessarily implies the deterioration of the art; and prophesies for the future a kind of poetry which, benefiting from modern phychological knowledge, will find a means of appealing simultaneously to *all* the senses.

That poetry has the power to do this is the basis for Graves's response to Haldane's work, the thesis of which resembles that of Thomas Love Peacock's a century before, to which Shelley had responded in *his* defense of poetry: that "Poetry is in decay because poetry has lost touch with science; and science is the chief interest of the average Englishman today" (p. 16); and that prose is a much more effective means of dealing with contemporary problems and interests than poetry.

Graves admits that modern poetry has little appeal for the modern Englishman, and that "prose is what people read, while poetry languishes"; but he argues that this need not be; that "there is no reason why modern verse should not become to modern prose what the airplane is to the motor car" (p. 24). For poetry has a number of intrinsic virtues which make it in-

herently superior to prose: its rhythms, rhymes, and texture have
"an actual toxic effect on the central nervous system"; and, most
importantly, "besides the greater vividness of image and strengthening of music, the heightening of receptivity and sensitivity
that verse properly handled brings, there is another great contri-
bution: that is the awareness of a whole region of hidden association and implication behind phrases that in prose would be accepted at their face value" (p. 25). Furthermore, Graves questions Haldane's premise that the public is really greatly concerned
with science, and suggests that the average Englishman not only
knows little about science, but also that he is actually incapable
of understanding more than the simplest rudiments of any scien-
tific system. The only literary way of "reaching" him with any
worthwhile knowledge must be through some vehicle which appeals primarily to his feelings; and it is for this reason that poetry
—sensuous, non-intellectual poetry, that is—is a better vehicle than
prose.

In *Another Future of Poetry* we see Graves once again as a
poet who is vitally concerned with the techniques of his craft, and
who is convinced that the pragmatic function of poetry is, potentially at least, a primary concern of the poet. He believes at
this stage in his career (even if his practice in the later *Whipperginny* poems and in *Mockbeggar Hall* does not correspond very
closely with his theories) that poetry's chief aim is to enhance the
mental and emotional health of its author and its readers; and his
concern is the development of a poetry which will perform this
function most effectively. In *Poetic Unreason* he attempts to
establish the importance to poetry of an understanding of modern
psychological theories, and to investigate the nature of the creative
process; and in *Another Future of Poetry* he is more specific about
the way in which the poet can utilize the technical devices available to him so that his poetry will accomplish its purpose. Why
Robert Graves should seem at this time in his career as a poet to
be turning his back on his own theories, to be in effect ignoring
the responsibility that he had set for the poet, is not entirely clear.
The most likely answer, as I have suggested above, is that the

popular and critical failure of his own subjective and sensuous earlier work, coupled with his suspicions that he was in danger of writing his way out of the very difficulties on which his strength as a poet depended, caused him to turn from the romantic attitude of his "true" poet to the more abstract and cerebral poetry he predicted for those writers who have lost the impulses of romance.

# 6

# Preparation for Departure

There were a number of reasons besides his failure as a public poet that caused the five years at Islip to be unhappy ones for Robert Graves; for they were, as he says in his autobiography, clouded by "many deaths and a feeling of bad luck" (*Good-bye to All That*, p. 405): Sir Walter Raleigh and W. H. R. Rivers had died in England, and George Mallory, his old Charterhouse master and friend, had been lost on the slopes of Mount Everest. With the exception of Siegfried Sassoon, there were few old army friends left. Edmund Blunden had gone to Tokyo as a professor of English literature; T. E. Lawrence was now in the Royal Tank Corps; and Basanta Mallik had returned to India. Their friends gone, Graves and Nancy became increasingly worried about their own financial insecurity, and Graves grew willing by 1925 to undertake almost any writing job that would bring in money. He wrote a series of rhymes which were to be part of an advertising campaign for a biscuit company; some "silly lyrics" for a light opera which was never staged; some translations of Dutch and German Christmas carols; rhymes for children's Christmas annuals; and edited three pamphlets of verse for Ernest Benn's series, *The Augustan Books:* selections from Skelton's poems, a collection of the less familiar nursery-rhymes, and a group of twenty-three poems culled from his own volumes.[1] He did some verse-reviewing for the *Nation* and *Athenaeum* until 1925, when he "found it more and more difficult to be patient with dud books of poetry" *(Good-bye to All That,* p. 408). He wrote a ballad-opera, *John Kemp's Wager,*[2] which was an "artificial simple play for performance by village societies," and which was performed only once, in California, where reviewers called it "delightfully English and quaint" *(Good-bye to All That,* p. 407).

Not everything that Graves wrote during the period of depression from 1925 to 1927 was for money's sake alone, however: there was, of course, *Another Future of Poetry;* and there were his contributions to the new and very radical quarterly, *The Calendar of Modern Letters,* in which he confirmed the suspicions aroused in *Contemporary Techniques of Poetry* that, in the controversy between the Conservatives and the Left-Wingers of poetry, he now stood definitely left-of-center. And, most importantly, there was another small volume of new poems: *Welchman's Hose,* published as a limited edition by the Fleuron Press of London in 1925, and containing several of the best poems of Graves's second period.

Although the concern with philosophical and psychological problems still informs much of the poetry of *Welchman's Hose,* there are signs that Graves was beginning now to effect a degree of fusion between his intellectual theories and his hitherto constrained impulses toward a poetry of primarily emotional appeal; that is, he was now attempting to apply his theories to life, to illustrate them—as he had begun to do in *The Feather Bed*—rather than to state them objectively. The result was a number of poems in this volume that have considerably more "body" to them than those of *Whipperginny* and *Mockbeggar Hall.*

The opening poem in *Welchman's Hose,* "Alice" (pp. 1-2), does not, however, go far in this direction, and indeed is another lesson in relativity and the inapplicability of reason and logic to

1. *Robert Graves: The Augustan Books of Modern Poetry, No. 13* (London: E. Benn, 1925).
2. Oxford: Blackwell, 1925; and New York: S. French, 1925.

certain important areas of experience; but it does at least suggest
that Graves had succeeded in reaching a point at which he no
longer feared that the true poet must necessarily immerse himself
totally in a world of irrationality and nightmare. The poem is,
as J. M. Cohen suggests, in part "a fresh and more successful
treatment of the 'North Window' theme,"[3] although written on
a lower emotional level: Alice, "that prime heroine of our nation,"
climbs through the Looking Glass into a world where reality
appears to be reversed. Unfettered by any conventional philosophical notions of correspondence, she refuses "with proper
British phlegm" to assume that the strange world beyond the glass
is necessarily analogous in any way to the "real" world of Victorian
England, governed by the traditional concepts of Time and Space.
The other world will be "queer," but it will be true to its own
rules; and Alice, filled with common sense and "simple faith in
human strategem," can learn those rules and in only six moves
win her crown in the Game of Chess:

> For Alice though a child could understand
> That neither did this chance-discovered land
> Make nohow or contrariwise the clean
> Dull round of mid-Victorian routine,
> Nor did Victoria's golden rule extend
> Beyond the glass: it came to the dead end
> Where formal logic also comes; thereafter
> Begins that lubberland of dream and laughter,
> The red and white flower spangled hedge, the grass
> Where Apuleius pastured his Gold Ass,
> Where young Gargantua made full holiday;
> But further from our heroine not to stray,
> Let us observe with what uncommon sense,
> Though a secure and easy reference
> Between Red Queen and kitten could be found,
> She made no false assumption on that ground
> (A trap in which the scientist would fall),
> That queens and kittens are identical.

3. *Robert Graves*, Writers and Critics, No. 3 (Edinburgh, 1960), p. 41.

While the domain of unreason may be the proper dwelling place of the poet, we can infer from "Alice" that the poet need not fear it as a limitless realm which must encroach on the boundaries of everyday reality. The world on the other side of the Looking Glass, if it is not controlled by Victorian logic, nevertheless is not chaotic or frightening; it has its own rules, and the poet may enter and leave it at will.

"From Our Ghostly Enemy" (pp. 5-7), a very Frostian narrative poem, is also a poem which one is tempted to take as symbolic autobiography.[4]  It is the story of a man who is haunted by a spectre that distorts and warps everything the man tries to do, and constantly tempts him to violent action.  He appeals to his wife, who gives him some simple but efficacious advice:

> "Husband, of this be sure,
> That whom you fear the most,
>     This ghost, fears you.
>
> "Speak to the ghost and tell him,
>     'Whoever you be,
> Ghost, my anguish equals yours,
> Let our cruelties therefore end.
>     Your friend let me be.' "
>
> He spoke, and the ghost, who knew not
>     How he plagued that man,
> Ceased, and the lamp was lit agin,
> And the dumb clock ticked again,
>     And the reign of peace began.

Once again, as Cohen points out, the theme is "the diversion of fear"[5]: when the ghost that has plagued us is faced, and a truce is made with him, then our fear evaporates and we can live in peace.

4. We are perhaps justified in doing this by the fact that Graves has admitted the autobiographical significance of his poems. See, for instance, his Foreword to *Poems and Satires, 1951* (London: Cassell, 1951), p. viii, in which he says that "A volume of collected poems should form a sequence of the intenser moments of the poet's spiritual autobiography. . . ."

5. *Robert Graves*, p. 43.

Luckily for Graves's career, however, his preoccupation with the supernatural and the irrational was not for long dispelled by any of his attempts to enter into a "reign of peace"; for in "The Presence" (p. 39), certainly the most moving poem in this period of his career, another man is driven almost to insanity by his grief over the survival of his departed wife's spirit. He will not accept her death, because "death" to him implies absolute extinction.

> Why say Death? for Death's neither harsh nor kind:
> Other pleasures or pains could hold the mind
> If she were dead; for dead is gone indeed,
> Lost beyond recovery and need,
> Discarded, ended, rotted underground.

And his wife's spirit is still all about him, occupying his mind, denying to it any room for "other pleasures or pains":

> But living still, barred from accustomed use
> Of body and dress and motion, in abuse
> Of loving-kindness (for our anguish too
> Denies we love her as we swear we do).
> She fills the house and garden terribly
> With her bewilderment, accusingly
> Enforcing her too sharp identity,
> Till every stone and flower, bottle and book,
> Cries out her name, pierces us with her look,
> "You are deaf, hear me!
> You are blind, see me!"
>           How deaf or blind,
> When horror unrelieved maddens the mind
> With those same pangs that lately choked her breath
> And changed her substance, but have brought no death?

The haunting here, like that in "From Our Ghostly Enemy," is an inward haunting, the function of a tormented imagination, the real source of man's greatest fears; and such poems as these prompt us to believe that there was more than a little justice in Graves's correlation between his neuroses and his best poetry.

This is not to say, however, that Graves could be effective only when dealing with his fear-theme. There are two poems in *Welchman's Hose,* one very simple and one very complex, that bear no relation to it, and that must be counted as among his most enduring achievements. One of these, a four-line diversion called "Love Without Hope" (p. 21), recalls the sentimental nursery-rhymes of the early volumes, but surpasses all of them by the economy and precision with which the poet communicates a complete experience, funny and yet touching at the same time:

> Love without hope, as when the young Bird-catcher
> Swept off his tall hat to the Squire's own daughter,
> So let the imprisoned larks escape and fly
> Singing about her head, as she rode by.

The second poem is "The Clipped Stater" (pp. 40-44), ad-dressed when first published[6] to T. E. Lawrence, in which Graves, equating Lawrence with Alexander the Great, tells the story of how Alexander, frustrated by his inability to find new worlds to conquer, throws away his crown and his divinity; and, carried away to a remote corner of the world by a djinn, enlists as a private in the army of an Oriental potentate. (The parallels with the life of Lawrence, who had now become plain Aircrafts-man Shaw, are obvious.) While serving as a guard along the barren north border of his adopted kingdom, Alexander is paid with a coin that bears his own profile upon it.

What is remarkable about this long (104 lines) poem is that its total effect is one of unity and coherence, in spite of the fact that Graves employs in it every mode of thought—except the themes of love and fear—that had governed his poetry up to this time. His initial attitude is one of playful irony, as he describes Alexander's discomfort as a God:

> He would not take a Goddess to his Throne
> In the elder style, remembering those disasters
> That Juno's jealous eye brought on her consort.
> Thaïs was fair; but he must hold his own.

6. *The Calendar of Modern Letters,* I, No. 1 (March, 1925), pp. 25-26.

Nor would he rank himself a common god
In fellowship with those of Ind or Egypt
Whom he had shamed: even to Jove his father
Paid scant respect (as Jove stole Saturn's Nod).

When Graves describes Alexander's being caught up by the djinn, the poem takes on the bemused and wondering tone of the early fairy-tale verses; and the mood changes yet again to one of matter-of-fact realism in the descriptions of Alexander's new life as an enlisted man.

And he grows grey and eats his frugal rice;
Endures his watch on the fort's icy ramparts,
Staring across the uncouth wildernesses,
And cleans his leather and steel; and shakes the dice.

And, finally, when Alexander sees his own head on the silver stater he is given, Graves turns the poem into a metaphysical disquisition on his favorite theme of this period: the relative nature of divinity. Can he really have been God, Alexander wonders, if his omnipotence could be limited—if God could be "by his own confines accursed"?

Was his lost Empire, then, not all-embracing?
And how does the stater, though defaced, owe service
To a God that is as if he had never been?

What gives the effect of unity to this potentially diffuse poem is something quite simple: the fact that, more than a consideration of man's mind and the nature of things, it is an organically bonded fiction—a narrative, complete with beginning, middle, and end, about a single man; and its strength as a poem lies not so much in the ingenuity with which the mood is varied, as in the mythic quality it gains from the character of Alexander, the presence of the supernatural elements, and the way in which its action spreads over so much time and space.

In January, 1926, Graves, Nancy, their four children, and the American poetess Laura Riding[7] sailed for Egypt, where the influence of Lawrence, Arnold Bennett, and others had gained Graves the post of Professor of English Literature at the newly-founded University of Cairo. His tenure there was brief; for after a year, irritated by the climate, the curriculum, and the faculty, he resigned and led his entourage back to England. Once resettled there (this time in a houseboat on the Thames, in London), and sensing that a major shift in the direction of his literary career was imminent, he began what he calls in his autobiography (p. 438) "a process of tidying-up" which resulted in the publication of the final work of his second poetic period: *Poems, 1914-1926*.[8] This process was not so much collective as it was selective, in that it amounted to a disavowal of almost half the poetry that Graves had so far published. *Poems, 1914-1926*, then, is the first instance of what was to become a series of frequent and ruthless excisions and revisions of the Graves canon.

He was harshest, as we might expect, on the volumes of his early period: out of the hundred and thirty-six poems of *Over the Brazier, Fairies and Fusiliers, Country Sentiment,* and *The Pier-Glass,* only fifty-one now survived. With those of the second period he was considerably more lenient: thirty-one of *Whipperginny's* fifty-two, eleven of *Mockbeggar Hall's* sixteen, and fourteen of *Welchman's Hose's* eighteen were kept. All of *The Feather Bed* except the Prologue and Epilogue was deleted. Graves appears to have been reasonably satisfied with poems he allowed to remain, for almost all of them appear in *Poems, 1914-1926* substantially as they had appeared at the time of their first publication.

There are also (counting the nine new pieces of *Poems, 1914-*

7. Because her connection with Graves is a complex one, and is one of the chief concerns of Part III, I refrain here from indicating more than Miss Riding's presence.
8. London: Heinemann, 1927. Some months later Heinemann also published *Poems, 1914-1927,* which was actually only a limited edition of *Poems, 1914-1926,* differing from it only in that it contained nine additional poems composed too late for inclusion in the earlier volume. Because of their near-identity, I shall consider the two volumes together.

*1927*) twenty-seven poems that had been written after the publication of *Welchman's Hose* and before the return from Egypt.
Anthony Thwaite, in his recent survey of contemporary poetry,[9]
while admitting that most of these poems have a "tart, individual
flavour," feels that they have little body—that they are "fragmentary . . . simply pieces of fancy or whimsy." While it is
certainly true that several are little more than semi-playful satiric
exercises in the Skeltonic style that Graves had cultivated from
the beginning of his career, Thwaite is quite inaccurate in stating
that Graves's inclination at this time was toward "pieces of fancy
or whimsy." For the majority of these poems of 1925 and 1926
suggest, on the contrary, that Graves was perhaps more despondent
at this time than at any other stage of his career, and that he was
disposed to display this despondency in his poetry.

Thwaite probably bases his generalization on a few poems like
"The Marmosite's Miscellany"[10] (*Poems, 1914-1926*, pp. 181-89)
and "The Philatelist-Royal" (*Poems, 1914-1927*, pp. 225-26), in
which Graves seeks for the most part only to display his considerable skill as a metrist and rhymester. Most of these, like
"The Philatelist-Royal," have only their cleverness to recommend
them:

> The Philatelist-Royal
> Was always too loyal
> To say what he honestly
> Thought of Philately . . .
> Must it rank as a Science?
> Then he had more reliance
> (As he told the Press wittily),
> In Royal Philately
> Than in all your geologies,
> All your psychologies,
> Bacteriologies,
> Physics and such.

9. *Contemporary British Poetry: An Introduction* (London, 1959), pp. 130-35.
10. Originally published, with Graves using the pseudonym of "John Doyle,"
in *The Calendar of Modern Letters*, II, No. 7 (Sept., 1925), pp. 1-14; later the
same year published separately by the Hogarth Press.

Of these lighter poems, only "The Marmosite's Miscellany," which Graves has called "a long reckless satire" (Foreword, *Collected Poems, 1938,* p. xxii), exhibits a concern with more than patter. Using a scholarly monkey on display at a World Exhibition as his mouthpiece, the poet comments scathingly on the state of modern literature. The marmosite first belittles the Georgians, led by Graves's old mentor, Edward Marsh (one suspects that an unwillingness here to be caught biting the hand that had fed him is what prompted Graves to use a pseudonym when he first published the poem), then goes on to attack the posturings of Yeats and Eliot, the philistinism of Arnold Bennett, the dark mutterings of D. H. Lawrence, and all the fashionable modernists whose practice it is to take

> A sniff at every flask
> And a lick at every stopper;

and finally concludes with a gloomy assessment of the way in which modern poets have lost their public:

> We serve a lost cause: does any pride remain
>    In prolonging tradition beyond its due time,
> Giving it lip-service, mumbling and vain,
>    With a measured metre and expected rhyme?
> Morning and evening our ancient bells chime,
> Yet the whole congregation could sit in one pew,
> The sexton, the verger, and old folk one or two.

If there is anger in "The Marmosite's Miscellany," it is of a playful sort, tempered by the absurdity of the garrulous monkey and by the jingle of the metre and rhyme. But in many of these later poems—the ones that Anthony Thwaite does not consider— anger predominates; and, in poems the moods of which range from despondency to fury and even near-despair, Graves directs his attacks at optimists, at sensualists, at devotees of poetry, at the corrupt use of language—and even at the failings of the poet himself.

"O Jorrocks, I Have Promised" (*Poems, 1914-1927*, pp. 221-
22), a bitter complaint against the impositions that are made
on a poet's time, concludes with a sardonic mock-prayer:

> O Jorrocks I have promised
> To serve thee to the end,
> To entertain young Indians,
> The pupils of my friend,
> To entertain Etonians
> And for their sake combine
> The wit of T. S. Eliot,
> The grace of Gertrude Stein.
> Be thou forever near me
> To hasten or control,
> Thou Literary Supplement,
> Thou Guardian of my soul.
> I shall not fear the battle
> While thou art by my side,
> Nor wander from the pathway
> If thou wilt be my guide.
>                    Amen.

In "Virgil the Sorcerer" (*Poems, 1914-1926*, pp. 174-77) Graves
cites the legend of how Virgil of Toledo, a magician of the
twelfth century, used his occult powers to charm himself and his
fellow-prisoners out of their dungeon. Then, having given this
instance of the tremendous force that is potential in magic,
Graves asks himself if he too has the ability to work such spells,
and concludes despairingly that for him even to hope for such a
thing is vanity: he, like most would-be magical poets, is a Virgil
at best "only one night in twenty," and lacks the resolution to
free himself and his readers from their cells:

> . . . Time the limiter wears us to rags
>    Aided by Doubt and Sloth, demons of spite
> Whose daily fouling soaks the dungeon flags
>    And splashes the long wall on which we write

> Till we at last grow filthy; we condone
>   The unmoving present: on a mound of mud
>   We loll red-eyed and wan, whittling a bone,
>     Vermined, the low gaol-fever in our blood.

The poet is here seen as corrupted by the decadence of his age; and in other poems of this final group Graves lashes out often at the banality and depravity of contemporary society. "Blonde or Dark?" (*Poems, 1914-1926*, pp. 208-9), which blames society's ills on sensualists who call for "women, drink, and snuff," is a surprisingly puritanical poem that evokes memories of the schoolboy's disgust with physical love Graves had long before expressed in "Oh and Oh!" of *Over the Brazier;* and "Hell" (*Poems, 1914-1927*, pp. 219-20) describes the glee with which the devil accumulates the lifeless, meaningless words and phrases by which society maintains itself, and stores them up in his great sack, along with "Husks, rags and bones, waste paper, excrement," to be fed to damned souls.

The way in which we use language to shield ourselves from the force of reality is treated with less phlegm and more philosophy in "The Cool Web" (*Poems, 1914-1926*, pp. 215-16).

> Children are dumb to say how hot the day is,
> How hot the scent is of the summer rose,
> How dreadful the black wastes of evening sky,
> How dreadful the tall soldiers drumming by.

We adults, however, have a "cool web of language" that we use to spell away the heat of the sun, the scent of the rose, the awesomeness of the night and the marching soldiers. Yet, though our volubility robs life of its savor, it is necessary if we are to preserve our sanity:

> But if we let our tongues lose self-possession,
> Throwing off language and its wateriness
> Before our death, instead of when death comes,
> Facing the brightness of the children's day,
> Facing the rose, the dark sky and the drums,
> We shall go mad no doubt and die that way.

We must choose, then, between a life of half-tones and a life of madness; our reason cannot cope with the force of existence unless that force is dissipated through a web of abstract, opaque verbiage. There is no suggestion here, as there was in "Alice," that it is possible—especially for the true poet—to survive in a world of unreason. The climax of all this negativism is reached in "The Dead Ship" (*Poems, 1914-1927*, p. 220),[11] in which life is seen as a hopeless voyage on an unseaworthy ship manned by a surly crew. The navigational charts are all blank, but this matters little; for we have absolutely no control over the ship's direction:

> Though you enlarge your angry mind
> Three leagues and more about the ship
> And stamp till every puncheon skip,
> The wake runs evenly behind.

And the destination to which we are so inexorably drawn is only

> The turning-point of wretchedness
> On an uncoasted featureless
> And barren ocean of blue stretch.

There are two love-poems in this final group, but as we have already noted, love is no longer taken by Graves to be more than a momentary, fleeting means of relief from the general bleakness of life. The first of these, "This is Noon" (*Poems, 1914-1926*, p. 207), returns to the themes of "Song of Contrariety" and "Full Moon": love is too fragile, too ephemeral to withstand either the full force of moonlight or of daylight—it hides from these, and the lovers' only hope is that it will reappear undiminished when darkness returns. In Graves's poetry it seldom does reappear, however; like most of the worthwhile things of life, he implies, love will be destroyed, and we must therefore make the most of it while it survives. The other love-poem, "Pure Death" (*Poems, 1914-1926*, p.

11. Retained in *Poems, 1926-1930*, as "Ship Master," and changed to "The Furious Voyage" in *Collected Poems, 1938*.

214), must surely stand as the high point of Graves's achievement
during the second period of his career.  All the horror a resurgence
of the old fear-theme can bring is here, heightened by the peculiar
yet highly effective diction that is one of the outstanding characteristics of Graves's mature poetry—a style that might be described as midway between Latinate and literary-colloquial, always precise, always restrained, sometimes almost dry, sometimes
almost elegant.

> This I admit, Death is terrible to me,
> To no one more so, naturally,
> And I have disenthralled my natural terror
> Of every comfortable philosopher
> Or tall dark doctor of divinity:
> Death stands again in his true rank and order.
>
> Therefore it was, when between you and me
> Giving presents became a malady,
> The exchange increasing surplus on each side
> Till there was nothing but ungivable pride
> That was not over-given, and this degree
> Called a conclusion not to be denied,
>
> That we at last bethought ourselves, made shift
> And simultaneously this final gift
> Gave.  Each with shaking hands unlocks
> The sinister, long, brass-bound coffin-box,
> Unwraps pure Death, with such bewilderment
> As greeted our love's first accomplishment.

That the ultimate gift in a love affair should consist of the mutual
surrender of their innermost selves, which the lovers had until
then held back from giving through pride, is an entirely fitting,
and perhaps rather conventional, point for a love-poet to make.
But that this surrender should reveal their terror of death, unabated by any philosophical or religious assurances, is a conclusion
that makes the poem unique—the sort of thing that only Robert
Graves would be likely to write.

What we find in this second period of Graves's career, then, is his attempt to make himself over into the sort of poet he was temperamentally disinclined to be.  He has always been a scholarly man (though admittedly of a type that is the despair of more conventional academicians), but he was at this time, as throughout his career, far too sanguinary and intense to deal objectively in his poetry with the psychological and metaphysical concerns that now intrigued him so.  As becomes apparent in the few completely realized poems of this period, Graves is at his best with subjects that allow him to exploit his fascination with the grotesque, the terrifying, even the disgusting.  In those poems in which he affects a cynical detachment or a mocking aloofness from the grosser aspects of love or fear, he is often clever and ingenious.  But there is a coldness about such poems that repels the reader.  They do not touch us, and we are somehow offended by our realization that they could not have touched him very deeply, either.  Perhaps we are too much like those readers Graves inveighs against in his Author's Note to *Whipperginny,* who "demand unceasing emotional stress in poetry at whatever cost to the poet"; but the best poems of this period—those in which the fear-theme leads Graves into his negative but moving considerations of love, pain, and death—are ample evidence that Graves attains full poetic stature only when the unceasing emotional stress is there.

# Part Three

## Self-exile to Majorca:
## The Influence of Laura Riding

7

# Graves and Riding:
# The Critical Collaborations

"In 1925 I first became acquainted with the poems and critical work of Laura Riding, and in 1926 with herself; and slowly began to revise my whole attitude to poetry."[1] Such statements as this by Robert Graves about what must surely be one of the most unusual partnerships in literary history are indeed provoking, because he seldom enlarges upon them: about the precise nature of his indebtedness to Miss Riding, as about most of his life since 1927—the date at which *Good-bye to All That* leaves off—Graves has been extremely reticent (and Miss Riding has never once made any direct reference publicly to her friendship with him). There is much, therefore, concerning the crucial thirteen years of Miss Riding's influence about which we can only guess.[2] But from the few statements, direct and indirect, that Graves has made from time to time about these years, and from what little of her autobiography Miss Riding has divulged, it is still possible at least to outline the main points of their association.

1. Foreword, *Collected Poems, 1938,* p. xxiii.
2. And we must be careful about our guessing. As Graves has written to me, "The trouble about these literary essays is that they have to leave out the most important things because libellous."

In the brief personal sketches she has submitted from time to time to Stanley Kunitz for inclusion in his valuable brief accounts of modern authors,[3] we learn that Laura Riding was born in New York City in 1901 "of Jewish (but not religiously so) parents" (*Twentieth Century Authors,* 1942, p. 1173); that, while a student at Cornell in 1923, she married Louis Gottschalk, a history instructor there; and that she and Gottschalk were divorced in 1925. We know that she began writing poems while at Cornell, and that in 1924 John Crowe Ransom and his Nashville colleagues awarded her a prize of $100 for her poems, some of which they published in their journal, *The Fugitive.* We are also told that in December, 1925, after having tried her literary fortunes in New York for a short period, she left for Europe, where she spent the next thirteen years, living chiefly in Egypt, England, Majorca, and France; that she returned to the United States in 1938; and that in 1941 she married Schuyler Jackson, "poet, farmer, and contributing editor of *Time*" (*Twentieth Century Authors,* 1942, p. 1173). She and Jackson now live in Wabasso, Florida, and make their living "by shipping and growing citrus fruits" (*Twentieth Century Authors,* 1955, p. 483).

It is, of course, those thirteen years in Europe that concern us most about Laura Riding's life; and it is Graves who supplies us with all the information we are likely to have on this period until the passage of time allows for a more exhaustive and less discreet study of their partnership.

From the concluding paragraphs of *Good-bye to All That,* and from a highly allusive and ambiguous "Dedicatory Epilogue to Laura Riding" appended to the first edition of that work, we can reconstruct a somewhat fragmentary record of the early years of the Graves-Riding alliance. It began in 1925 when Graves and Nancy, having been impressed by a Riding poem they had read in *The Fugitive* (Graves cited this poem, "The Quids," as a superior example of Leftist verse in *Contemporary Techniques of*

---

3. *Authors Today and Yesterday* (New York, 1933), pp. 564-66; *Twentieth Century Authors* (New York, 1942), p. 1173; *Twentieth Century Authors* (New York, 1955), pp. 482-83.

*Poetry,* pp. 19-20), invited its author to visit them in England.[4] Fresh from her divorce, and apparently not faring well financially in New York, Miss Riding accepted the invitation, and arrived in London early in 1926.[5] Once they had met, there was an immediate rapport between the two poets ("a unity to which you and I pledged our faith and she [presumably, Nancy] her pleasure");[6] and when the Graves family left for Egypt that spring, Laura Riding went along.

On their return to England in 1927 Graves and Miss Riding began learning the technique of hand-printing, and soon founded the Seizin Press, by which they proposed to publish works by themselves and by other writers who shared their own rather iconoclastic views of literature and society.   (The first fruits of their literary collaboration were not, however, published by the Seizin Press: *A Survey of Modernist Poetry* was brought out in 1927 by Heinemann, and *A Pamphlet Against Anthologies* was published in 1928 by Jonathan Cape.)

In April, 1929, Miss Riding almost died from injuries sustained in a fall from a fourth-story window; and the following month Nancy separated from Graves, taking the children with her. Three months later *Good-bye to All That* was completed, and Graves left England for good.   This much we know from his autobiography.[7]

From subsequently published references to this phase of his life we learn that, on the recommendation of Gertrude Stein (whom he met in Paris soon after leaving London),[8] Graves went

4. Louise Cowan, in *The Fugitive Group* (Baton Rouge, 1959), p. 146, states that Graves at this time also offered Miss Riding a teaching position at the University of Cairo.

5. From Philip Horton, in his *Hart Crane: The Life of an American Poet* (New York, 1937), p. 181, we learn that before her association with the Graves family she spent some time as the close companion of Crane.

6. *Good-bye to All That,* p. 444.

7. In his Prologue to the 1957 edition of his autobiography, Graves says of the initial version of *Good-bye to All That* that "it was my bitter leave-taking of England where I had recently broken a good many conventions; quarreled with, or been disowned by, most of my friends; been grilled by the police on a suspicion of attempted murder; and ceased to care what anyone thought of me."

8. Cf. "Why I Live in Majorca," *5 Pens in Hand* (New York: Doubleday, 1958), p. 15.

to the island of Majorca and settled in Deyá, a small fishing and olive-producing village on the mountainous northwest coast of the island.   Still an invalid, Laura Riding went with him; the Seizin Press was re-established; and the literary partnership was taken up where it had been left off in England.

The next nine years were highly productive ones for both of them.  Between 1929 and 1938 Graves published six volumes of poetry[9]; five novels, mostly historical (which, of course, brought him far more fame and money than any of his poetry and criticism had)[10]; a short play, never produced[11]; as well as several short stories and a number of essays on various non-literary subjects.

In addition to *A Survey of Modernist Poetry* and *A Pamphlet Against Anthologies,* Graves cooperated with Laura Riding on two other ventures: a satirical novel entitled *No Decency Left,* written under the joint pseudonym of "Barbara Rich" and printed by the Seizin Press in 1932; and in the founding and editing of an eccentric literary annual which they called *Epilogue: A Critical Summary,* and which, as Graves has said, "commended increasing inattention in literary circles"[12] during its three years of existence.[13]

The coming of the Spanish Civil War in 1936 caused Graves and Miss Riding to disband the Seizin Press and to leave Majorca. They travelled for some time on the Continent until, in 1938, Miss Riding returned to America and Graves to England, where he soon published his *Collected Poems, 1938*—the work which stands as a summation of and farewell to his third poetic period, as *Poems, 1914-1926,* had done for his second.

9. *Poems, 1929* (Deyá, Majorca: Seizin Press, 1929); *Ten Poems More* (Paris: The Hours Press, 1930); *Poems, 1926-1930* (London: Heinemann, 1930); *To Whom Else?* (Deyá, Majorca: Seizin, 1931); *Poems, 1930-1933* (London: A. Barker, 1933); and *Collected Poems, 1938* (London: Cassell, 1938).

10. *The Real David Copperfield* (1933), *I, Claudius* (1934), *Claudius the God and His Wife Messalina* (1934), *Antigua, Penny Puce* (1936), and *Count Belisarius* (1938).

11. *But It Still Goes On* (1930).   Reprinted in Graves's *Occupation: Writer* (New York: Farrar, Straus and Cudahy, 1950), pp. 121-94.

12. *The Common Asphodel* (London: Hamish Hamilton, 1949), p. 224.

13. Vol. I (Autumn, 1935), Vol. II (Summer, 1936), and Vol. III (Spring, 1937) published simultaneously in Majorca by Seizin and in London by Constable.

It is not, then, until we examine their work during these thirteen years that we gain any real insight into the nature of the relationship between Graves and Miss Riding. When we do this we are struck by the fact that, although Graves was the elder (by six years) and better known poet, it was obviously Laura Riding who was the dominant partner. There are probably at least two reasons for this condition: first, the unusually aggressive and forceful personality of Miss Riding; and, second, Graves's extraordinary receptivity to the ideas and enthusiasms of others— the same trait which had caused him earlier to come so strongly under the successive influences of George Mallory, W. H. R. Rivers, T. E. Lawrence, and Basanta Mallik. In other words, the relationship between Miss Riding and Graves was determined by her desire to teach, and by his willingness to learn.[14] Miss Riding was, moreover, an ardent feminist, and felt that the traditional superiority of the male was an illusion that must be dispelled:

I like men to be men and women to be women; but I think that bodies have had their day. The fundamental relation which has to be made is between the male mind and the female mind, and in this relation the female mind is the judge, and the male mind the subject of judgment. But the male mind has now had all the time there is for working up case.[15]

14. Louise Cowan (*The Fugitive Group*, pp. 184, 223), takes note of Miss Riding's aggressiveness in her dealings with Messrs. Ransom, Tate, Davidson, *et al.*: "She was not really influenced by the Fugitive approach to poetry; indeed, some of the men were later to feel that, far from being a disciple, she would have liked to take the Fugitives over and influence *them*." Later, when Tate and Edmund Wilson began planning a poetry series to be brought out by the Adelphi Press, which was to include the works of Miss Riding, Phelps Putnam, Tate, Malcolm Cowley, Hart Crane, Wilson, and John Peale Bishop, Miss Riding tried to assume the leadership of the project "and ended by causing some little dissension." The idea for the poetry series was abandoned after Miss Riding sailed for England (a departure doubtless accompanied by sighs of relief from the gentlemanly Fugitives).

15. Quoted in Kunitz, *Authors Today and Yesterday*, 1933, p. 565. Horace Gregory and Marya Zaturenska, in their *A History of American Poetry, 1900-1940* (New York, 1942), p. 381, recall the rumor that in her house in Deyá the following inscription was written in large gold letters on her bedroom wall: "GOD IS A WOMAN." Graves denies this rumor: the only inscription, he claims, was "Here is escape then, Hercules, from empire," written in blue chalk.

Graves had displayed in several of his earlier poems an already
firm conviction that women deserved to be taken as the equals, at
least, of men (see especially "Ovid in Defeat" in *Welchman's
Hose,* and "Pygmalion to Galatea" in *Poems, 1914-1926*); and
Laura Riding's aggressive intellectuality must have strengthened
conviction even further.[16]

Whatever the psychological motivations behind this curious
relationship, there is little doubt that Laura Riding caused
Graves substantially to modify his poetic practice, and that his
influence on her work was negligible (she ceased, in fact, to write
poetry altogether by 1938). In *Epilogue,* too, for which she was
the editor and Graves the assistant, Miss Riding's voice, always
positive and often downright arrogant, was the stronger. And
in the critical works on which the two collaborated one recognizes
that same strident voice, only occasionally tempered by the humor
and generosity which had been redeeming factors in Graves's
earlier studies of poetry.

Because the two insist in their prefatory note to *A Survey of
Modernist Poetry,* and again in their Foreword to *A Pamphlet
Against Anthologies,* that these works were the products of a
"word-by-word collaboration," we must assume that Graves gave
his wholehearted support to the arguments and assertions of these
works, even if they seemed occasionally at variance with his earlier
views. We shall therefore consider these two volumes as expressive
of what Graves felt at this time about the profession of poetry.

*A Survey of Modernist Poetry* is a statement of their opinions
about the present condition of poetry and of poetry criticism in
England and America. The purpose of the work is to consider
the then popular notion that modernist poetry is willfully and
needlessly obscure; that the rights of the plain reader (whoever
that is) are being violated by poets who have apparently no feel-

16. One is tempted by these reflections to speculate about the reasons why, in
all of his novels of this period (and, for that matter, in his later ones as well),
Graves's women are invariably stronger—more masculine, in fact—than his men.
And Randall Jarrell, in "Graves and the White Goddess," *Yale Review,* XLV
(Winter, Spring, 1956), pp. 467-78, asserts confidently that the White Goddess is
little more than a transmogrification of Laura Riding. There is, as we shall see,
at least a partial justification for this notion.

ings of obligation to them.  Graves and Miss Riding feel that the crux of the argument between the reading public and the modernist poet is their different definition of *clarity*.  Both groups, they say, agree that perfect clarity is the end of poetry; but the reading public insists that no poetry is clear except that which it can understand at a glance, while the modernist poet insists that the clarity of which the poetic mind is capable demands thought and language of a far greater sensitiveness and complexity than the reading public will permit it to use.  Poetry obviously demands a more vigorous imaginative effort than the plain reader is willing to apply to it; and, if the poet is to remain true to his conception of what poetry must be, he has to run the risk of seeming obscure and freakish, and of having no reading public.  The modern obscurists do not *mean* to keep the public out of their poetry; but for them to write to suit public taste would require them to violate the integrity of their art.  The responsibility for communication is as much the reader's as the poet's: "The reader's rights to the poem are, presumably, like the poet's, whatever his intelligence is able to make of them" (*A Survey of Modernist Poetry*, p. 25).

The authors make a distinction between "modernist" and "modern."  The "modern" poet, who makes his claim for originality solely on the basis of his historical contemporaneity, his use of current mannerisms and public devices, is no real poet: he is only catering to public tastes, or at the least playing for a fleeting notoriety.  "A poet of today who considers himself a modernist because he is successfully keeping up his date is, however low his opinion of Tennyson may be, merely an earnest Tennysonian" (p. 150).

The true "modernist" poet, on the other hand, places his faith not in history but in the immediate performances of poems not necessarily derived from history.

A strong distinction must be drawn between poetry as something developing through civilization and as something developing organically by itself. . . .  Poetry does develop in the sense that it is contemporaneous with civilization; but it has to protect itself from contemporaneous influences rather than woo them, since there is no merit in believing in modernism for modernism's sake. One must always therefore keep this distinction in mind: between what is historically new in poetry because the poet is acting as a barker for civilization, and what is intrinsically new in poetry because the poet is an original interpreter of the fortunes of mankind.  (p. 154)

Modernism for Graves and Miss Riding implies independence, not relying on any of the traditional devices of poetry-making or on any of the effects artificially achieved by using the atmosphere of contemporary life to startle, or to convey reality.  Obviously, then, in making their defense of the reaction from the Georgian poetry of the first two decades of the twentieth century, they are not saying that modernist poetry is necessarily good because it is *new*.  Their attacks on poetry which has only newness to recommend it are contained in their discussion of "dead movements."

A dead movement is one which never had or can have a real place in the history of poets and poems.  It occurs because some passing or hitherto unrealized psychological mood in the public offers a new field for exploitation, as sudden fashion crazes come and go, leaving no trace but waste material.  (p. 116)

Imagism is one of the earliest and the most typical of these twentieth-century dead movements.  Originally, "it had the look of a movement of pure experimentalism and reformation in poetry" (p. 116); but by issuing its public manifesto, by organizing itself as a literary party with a defined political program, by anthologizing itself, Imagism revealed itself to be a "stunt of commercial advertisers of poetry to whom poetic results meant a popular demand for their work, not the discovery of new values in poetry with an indifference to the recognition they received" (p. 117).  They decided beforehand the kind of poetry that was wanted by the time, and they wrote to satisfy the demand; they wanted to be *new* rather than to be poets.  Their forms of modernism, which were supposedly undertaken in the interests of the plain reader, with their aims of simplicity ("the use of the language of everyday speech") and discarding of poetical padding which had prevailed in earlier fashions of poetry, sacrificed matter for the sake of new manner. So with Georgianism, another dead movement. As a reaction from Victorianism, it sought to discard all archaic diction and all formally religious, philosophic, or "improving" themes. It was to be English yet not aggressively imperialistic; pantheistic rather than atheistic; and "as simple as a child's reading book" (p. 119). This was all to the good, perhaps, but the final result was that Georgianism could better be praised for what it was not than for what it was. Eventually, the poets and the plain readers both became tired of it at about the same time.[17]

The poets whom Graves and Miss Riding do not like (and there are many of them) are either those members of dead movements who, like Carl Sandburg, write poetry which "will be preferred by readers because it can give them as much innocent enjoyment as a good short story or their newspaper or an up-to-date jazz orchestra" (p. 100); or those who, like Wallace Stevens, Ezra Pound, and "H. D.," are so concerned with questions of form—or rather, of formlessness—that their poetry lacks meaning.

In their discussion of the characteristics of true modernist poetry, we see some of the poets to whose work they are willing to grant at least grudging approval. These are Edith and Sacheverell Sitwell, who have written good poetry in spite of their exploitation of modern painting theory; Herbert Read and Archibald MacLeish, who have not been entirely impeded by their penchant for psychological theorizing (a curious qualifica-

---

17. It is interesting to note that Roy Campbell, whose career paralleled Graves's in several respects, published the following year a catechism for Georgian poets which was an even more succinct *coup de grâce* to the movement than that of Graves and Miss Riding:
1. Have you ever been on a walking tour?
2. Do you suffer from Elephantiasis of the Soul?
3. Do you make friends easily with dogs, poultry, etc.?
4. Are you easily exalted by natural objects?
5. Do you live in one place and yearn to live in another place?
6. Can you write in rhyme and metre?
As prime examples of poets who should answer these questions affirmatively, Campbell suggests Walter de la Mare and Robert Graves. Cf. Roy Campbell, "Contemporary Poetry," *Scrutinies, By Various Writers* (London, 1928), pp. 161-80.

tion, coming from the author of *On English Poetry* and *Poetic Unreason*); D. H. Lawrence, a genuine poet in spite of his clumsy sex-engrossment; T. S. Eliot, whose desire to display his encyclopaedic learning does not always hide his real talent as a lyricist; and E. E. Cummings, whose typographical and organizational outrages are sincere attempts to force the lazy plain reader to pay attention to the serious themes of his poetry.

Not all, however, of the poets the authors respect are, in the authors' sense, "modernist" poets. There are some of whom "modernism" is used merely to describe a certain independence of mind, without definitely associating them with modernism as a cause: "though content to stay in the main stream of poetry they make judicious splashes to show they are aware of the date" (p. 160). Of this group are Siegfried Sassoon, John Crowe Ransom, and—most especially—Robert Frost, whose nature poems are "perhaps the only unaffected ones of our period" (p. 161).

Yeats is their example of that class of poets who "have had neither the courage nor the capacity to go the whole way with modernism and yet do not wish to be left behind." They note how Yeats, who, "observing that his old poetical robes had worn rather shabby, recently acquired a new outfit" (p. 161).

The commentaries on the state of contemporary poetry in 1927 are for the most part very apt and timely; and the dissections of the dead movements show a shrewd and relatively objective attitude toward literary fashion. In their evaluations of individual poets, however, Graves and Miss Riding are led by their own somewhat idiosyncratic tastes and their self-imposed roles as disgruntled exiles to give way too often to extreme subjectivity. They are heavily partisan: willing to praise their favorite poets unabashedly, they can only with the greatest difficulty find anything positive to say about a poet who has for some reason offended them. In partial extenuation of this subjectivity, one must remember that Cummings and Ransom, at least, were new stars in the poetic firmament at this time, and that Graves and Miss Riding, being the first to spot them—for English readers, at any rate—

might naturally be expected to have a proprietary interest in them. In any case, the doctrinaire ardor of the authors, even while expressing itself in a wholesale demolition of contemporary reputations, does not prevent them from saying a number of fresh and pertinent things about poetry—most of which occur in the handling of individual poems.

Indeed, what has made *A Survey of Modernist Poetry* a work of importance to literary criticism has been the analysis of Shakespeare's Sonnet 129 ("Th' expense of Spirit in a waste of shame") as compared with the poetic practice of E. E. Cummings. By means of a brilliant and intricate close analysis of the sonnet, the authors demonstrate how much of its meaning is distorted and lost by modernization of spelling and punctuation.

Shakespeare's emendators, in trying to make him clear for the plain man, only weakened and diluted his poetry. Their attempts to make Shakespeare easy resulted only in depriving him of clarity. There is but one way to make Shakespeare clear: to print him as he wrote or as near as one can get to this. Making poetry easy for the reader should mean showing clearly that it is difficult. (p. 75)

Cummings' poems share with Shakespeare's a "deadly accuracy": Cummings "expresses with an accuracy that is peculiar to him what is common to everyone"; Shakespeare "expresses in the conventional form of the time, with greater accuracy, what is peculiar to himself" (p. 63). And, as it is ruinous to alter Shakespeare's very conscious spelling and punctuation in his sonnet, so it would be harmful to tamper with the textual and syntactical irregularities of any Cummings poem.

The method of explication Graves and Miss Riding use here and elsewhere in *A Survey of Modernist Poetry*—precise and meticulous scrutiny of the logical, rhetorical, and grammatical aspects of poems considered as autonomous—made a great impression on the youthful William Empson, and provided him with the technique he was to develop two years later in *Seven Types of*

*Ambiguity.*[18]   It is no wild claim to make, therefore, that the
Graves and Riding system of *explication de textes* as employed in
*A Survey of Modernist Poetry* is one of the cornerstones on which
the New Criticism rested.

Although many of their fellow-poets are set up as targets in
their first collaborative venture, Graves and Miss Riding make the
chief villain of the work the poor "plain" reader, who they say
has become so slothful and dull that he can respond only to the
simplest, blandest poetic gruel, stocked with clichés and obsolete
poetic diction, and absolutely free from any disturbing qualities
that might force him to use his brain.

We have already noted, in Part II, Graves's growing scorn
for the public that refused to recognize him and to accept the
therapy his poems offered; and we have seen, in *Another Future
of Poetry,* how little faith Graves had by that time in the public's
ability to comprehend anything much above the most elementary
levels of complexity.   His exasperation with the plain reader in
*A Survey of Modernist Poetry* should hardly surprise us, then—
especially when we learn that this was an attitude which Laura
Riding shared equally with him.   In the preface to her *Collected
Poems,*[19] she explains how the backward and lazy reader must be
led by the hand through her poems if he is to understand them at
all:

My poems would, indeed, be much more difficult than they have
seemed if I did not in each assume the responsibility of education
in the reasons of poetry as well as that of writing a poem.   Because
I am fully aware of the background of miseducation from which
most readers come to poems, I begin every poem on the most

18. Stanley Edgar Hyman, in *The Armed Vision* (New York, 1955), p. 263, quotes
from the Spring, 1940, issue of *Furioso,* in which I. A. Richards gives an account of
the genesis of *Seven Types.*   Empson "brought up the games of interpretation
which Laura Riding and Robert Graves had been playing with the unpunctuated
form of 'The expense of spirit in a waste of shame.'   Taking the sonnet as a
conjurer takes his hat, he produced an endless swarm of lively rabbits from it and
ended by 'You could do that with any poetry, couldn't you?' . . . So I said, 'You'd
better go off and do it, hadn't you?' "   Hence, *Seven Types of Ambiguity.*   Empson
himself acknowledges, in his prefatory note to *Seven Types* (London, 1930), that his
method derived from that of Graves and Miss Riding in *A Survey of Modernist
Poetry.*

19. London: Constable, 1938; and New York: Random House, 1938; p. xvii.

elementary plane of understanding and proceed to the plane of poetic discovery (or uncovering) by steps which deflect the reader from false associations, false reasons for reading. No readers but those who insist on going to poems for the wrong reasons should find my poems difficult; no reader who goes to poetry for the right reasons should find them anything but lucid; and with few other poets are readers so safe from being seduced into emotions or states of mind which are not poetic.

Laura Riding thus throws the blame for any failure in communication entirely on the reader: if one of her poems seems impenetrable to him, it is because of his own ignorance or "false reasons for reading." Implicit in Miss Riding's statement is the point she and Graves had made in *A Survey of Modernist Poetry:* that, while the poet may contrive to force-feed his poems to a reluctant reader, he must on no account demean himself or his art by diluting those poems so that they are palatable to the ignorant public.

This same point is part of the thesis of *A Pamphlet Against Anthologies,* the second Graves-Riding collaboration, which is that popular anthologies subvert the cause of true poetry by pandering to the childish public taste—by including only old favorites which the reader must have learned in school; by revising, editing, and bowdlerizing originally true poems until they too hold out no challenge; and—perhaps worst of all—by directing the reader to modern poets who are currently fashionable, or to bygone poets whose stock is in the ascendant at the time of the anthology's publication. This sort of thing, Graves and Miss Riding claim, is what the reader wants, and they mock him for his simple-mindedness; but their greatest scorn is for the anthologist, who strives to reap financial benefits from the public's insipidity, instead of offering it poems which will make it sharpen its intelligence and sensibility.

Not *all* anthologies are bad, however; there are the occasional "true" anthologies, which can be one of two types: the rescue-anthology, which confines itself to the collecting of poems that would otherwise be lost—"popular ballads, epigrams, epitaphs, squibs, stray lyrics, and even longer poems that have irretrievably lost author and date" (*A Pamphlet Against Anthologies,* p. 11); or the strictly non-professional, non-purposive collection, such as the poet's or amateur's scrap-book, which is not intended for any but the smallest amount of circulation. As examples of the first type the authors mention Child's *English and Scottish Ballads,* Lomax's *Cowboy Songs and Frontier Ballads,* and Bullen's *Lyrics from the Elizabethan Songbooks*; and as an example of the second type, the Commonplace Book kept by Woodhouse, Keats's friend.

Any sort of collection that falls outside these two categories is a "trade" anthology, and as such merits the scorn of the authors. After tracing the history of this type from the numerous *Beauties of the Poets* collections of the late 1700's, through Palgrave and Quiller-Couch in the nineteenth century, to Untermeyer in the twentieth, Graves and Miss Riding examine the "ideal" trade anthologist, and speculate on his methods of choosing and editing his poems. First of all, he must be an expert in literary booms.

He will have to know, for instance, the exact upward popularity curve of Donne, Marvell, Skelton, Blake, Clare and others, and the exact downward curve of Burns, Byron, Tennyson, Browning, Swinburne, as revealed by an exhaustive historical chart of previous booms and depressions in poets. (p. 51)

The ideal anthologist must then, having chosen his poets, select from their works the simplest poems he can find, never considering whether they are in the least representative of their authors. He must not hesitate to delete passages that are likely to disturb his readers, or to retitle and repunctuate the poems as he sees fit. He must be modest, "as tender of the virgin mind of his putative public as an old-fashioned mother of her daughter's, or a new-fashioned daughter of her mother's." And to this modesty he must add a great gift for stupidity in the face of any difficult passage in a poem: "At the first glimmer of any possible obscurity he must shut his eyes tight and pass on in search of something easier" (p. 59).

After alloting his page-space to his poets in descending order of generosity according to their current reputations, the ideal anthologist must draw up a list of subjects from which to choose his poems, always including Love (of which there are three sorts: Triumphant, Renunciatory, and Christian Mystic), Hunting, Farm Life, a Sea Piece, a Spring Piece, a Poem about a Train, a Poem about England and/or the Stars and Stripes, a Poem about a Dead Child, etc. Finally, his collecting and sorting done, the ideal anthologist writes a preface which is either cute or pompous, depending on the tone of his volume, and the anthology is complete.

*A Pamphlet Against Anthologies* exhausts its rather slender thesis in the first three of its nine chapters, and continues on in the same raffish and flippant mood through the remaining six, which are devoted mostly to even more outrageous attacks on the weaker poems of their contemporaries than the authors had made in *A Survey of Modernist Poetry*. Their study of Yeats's "Lake Isle of Innisfree,"[20] in particular (ostensibly chosen because of its popularity as an anthology-piece), is a comic masterpiece of malicious criticism. Taking the poem apart line by line, and scrutinizing each segment with mock-objectivity, Graves and Miss Riding succeed in making it and its author look foolish. They even compose a little epigram called "Inisfree on its Author" to serve as a tail-piece to their critique:

> In the Senate house in Dublin
> My old honest author sits
> Drinking champagne on the proceeds
> Of his early loss of wits.

Graves has, we see, come a long way from the days when he was so fond of *The Wanderings of Oisin*.

For all its cleverness, *A Pamphlet Against Anthologies* is light stuff, almost certainly not intended to be taken very seriously. It is, however, an indication of the scorn felt by Graves and Miss Riding for almost all authors, publishers, and readers of poetry. Graves made his attitude even clearer in an address to the Teacher's Union in London, delivered on Guy Fawkes' Day, 1928, shortly after the publication of *A Pamphlet Against Anthologies*:

20. Which the authors, linguistic purists, consistently misspell "Inisfree."

. . . people have not realized that it is now several years since I considered you, the aggregate public.   When I write now, I write only to please one thing, and that is the sense of what the poem I am writing ought to be intrinsically, and I don't care at all whether you, the aggregate public, like it or not. . . .   The aggregate public is an aggregate disorder without seriousness or truth—its members are concerned only in *doing the right thing.*[21]

We find, then, that in 1927 and 1928 Graves's theory of poetry had caught up with what his own poetic practice had been (or, rather, what it had aimed at being) since 1923, when he sought to turn his back on his public and write only for himself and those few who shared his psychological and philosophical concerns.   In his "November 5th Address" he says that there are "two familiar ways of not writing poetry": one is through "fantasia"—that poetry which is analogous to dreaming, in that it is "fully intelligible only in a limited personal context, though the unconscious recognition by its readers of common pathological symbols occurring in it may give it wide currency."   Its chief weakness is that it is "not fully removed from the author."   The other sort of non-poetry is "classicism," which still denotes for Graves that poetry which is deliberately and rationally conceived, independently of any inspiration on the part of the poet.

"Fantastic" poetry is, of course, what Graves had earlier championed in *On English Poetry* and *Poetic Unreason,* and what he had tried to write before 1923; and "classical" poetry is what, in effect, most of his practice amounted to in the second period of his career—although, as we have noted, he was not always successful in suppressing the metamorphic, romantic element.

The critical work of Robert Graves's third period is, then, a repudiation of the theories he had espoused in his preceding studies of poetry, and a rejection of both of his earlier modes of composition.   What sort of poetry he proposed to write now, and how much he was guided in his choice by Laura Riding, is the subject of the next two chapters.

21. "November 5th Address," first printed in *X: A Quarterly Review,* I, no. 3 (June, 1960), pp. 171-76.

# 8

# Poetry of the
# Laura Riding Years (I)

In the conclusion to *Good-bye to All That,* as we have noted, Robert Graves gives the impression that his association with Laura Riding led him to a sort of poetic rebirth, a change of heart in which he discarded one set of values and adopted another. In the Foreword to *Collected Poems, 1938,* after confirming this impression, he ends by saying (p. xxiv), "I have to thank Laura Riding for her constructive and detailed criticism of my poems in various stages of composition." Such admissions of indebtedness have led almost all of Graves's critics to assume that the influence of Laura Riding on both his attitude toward poetry and his poetic practice was indeed great. An anonymous reviewer in the *Times Literary Supplement* for Friday, 5 June, 1959, says of Graves that there is "little doubt" that it was through his association with Miss Riding "that he reached full stature as a poet." Roy Fuller has stated that "One may guess that it was Miss Riding's stern critical standards that finally expunged from his verse not only the remains of the anodynic tradition, but also those extended and sterile satirical versifications, the chummy literary verse letters, the imitations of Skelton, and so forth, that

he was still writing up to 1925"; and that the poems he wrote
during the time of Miss Riding's influence "constitute . . . Graves's
real achievement."[1] Generally agreeing with this view is Geoffrey
Bullough, who feels that during this time Graves's work grew
"more stable, terse, and controlled in form."[2]

Only three critics have felt that Laura Riding's influence was
at all harmful to Graves. Horace Gregory, while admitting that
it has ultimately proved beneficial, suggests that the first results
of the partnership "cramped Graves's style"[3]; Nelson Algren believes that Miss Riding's direction caused Graves's poetry to become introverted ("He seems to be speaking . . . more and more
to himself")[4]; and J. M. Cohen states that her "puritanical"
theories produced in Graves a tendency to "turn away from
feeling . . . to the neglect of all emotional or spiritual overtones."[5]

Without more tangible evidence of the exact nature of Miss
Riding's influence, it is impossible to determine precisely the
extent of that influence. How much of Graves's development
during this period is due to Miss Riding, how much is the result
of other factors, and how much may be taken as a logical and
predictable extension of his earlier work? A brief glance at Miss
Riding's own work will help us answer these questions.

First of all, her concepts of the nature and function of poetry
were indeed, as Cohen says, "puritanical": she believed poetry to
be ideally nothing less than the last repository of Truth, the only
vehicle for the display of human thought in its pure form.
Poetry should be freed from extrinsic decoration, superficial contemporaneity, and—above all—didactic bias. It should not be
expressive of any religious or philosophical belief, for all such
beliefs are corrupt; neither should it be used to preach any political or social goals—that is the function of prose. The real poet's
only concern is for the poem itself.

1. "Some Vintages of Graves," *The London Magazine*, V, No. 2 (February, 1958),
pp. 56-59.
2. *The Trend of Modern Poetry* (London, 1949), p. 77.
3. "Robert Graves: A Parable for Writers," *Partisan Review*, XX, No. 1
(January-February, 1953), pp. 44-54.
4. "Sentiment With Terror," *Poetry*, LV (1939), pp. 157-59.
5. *Robert Graves*, Writers and Critics, No. 3 (Edinburgh, 1960), p. 51.

The right reasons for going to poetry cannot be very different from those that a poet must have if the poem is to be a poem and not reading-matter interesting on other grounds than those of poetry. A poem is an uncovering of truth of so fundamental and general a kind that no other name besides poetry is adequate except truth. Knowledge implies specialized fields of exploration and discovery; it would be inexact to call poetry a kind of knowledge.[6]

Poetry, for Miss Riding, is literally the good life:

Our own proper immediacies are positive incidents in the good existence which is poetry. To live in, by, for the reasons of, poems is to habituate oneself to the good existence. When we are so continuously habituated that there is no temporal interruption between one poetic incident (poem) and another, then we have not merely poems—we have poetry; we have not merely immediacies—we have finality. Literally. . . . And so I say, not within the suppositious contexts of religion but within the personally actual contexts of poetry: literally, literally, without gloss, without gloss, without gloss. So read, so exist: with your very best reasons. (*Collected Poems*, pp. xxvii, xxviii)

Perhaps because of this pursuit of literal perfection, Miss Riding was led in her own practice to produce poems that were entirely abstract and lifeless: intent on excluding whatever seemed to her to be "unpoetic," she composed, after much thinning, straining, and refining of words and feelings, poems that were often delicate, but more often only dryly cerebral and coldly theoretical:

The rugged black of anger
Has an uncertain smile-border.
The transition from one kind to another
May be love between neighbor and neighbor;
Or natural death; or discontinuance
Because, so small is space,
The extent of kind must be expressed otherwise;

6. Preface to her *Collected Poems* (London, 1938), p. xviii.

> Or loss of kind when proof of uniqueness
> Confutes the broadening edge and discourages.
>
> *(Collected Poems,* p. 59)

Such lines as these, moreover, so lacking in verbal discipline and
rhythmic pattern of any kind, cause one to disbelieve that Miss
Riding could have taught Graves, from the earliest days of his
career a highly skilled technician, much about prosody. And even
in her most "experimental" verse Miss Riding seems to do little
more than emulate Gertrude Stein:

> What to say when the spider
> Say when the spider what
> When the spider the spider what
> The spider does what
> Does does dies does it not . . .
>
> *(Collected Poems,* p. 86)

Unless Miss Riding was better able to advise Graves than herself, then, it is unlikely that she did much to improve his technical
performance.[7]

   There are, however, certain aspects of Graves's poetry during
this period that probably reflect the practical influence of Miss
Riding. She was, for one thing, given to composing whimsical
fantasies in which the actions of sub-human figures were intended
to provide a satiric commentary on mankind's failings. Her
"Quids" *(Collected Poems,* p. 30), identically fuzzy atomic particles of the great "Monoton," long for individuality and independence of action.

> The quids, that had never done anything before
> But be, be, be, be, be—
> The quids resolved to predicate,
> To dissipate in grammar . . .

7. I ought to note here that Graves agrees not at all with my brief evaluation
of Miss Riding's achievement as a poet. For him, still, "she was the arch poet of
her generation"; and he prophesies that by 1983 readers of this book will see as its
greatest flaw my blindness to Miss Riding's worth. Perhaps he is right.

A quid here and there gyrated in place-position,
While many turned inside-out for the fun of it . . .
By ones, by tens, by casual millions,
Squirming within the state of things,
The metaphysical acrobats,
The naked immaterial quids,
Turned in on themselves
And came out all dressed—
Each similar quid of the inward same,
Each similar quid dressed in a different way,
The quid's idea of a holiday.

But

Oh, the Monoton didn't care,
For whatever they did—
The Monoton's contributing quids—
The Monoton would always remain the same.

The implications are that we are all quids, our petty distinctions only covering a basic sameness, and that whatever we do has no effect at all on the Monoton—God or the Universe, we must suppose.

Miss Riding satirizes the insensitive and timorous in her poem about the "Tillaquils" (*Collected Poems*, p. 22), a little couple, "nearly a man and a woman," who are afraid to love, and who avoid facing life—and death—by engaging on a ceaseless round of delicate and wistful dancing which takes them

To nothingness and never;
With only a lost memory
Punishing this foolish pair
That nearly lived and loved
In one nightmare.

Such poems as these probably prompted Graves to revive his early fondness for the grotesque, for we find him turning often during this period to wry accounts of the more disreputable supernatural creatures. But where Laura Riding's fantasies are brittle and abstract, Graves's are tough-minded, concrete, and often coarser than anything he had done before.

In "Railway Carriage" (*Poems, 1929,* pp. 16-17), for example, he tells of a religious revival on a beach near a Welsh village that is interrupted by a procession of ectoplasmic creatures who issue silently from the caves nearby. As these ghostly figures move slowly (out of time with the revivalists' band) toward the sea, they are approached by the pompous mayor of the village, who attempts to address them. Only the last apparition stops to hear him, after which it makes a terse rejoinder: a loud belch. Then, having issued this brief evaluation of Welsh stuffiness and religious fundamentalism, it fades into the sea.[8]

In "Ogres and Pygmies" (*Poems, 1930-1933,* p. 13), Graves sets up a contrast between "Those famous men of old, the Ogres" and effete, effeminate modern man, represented by the Pygmies. The Ogres were marvelous creatures indeed:

> They had long beards and stinking arm-pits.
> They were wide-mouthed, long-yarded, and great-bellied . . .
> With their enormous lips they sang louder
> Than ten cathedral choirs, with their grand yards
> Stormed the most rare and obstinate maidenheads,
> With their strong-gutted and capacious bellies
> Digested stones and glass like ostriches.

But the Ogres are gone now, and in their place are

> . . . the sweet-cupid-lipped and tassel-yarded
> Delicate-stomached dwellers
> In Pygmy Alley.

We ought, says Graves, to laugh heartily at the spectacle provided by both extremes—by the noisome violence of the Ogres, and the fragrant prissiness of the Pygmies—but it is a measure of our own "disproportion" that we do not.

8. In *Collected Poems, 1938* (p. 114), Graves retitled this poem "'Welsh Incident," and, moved by an inexplicable and uncharacteristic niceness, changed the belch to "a very loud, respectable noise—like groaning to oneself on Sunday morning in Chapel"—thereby robbing the poem of a large degree of its humor.

Another playful grotesque of this period is the priapic "Down, Wanton, Down" (*Poems, 1930-1933*, p. 5), in which Graves admonishes, with affectionate contempt, an intractable part of himself (to use G. S. Fraser's euphemism):

> Down, wanton, down! Have you no shame
> That at the whisper of Love's name
> Or Beauty's, presto! up you raise
> Your angry head and stand at gaze?
>
> Poor bombard-captain, sworn to reach
> The ravelin and effect a breach,
> Indifferent what you storm or why
> So be that in the breach you die!

Graves's renewed impulse toward the *outré* does not always, however, lead to humor. In "The Beast" (*Ten Poems More*, pp. 6-8),[9] perhaps his grisliest piece, Spenser's Blatant Beast refuses to die after being overcome by the Red Cross Knight, and lives on to torment his opponent. Although everyone publicly rejoices at what they think to be the destruction of the Beast— here, the necessary evil in the Universe—secretly their hearts are full of "doubt and rue." Because of their regret at his death, the Beast will not stay dead:

> Therefore no grave was deep enough to hold
> The Beast, which after days came thrusting out
> Wormy from rump to snout,
> His draggled cere-cloth foul with the grave's mould.

The villagers tie stones about him and toss him into the sea; but he paddles back to shore, "With deep-sea ooze and salty creaking bones." They attempt to burn him; but "With stink of singeing hair/ And scorching flesh" the dragon's corpse rolls from the pyre. The Knight is overcome by shame because of his failure to kill the Beast, not realizing in his saintliness that the people do

9. Changed to "Saint" in *Poems, 1926-1930;* in *Collected Poems, 1938,* and in all subsequent collections, the first three verses, in which Graves explains the function of the Blatant Beast in the *Faerie Queen,* are deleted.

not really want the Beast to die.  Daily growing more horrible, it attaches itself to the Knight and will not leave him; and finally, when the Knight dies, it creeps into his bed beside him.

Graves's point in this poem seems to be that evil is necessary to man because, as long as it exists, they can hope for salvation if they overcome it.  If it *is* ever overcome, however, the hope is gone, for there is no salvation—the Beast does not disappear, but becomes "carrion and a worse/ Than carrion."

Many of Graves's poems during this period also reflect Laura Riding's fondness for ingenuity and the exercise of wit.  But where she too often sacrificed logical coherence for the sake of verbal cleverness, Graves always maintains a tight control of his meaning.  In "Warning to Children" (*Poems, 1929,* p. 5), for example, his argument is that all purely speculative thought can only set in motion an endless pattern of meaningless though not unattractive nonsense; and the pattern of his verse illustrates very aptly the way in which such speculations lead one into a series of ever-contracting and expanding cycles that end always where they had begun:

> Children, if you dare to think
> All the largeness, smallness,
> Fewness of this single only
> Endless world in which you say
> You live, you think of things like this:—
> Lumps of slate enclosing dappled
> Red and green, enclosing tawny
> Yellow nets, enclosing white
> And black acres of dominoes.
> In the acres a brown paper
> Parcel, then untie the string.
> In the parcel, a small island,
> On the island a large tree,
> On the tree a husky fruit,
> Strip the husk and cut the rind off,
> In the centre you will see
> Lumps of slate enclosed by dappled

> Red and green, enclosed by tawny
> Yellow nets, enclosed by white
> And black acres of dominoes.
> In the acres a brown paper
> Parcel, leave the string untied.
> If you dare undo the parcel
> You will find yourself inside it . . .

In "The Tow Path" (*Poems, 1929*, p. 21),[10] which seems at first to be more nonsensical than "Warning to Children," Graves nevertheless manages to emerge from a series of puns, neologisms, and anagrams with a commentary on the relationship between art and sin:

> Anagrammatising
> Transubstantiation,
> Slily deputising
> For old copopulation
> SIN SAT ON A TIN TAR TUB
> And did with joy his elbows rub.

> Art introseduced him
> To females dull and bad,
> Flapper flappings, limb-slim,
> From his blonde writing-pad,
> The river girlgling drained of blood—
> Post-card flower of kodak mud.

> By such anagrammagic
> And mansturbantiation
> They fathered then this tragic
> Lustalgia on the nation,
> And after that, and after that,
> ON A TIN SIN TUB ART SAT

Where Graves is most like Laura Riding, however, is in his "In Broken Images" (*Poems, 1929*, p. 3), an intellectual exercise

10. Changed to "Anagrammagic" in *Poems, 1926-1930*, and afterwards deleted from the canon.

in which the argument is elaborated solely for the establishment
of a pattern of opposites.

> He is quick, thinking in clear images;
> I am slow, thinking in broken images.
> He becomes dull, trusting to his clear images;
> I become sharp, mistrusting my broken images.
> Trusting his images, he assumes their relevance;
> Mistrusting my images, I question the fact.

The poem goes on to construct four more steps out of statements
and counter-statements, and one is left with the impression that
he has read something clever, but something which is not about
anything in particular.  As Ronald Hayman has said, "its development is quite haphazard: its only incentive to go on seems to be
the hope of finding chances to echo phrases or balance their
opposites against them."[11]  In spite of its pattern, its poise, and
its cleverness with words, it is a slight poem, the total abstraction
of which marks it as uncharacteristic of Graves.

There is one other note in Graves's poetry during this third
phase of his career which seems derived from Laura Riding: a
scorn for society in general, and the reader in particular, which
often borders on arrogance.  In "Pavement" (*Poems, 1929*, p.
25),[12] Graves presents a straight-facedly romanticized portrait of
a "Practical Chimney Sweep" as seen through the eyes of the
children who fondly follow him about town, marvelling at his
black hands and face, and admiring the twinkling brass ornaments
on his pony's harness.

> "Isn't that pretty?"  And when we children cried
> "Hello, Wm. Brazier, how are you, Wm. Brazier?"
> He would crack his whip at us and smile and bellow
> "Hello, my dears!"

Then, having made his sentiment as thick as possible, Graves
abruptly shifts his tone, and adds in brackets:

11. "Robert Graves," *Essays in Criticism*, V (January, 1955), pp. 32-43.
12. Retitled "Wm. Brazier" in *Collected Poems, 1938*.

>   . . . [if he was drunk, but otherwise
> "Scum off, you dam young milliners' barstards you!"
> Let them copy it out on a pink page of their albums,
> Carefully leaving out the bracketed lines.
> It's an old story—f's for s's—
> But good enough for them, the suckers.]

If we leave out the bracketed lines, then, we have a cloying little piece tailor-made for the "trade" anthologies Graves detested so heartily; and if we include them we have a savage and derisive attack on the people who read such anthologies.

In "Front Door" (*Poems, 1929,* p. 20),[13] Graves announces that, as the legitimate heir of the "reigning house" of poetry, he is entitled to preserve the vices of his ancestors, and even to react against their poetic tradition if he so wishes—or, as he puts it, to "dung on my grandfather's doorstep"—

> Which is a reasonable and loving due
> To hold no taint of love or vassalage
> And understood only to him and me. . . .

All others, since they do not understand their betters' conduct, had better be cautious in their dealings with this barbarously proud royal family:

> But you, you bogratwhiskered, mean, psalm-griddling
> Lame, rotten-livered this and that canaille,
> You when twin lacqueys, with armorial shovels
> Unbolt the bossy gates and bend to the task,
> Keep well beyond the railings if you must watch
> Lest they mistake you this for that you are.[14]

In "Bay of Naples" (*Poems, 1926-1930,* p. 29), the "plain" reader's response to poetry is likened to that of a

> blind man reading Dante upside down
> and not in Braille. . . .

13. Retitled "Front Door Soliloquy" in *Collected Poems, 1938.*
14. In *Poems, 1926-1930,* Graves revises the conclusion somewhat, and adds a new final line: "This house is jealous of its nastiness."

But in "To the Reader over My Shoulder" (*Ten Poems More,*
p. 39), Graves's complaint is that the reader may see too much—
may, in fact, point out to the poet faults of which the poet himself
is only too well aware:

> All the saying of things against myself
> And for myself I have well done myself,
> What now, old enemy, shall you do
> But quote and underline, thrusting yourself
> Against me, as ambassador of myself,
> In damned confusion of myself and you?

Occasionally Graves's derisive spirit at this time shifts from
its attacks on the plain reader to other subjects.  An example of
this shift is "Landscape" (*Poems, 1929,* p. 23), which G. S. Fraser
has called "one of the rudest poems ever written about nature."[14]
Here Graves notes the way in which mountain rocks, leafy trees,
and clouds often gracelessly caricature the human face, drawing it
with bulbous nose, sunken chin, and cretinous grin.  This sort of
grossness is typical of all nature, says Graves:

> Nature is always so, you find
> That brutal-comic mind,
> As wind,
>
> Retching among the empty spaces,
> Ruffling the idiot grasses,
> The sheep's fleeces.
>
> Whose pleasures are excreting, poking,
> Havocking and sucking,
> Sleepy licking.
>
> Whose griefs are melancholy,
> Whose flowers are oafish,
> Whose waters, silly,
> Whose birds, raffish,
> Whose fish, fish.

14. "The Poetry of Robert Graves," *Vision and Rhetoric: Studies in Modern
Poetry* (London, 1959), p. 143.

Although this indictment of nature's coarseness is as extreme a one as we are likely to find anywhere, and would seem to support Roy Fuller's contention, noted earlier, that Laura Riding's influence caused Graves to make a final break with the bland nature-poetry of his anodyne period, there is still an element of fond jocularity here that takes some of the edge off Graves's attack. Much of Graves's poetry of this period, indeed, while often superficially bitter, is qualified by this jocularity—which indicates that, unlike Miss Riding, Graves is seldom so carried away by spleen that his sense of humor leaves him completely. He may have been influenced by Miss Riding's intractable negativism during this time, but—except for the obvious sincerity of his dislike for the public, which had so far either misunderstood or neglected him—he is seldom totally committed to such an attitude. His ogres, pygmies, belching ghosts, and brutish nature may be outrageous, but they are also laughable. In his crabbed way, he likes them all.

If we gauge Graves's performance during this period solely by the poems we have thus far examined, we are likely to agree that Laura Riding's influence was a substantial factor in determining the course Graves took at this time in his poetry. Most of the scorn, the derision, and the arrogance of these poems are probably traceable—in part, at least—to Miss Riding, as are all the clever displays of verbal ingenuity, all the intellectual jokes.

Yet, when we consider that most of these poems were written between 1929 and 1933—the early years of the Graves-Riding alliance—and when we recall that Graves had already shown a tendency toward the writing of such *jeux d'esprit* during the second phase of his career, we begin to wonder if Graves's attitude during these six years was not just as much an extension of his prevailing mood in the late Twenties, as it was a reflection of his total subservience to Miss Riding's personality. To be sure, his negativism in these poems is more intense than it had formerly been, and Miss Riding might have helped it become so; but might not the events of these hectic years—his separation from Nancy, the death or estrangement of most of his friends, his self-exile to Majorca—have been factors of equal importance? More-

over, as we have noted, Graves's fascination with the grotesque
is not new here, but only a renewal of a former interest.

We cannot, then, assume with finality that Miss Riding's poetic
techniques or subjects had any very great impact on Graves's
practice. But we can certainly agree with Roy Fuller that, from
1929 on, Graves ceased to indulge in many of the more digressive
and derivatory forms of poetry that had appealed to him earlier
in his career, and that the poems he wrote during the early
Thirties display a degree of control and discipline that he had
heretofore exhibited only occasionally. Again, we cannot say
with certainty how much of this greater strictness is directly
attributable to Miss Riding's influence; but from what little
Graves has said about her, and from our knowledge of her per-
fectionist theories about poetry, it seems likely that her influence
in this respect was considerable. Their alliance began at a point
when Graves's career was at its lowest point: the public, when it
thought of him at all, remembered him as a soldier-poet who had
written some charming love and nature poems; his poetic excursions into metaphysics and psychology had proved to be dead
ends; and he had begun to entertain serious doubts both about
his worth as a poet and about the social usefulness of poetry.
Then he met Miss Riding, who maintained with no little ferocity
that the public was too cloddish to recognize real poetry when it
saw it, and who made great claims for poetry as the only hope for
the expression of truth left to man. The poet's sole obligations,
she said, were to himself and his poems—every other consideration
was irrelevant.

The effect of such a martial spirit was immediate and drastic
on Graves, whose faith in himself and his vocation was straightway
renewed. He now had all the audience he required: himself and
Laura Riding. Paradoxically, however, Miss Riding's influence
simultaneously aided and impeded his progress. He had begun,
in the final months of his second period, to write the sort of
poems that have caused critics to recognize his voice as one of
the most distinctive and compelling in modern literature; and one
suspects that it was Miss Riding's example that led him for a time

to ignore the impulses that had caused him to write these few promising verses, and to compose instead the half-serious, mocking poems that we find scattered throughout the early volumes of his third period. Thus, while her forceful personality led Graves to a reaffirmation of his poetic faith, her example led him for a time to devote himself to the satires and grotesques that he has always taken up when not impelled by any great sense of poetic urgency.

# 9

# Poetry of the
# Laura Riding Years (II)

Fortunately for Robert Graves, Laura Riding's example was of shorter influence on his poetry than were her stern precepts; and we find him now, for the first time in his career, giving his almost undivided attention to serious considerations of the themes that have always come most naturally to him: those that treat of the unresolved conflicts between love, lust, and time, between spirit and body, between reason and unreason. The poems of this period which he devotes to these themes (and there are many such poems) are, moreover, those which bear the stamp of his personality alone, and which owe perhaps only their intensity to the influence of Miss Riding. This personality, which had heretofore revealed itself for the most part only in those poems in which Graves's primary intention had not been the expression of his various psychological or philosophical theories, is that of a man whose vision of life is essentially pessimistic, but who is stoically determined to make the most of whatever good he can find. For the mature Graves, existence is godless, disordered, brutish, and even terrifying; and it is only through love and the maintenance of a rigid and disciplined adherence to a graceful ideal he calls "excellence"[1] that man can retain his integrity in such a chaotic universe. This is not to say, however, that Graves had become an ascetic: self-denial or withdrawal from the grosser facts of reality have always seemed unnatural to him.

While he is always repelled and disgusted by the excesses of the flesh, his fastidiousness never prevents him from indulging his often morbid fascination with such excesses. As he says in his crucial foreword to the *Collected Poems, 1938* (p. xxiv), "To manifest poetic faith by a close and energetic study of the disgusting, the contemptible, and the evil, is not very far in the direction of poetic serenity, but it has been the behavior most natural to a man of my physical and literary inheritances." It is, in fact, this simultaneous contempt of and fascination with the darker aspects of life that lies at the roots of all his best poetry, and that has made Graves's voice so distinctive. It has made his poetry a peculiar blend of toughness and fear, of sentiment and cynicism, of emotional involvement and aloofness. It has made his love poetry, in particular (and Graves is from this time on primarily a love poet), so unconventional that one must go back perhaps as far as Donne's *Songs and Sonets* before he finds anything remotely like it.

Like Donne, Graves is as much concerned with lust as with love; but unlike Donne he cannot treat lust lightly. Lust, for Graves, is an almost inevitable partner of love; but, always the angry moralist in such matters, he cannot on that account reconcile himself to its presence. Although never an advocate of a chaste, platonic love (not even with tongue in cheek, like Donne), Graves cannot bring himself to an easy acceptance of the body's role in a love affair. His own body, in fact, is most often taken in his poetry to be a prison from which his spirit can never escape.

Such a view informs "Castle" (*Poems, 1929,* p. 15), a nightmarish poem in which the spirit is likened to a prisoner who can find no means of climbing the walls of the fortress in which he is trapped:

1. Cf. "The Worms of History," *Work in Hand* (London: The Hogarth Press, 1942), p. 47.

There's no way out, no way out—
Rope-ladders, baulks of timber, pulleys,
A rocket whizzing over the walls and moats—
Machines easy to improvise.  No escape,
No such thing; to dream of new dimensions,
Cheating checkmate by painting the king's cheek
So that he slides like a queen.
Or to cry nightmare, nightmare,
Like a corpse in the cholera-pit
Under a load of corpses.

Even if he tries to ignore his condition by the construction of dream-like fantasies, he will only

wake up sweating in moonlight
In the same courtyard, sleepless as before.

At the same time Graves is scornful of any suggestion that the prisoner should become reconciled to his fate.  In "Certain Mercies" (*Collected Poems, 1938,* p. 54), he asks if we should be grateful

That the rusty water
In the unclean pitcher
Our thirst quenches?

That the rotten, detestable
Food is yet eatable
By us ravenous?

That the prison censor
Permits a weekly letter?
(We may write: 'we are well.')

That with patience and deference
We do not experience
The punishment cell?

That each new indignity
Defeats only the body,
Pampering the spirit
With obscure, proud merit?

The emphatic answer is that we should *not* be grateful; that, even though our spirit's fate is lifelong imprisonment in our vile and craven body, we ought on no account meekly accept the meagre recompenses for such a fate, but ought instead to maintain an implacable hatred for our jailer. As G. S. Fraser comments, Graves's "common attitude to the body, to its lusts, to its energies, to its mortality, to the clogging foreign weight that it hangs about him, is a . . . somber one."[2]

This attitude, when carried over into his love poetry, often causes Graves to view the sex act as a graceless and even bestial expression of lust. It is interesting to contrast this emphasis as it occurs in his "Leda" (*Collected Poems, 1938,* p. 123) with Yeats's in his poem on the same subject. Yeats treats Leda's rape by Zeus as primarily a mystical or religious experience, and describes the act in a manner which, while highly sensuous, is purposely vague and suggestive:

> A sudden blow: the great wings beating still
> Above the staggering girl, her thighs caressed
> By the dark webs, her nape caught in his bill,
> He holds her helpless breast upon his breast.
>
> How can those terrified vague fingers push
> The feathered glory from her loosening thighs?

The emphasis here, we see, is really not so much upon the act itself as an expression of lust, as upon the real and awesome majesty of the experience: Zeus, the Father, is using Leda to found a new civilization. Yeats's poem, insofar as it concerns itself with Leda, is an attempt to portray her mystification and bewilderment during the event. But Graves is hardly concerned with the unusual circumstances of the rape. For him, Leda is only one of the participants in an ugly occurrence:

> Then soon your mad religious smile
> Made taut the belly, arched the breast,
> And there beneath your god awhile
> You strained and gulped your beastliest.

2. "The Poetry of Robert Graves," *Vision and Rhetoric: Studies in Modern Poetry* (London, 1959), p. 137.

For Yeats, Leda's rape is terrifying, yet beautiful; for Graves, it is only a sordid and disgusting exhibition of lust.

In "Sandhills" (*Poems, 1929*, p. 24), Graves rejects physical love as a pointless striving by the lovers for unity—pointless because sexual union results only in an endless and meaningless multiplication:

> The beast with two backs is a single beast,
> Yet by his love of singleness increased
> By two and two and two again
> Until instead of sandhills is a plain
> Disposed in two and two, by two and two,
> And the sea parts in horror at the view.

A much stronger manifestation of Graves's disgust with the demands of the flesh is "Succubus" (*Poems, 1930-1933*, p. 7), in which he wonders why the demoness who comes to him in his sleep never manifests herself as a beauty "slender and cool, with limbs lovely to see," who will

> toss her head so the thick curls fall free
> Of nippled breast, firm belly, and long slender thigh.

Why, he asks, must she always come instead as a loathsome apparition?

> Why with hot face,
> With paunched and uddered carcase,
> Sudden and greedily does she embrace
> Gulping away your soul, she lies so close,
> Fathering you with brats of her own race?

The answer comes in the form of a final question he puts to himself: "Flesh, is she truly more gross than your lust is gross?" The succubus, then, is nothing more than the imagined product of his own lust, and as such cannot help but be as ugly as the feeling that has created her.

Often in these poems the poet longs for a love that will be unsullied by physical desire. Such a longing is doomed to disappointment, for man is incapable of any attachment in which sensual gratification plays no part. In "The Stranger" (*Collected Poems, 1938*, p. 87), for instance, Graves tells of a man who becomes excited by the approach of an unfamiliar woman. He is struck first by her "sure and eager tread," and cynically supposes that such bodily grace must denote an effort on her part to make up for her homeliness. But, as she draws closer, he discovers that she is as lovely as she is graceful. Her beauty must be only a cloak for foolishness, he reasons next.

> But there was wisdom in that brow
> Of who might be a Muse.

Then, as this paragon reaches him, he suddenly drops his head, overcome with shame;

> For in his summer haughtiness
> He had cried lust at her for whom
> Through many deaths he had kept vigil,
> Wakeful for her voice.

He had long sought an ideal love; but, when a woman worthy of such love finally appears, his lust arises to prohibit the attainment of an ideal union.

Similarly, in "Ulysses" (*Poems, 1930-1933*, pp. 3-4), Graves depicts the Homeric hero as a man tormented by his inescapable sensuality. The poem begins in that smooth and workmanlike manner which is characteristic of the mature Graves:

> To this much-tossed Ulysses, never done
> With women whether gowned as wife or whore,
> Penelope and Circe seemed as one:
> She like a whore made his lewd fancies run,
> And wifely she a hero to him bore.

G. S. Fraser, who has detected in Graves's style a kinship with Ovid and other Augustan poets, points out the manner here in which the "she" and "she," standing for *illa* and *haec*, "reproduce in a neat inverted antithesis (it is Penelope, though she is his wife, who makes his lewd fancies run, and Circe, though she is his whore, who bears a hero to him) the effect of an Ovidian elegiac couplet" (*Vision and Rhetoric,* pp. 135-36). But if the reader is led by such a device to expect a smooth Ovidian treatment, he will be disturbed in the next stanza by two lines of startlingly romantic imagery: for Penelope and Circe,

> Now they were storms frosting the sea with spray
> And now the lotus orchard's filthy ease.

Moreover, with the epithet "filthy," Graves allows his contempt for sensuality (an attitude hardly compatible with Ovid) to intrude.[3] From this point the poem becomes another sermon against lust:

> One, two, and many: flesh had made him blind.
>     Flesh had one purpose only in the act,
>     Flesh set one purpose only in the mind—
>     Triumph of flesh and the continuance kind
> Of those same terrors with which flesh was racked.

In all of his travels, Ulysses, the great hero, the successful amorist, was only fleeing from self-contempt for his overriding sensuality. He was disgusted by his weakness, yet powerless to conquer it: "He loathed the fraud, yet would not bed alone."

There are for Graves, during most of this third phase, only two means of escape from the degradation of lust and the imprisonment of the spirit by the body, and both means are equivocal. The first lies in an acceptance of sensuality, and a realization that it will, when allied with the passage of time, kill love. Once such concessions are made, Graves feels, it is possible for one to concentrate on the beauty of love itself, to draw solace from the fact that, fleeting as it is, real love can exist. A notable expression of this partial resolution is the poignant "Between Dark and Dark" (*Poems, 1929,* p. 1),[4] a poem of advice to young lovers.

---

3. Perhaps feeling that "filthy" was too blatant an expression of revulsion, Graves substituted "drunken" for it in *Collected Poems, 1914-1947.*

4. Retitled "O Love in Me" in *Poems, 1926-1930;* and changed again to "Sick Love" in *Collected Poems, 1938.*

> O Love, be fed with apples while you may
> And feel the sun, and go in warm array,
> A smiling innocent on the heavenly causeway.
>
> Though in what listening horror for the cry
> That soars in outer darkness dismally,
> The dumb blind beast, the paranoiac fury,
>
> Be warm, enjoy the season, lift your head,
> Exquisite in the pulse of tainted blood,
> That shivering beauty not to be despised.
>
> Take your delight in momentariness,
> Walk between dark and dark, a shining space
> With the grave's narrowness, though not its peace.

Since Chaos, the "dumb blind beast, the paranoiac fury," lies all about the loved one, her only solace must come from the "delight in momentariness' that she can gain during her brief time in the sun's warmth. The "tainted blood" (blood roused by passion), the "shivering glory" (presumably the uncontrollable shivering of the body in the throes of passion), are, since an inevitable part to love, "not to be despised." Since it is so fleeting, and since it is a moment of sunshine surrounded by darkness, love must be accepeted on its own terms, and enjoyed for what it is. Lust may be an unpleasant element, but we have no time to spend in trying to rid ourselves of it. There is in this poem, as in many of Graves's love poems, a great deal of wistful tenderness which almost obscures the poet's basically cynical attitude toward life. (One is reminded by this of a similar quality in the love poems of W. H. Auden, whose debt to Graves is perhaps greater than has yet been recognized.)

The second means of escape from the conflict between love and lust, or between spirit and body, is less satisfactory: it requires a withdrawal from reality into the sort of inside-out dream world Graves had earlier described in "Alice." In "The Terraced Valley" (*Ten Poems More*, p. 12), the poet tells how, once while brooding about his love, he suddenly found himself wandering in a "new region":

> The unnecessary sun was not there,
> The necessary earth was without care,
> Broad sunshine ripened the whole skin
> Of ancient earth that was turned outside-in.

The features of the world seemed to him to be in reversed relationship: sun and sky had disappeared from their customary locations overhead, and light and warmth seemed now to come from the earth beneath him.  All things, indeed, appeared to possess the qualities of their natural opposites:

> Neat this-way-that-way and without mistake:
> On the right hand could slide the left glove.
> Neat over-under: the young snake
> Through an unbreaking shell his path could break.
> Singing of kettles, like a singing brook,
> Made out of doors a fireside nook.

There was only one thing wrong about this tranquil land where experience was inverted: he knew that his lover must be near him, but he could not see her.

> I knew you near me in that strange region,
> So searched for you, in hope to see you stand
> On some near olive-terrace, in the heat,
> The left-hand glove drawn on your right hand,
> The empty snake's egg perfect at your feet.

But he could find her nowhere, and cried disconsolately until

> you spoke
> Close in the sunshine by me, and your voice broke
> That antique spell with a doom-echoing shout
> To once more inside-in and outside-out.

The poet had succeeded in divorcing himself from the real world, but had found that his love could not accompany him into his inner world—that she could exist for him only in the present (in the revised version of this poem in *Collected Poems, 1938,* "That antique spell" is changed to "This trick of Time"), the world of cause and effect, where logic rules and where love affairs are subject to the cruel demands of time.

It should have become apparent by now that, while Graves makes frequent use of landscapes in his poetry, he is not primarily interested in them as landscapes: he uses them rather as symbols that express, or correspond to, certain emotional or physiological states. In the early "Rocky Acres" the harsh Welsh countryside had been used to convey the poet's contempt for the soft life; in "The Dead Ship" the trackless and empty sea had symbolized the pointlessness and blankness of existence; and such magical landscapes as the box-in-a-box, inside-out worlds of "Warning to Children" and "The Terraced Valley" illustrate Graves's belief that excursions into the irrational are, while fascinating, no very satisfactory way of eluding the demands of reason and time: the prisoner cannot hope to escape from the castle by refusing to accept its existence.

That his landscapes are used chiefly as objective counterparts for subjective feelings does not, however, prevent Graves from being one of the few modern poets capable of realistic descriptions of nature; for, like his favorites Hardy and Frost, he has always prided himself on his accuracy of observation (in *A Pamphlet Against Anthologies* it was part of his bludgeoning of Yeats to note that, in "The Lake Isle of Innisfree," the Irish poet had been guilty of putting his bee-hives in his "nine bean-rows," instead of in trees at some distance from his cabin; and of having his linnets, properly daytime birds, swarming about in the evening). Graves's power of description is perhaps best illustrated by "Flying Crooked" (*Poems, 1926-1930,* p. 41), in which he whimsically makes an analogy between his own waywardness and the aerial eccentricity of the butterfly:

> The butterfly, the cabbage-white,
> (His honest idiocy of flight)

> Will never now, it is too late,
> Master the art of flying straight,
> Yet has—who knows so well as I?—
> A just sense of how not to fly:
> He lurches here and here by guess
> And God and hope and hopelessness.
> Even the aerobatic swift
> Has not his flying-crooked gift.

The poem is, to be sure, primarily a humorous commentary on the butterfly's "Honest idiocy of flight"; but, like all of Graves's nature poetry, it is also a statement about himself (like all true romanticists, Graves is strongly self-absorbed), and perhaps a statement about the art of poetry, too.  The impression we receive from it is that Graves had by now become reconciled to his position outside poetic fashion, and that he could even pride himself on his inability to perform the smooth mental and verbal aerobatics of his more favored contemporaries.

There are, indeed, several indications at this stage of his career that, although he would continue to exercise a classical discipline and restraint in manner, he was moving toward a romantic conception of himself as a poet dedicated to the service of a mysterious and supra-rational Muse.  This shadowy figure to whom he now begins to pay his homage appears for the first time in "On Portents" (*Poems, 1930-1933*, p. 33):

> If strange things happen where she is,
> So that men say graves open
> And the dead walk, or that futurity
> Becomes a womb and the unborn are shed,
> Such portents are not to be wondered at,
> Being tourbillions in Time made
> By the strong pulling of her bladed mind
> Through that ever-reluctant element.

This Muse, who possesses such frightening power, and who is superior to Time, is not an easy mistress to serve; but the poet who does so becomes temporarily invested with her magical gifts, and is superior to those not inspired by her. In "The Bards" (*Poems, 1930-1933*, p. 1), Graves shows how violent her inspiration might be, and suggests that it is most likely to come to poets who, though their speech may be halting and rough, are honest in their emotions.

> It is a something fearful in the song
> Plagues them, an unknown grief that lies like a churl
> Goes common-place in cowskin
> And bursts unheralded, crowing and coughing,
> An unpilled holly-club twirled in his hand,
> Into their many-shielded, samite-curtained
> Jewel-bright hall where twelve kings sit at chess
> Over the white bronze pieces and the gold.

The formal and static beauty of the "twelve kings at chess" is a dead thing[5] and cannot withstand the honest inspiration of the bards—personified by the brutish intruder—that

> by a gross enchantment
> Flails down the rafters and leads off the queens—
> The wild-swan-breasted, the rose-ruddy-cheeked
> Raven-haired daughters of their admiration—
> To stir his black pots and to bed on straw.

It is perhaps not surprising that Graves, with his fondness for the grotesque, should choose to represent true poetic inspiration as a rapacious and frenzied ogre, thrusting aside his more polished rivals to carry off their beautiful wives and daughters; and in the fourth phase of his career we shall see Graves returning often to this sanguinary view.

For the most part, however, Graves's notions about his inspiration by the Muse are at this time considerably more restrained than he suggests in "The Bards"; and in those poems in which he announces his dedication to her, his tone is one of quiet respect.

5. Cohen, *Robert Graves*, p. 62, speculates incorrectly that Graves might be making a side reference here to the Yeats of the Byzantium poems; in fact (Graves tells me), the reference is to the terrifying Irish myth of the *Gila Dacha*.

She is seen not as a destroyer, but rather as someone who has
calmed his fears and set him on the right poetic path.  In the
title poem from *To Whom Else?* he asks:

> To whom else other than,
> To whom else not of man
> Yet in human state,
> Standing neither in stead
> Of self nor idle godhead,
> Should I, man in man bounded,
> Myself dedicate?
> To whom else momently,
> To whom else endlessly,
> But to you, I?
> To you who only,
> To you who mercilessly,
> To you who lovingly,
> Plucked out the lie? . . .
> With great astonishment
> Thankfully I consent
> To my estrangement
> From me in you.

It is quite possibly not at all a coincidence that the phrasing
of this poem should call to mind the patter of Laura Riding's
brittle verse; for there is little doubt that she seemed to Graves
the embodiment of his new-found Muse.  She had restored his
confidence in himself and his profession, and had forced him to
give his whole concentration to the perfection of his poems.  All
his poems, moreover, now were addressed to her, as his only fitting
audience.  He seems at times almost to have viewed her as something more than mortal: in the cryptic "As it Were Poems" with
which he concludes *Poems, 1930-1933*, he associates her with Isis,
the Egyptian vegetation goddess, and himself with Osiris, her
subservient mate.[6]  It is certain, at any rate, that Graves saw

6. This curious notion, which points us directly toward Graves's later studies of
the connection between myth and poetry, was suggested to Graves by his and Miss
Riding's reading of Plutarch's *On Isis and Osiris;* and we are led by it to agree

Laura Riding as his deliverer from the evils that had pursued him
before his retreat to Majorca; and that it is Miss Riding he addresses in one of the last poems of this period, "Fiend, Dragon,
Mermaid" (*Collected Poems, 1938,* p. 103),[7] where, after stating
that he is no longer haunted by his three old adversaries, the
Fiend (False Religion), Dragon (Despair), and Mermaid (Lust),
he announces that he has "turned his gaze" to

> the encounter
> The later genius, who of my pride and fear
> And love
> No monster made but me.

The final poems of his third period reveal, like the one mentioned above, that Graves had gradually come to feel it was possible for love to exist free of lust, and that one might live peace-
fully and with dignity, aloof from the furor of the outside world.
These last poems seem indeed to indicate that his self-exile with
Miss Riding had had the cathartic effect on his old neuroses that
he had hoped for: the old fear-theme seemed now to have been
replaced by a feeling of tranquillity. "End of Play" (*Collected
Poems, 1938,* p. 185) and "No More Ghosts" (*Collected Poems,
1938,* p. 189), especially, illustrate this feeling. In the former,
Graves announces with simple directness that he has "reached
the end of pastime," that he has "at last ceased idling," that he
will "tell no lies now," and that

> No more shall love in hypocritic pomp
> Conduct its innocents through a dance of shame
> From timid touching of gloved fingers
> To frantic laceration of naked breasts.

Yet, he concludes, love survives in spite of the removal of lust,
even if only as

---

with Randall Jarrell's theory that Graves's conception of the White Goddess as the
source of poetic inspiration is in large measure a symbolic recreation of his earlier
veneration of Laura Riding.

7. Not to be confused with "Old Wives' Tales" of *Whipperginny,* which was
subsequently (in *Collected Poems, 1938*) retitled "Mermaid, Dragon, Fiend."

the word carved on a sill
Under antique dread of the headsman's axe.

In "No More Ghosts," however, he is more positive in his assertion that love will prevail, and that it need no longer be seen as
necessarily doomed by the passage of time. The old ghosts who
had tormented him in the past are gone, he says to his lover, and

We are restored to simple days, are free
From cramps of dark necessity,
And one another recognize
By an immediate love that signals at our eyes.

No new ghost can appear. Their poor cause
Was that time freezes, and time thaws;
But here only such loves can last
As do not ride upon the weathers of the past.

Love may be threatened by time; but a love that is divorced from
the problems that time brings will last.

Graves's new serenity was not to be permanent, for his sanguinary temperament was shortly to create new conflicts which would
make him as crabbed and aggressive as ever; but it is safe to say
that the old moodiness and black pessimism, which had been an
integral part of his serious work up to this time, were exorcised
completely during the third phase of his career. How much of
this exorcism was due to Laura Riding's influence cannot be
precisely determined. But we know from Graves's statements
that she had a part in the alteration of his attitude toward his life
and his work; and, from what his poetry reveals about his sense
of dedication to her, we are justified in supposing that her part
was a large one.

At any event, we find that Graves's prevailing mood at the beginning of his third poetic period was one of bleak negativism;
that, during the early years of his partnership with Laura Riding,
he alternated between humorous and often coarse satires on the
foibles of society and darkly serious poems in which he depicted
man as adrift in a disordered and brutal world, and constantly

foiled in his search for pure love and spiritual freedom because of his inability to overcome the demands made on him by his body; and that he was able, in the closing years of this period, to arrive at what was at least a partial affirmation of his faith in the possibility of man's attaining a degree of love and order in his life. And, most importantly, we see that it was during these thirteen years that Graves became the master of his art. Whether through Laura Riding's influence or not, his poems now consistently possessed the terseness, the control, and the effect of complex and intense feelings expressed with simplicity and restraint that he had been able to achieve only occasionally in his early work, and that from now on were to inform almost everything he wrote. It had taken Robert Graves longer to find himself than it does most poets (he was now forty-three and had been writing for twenty-eight years), but he had at last done so.

# Part Four

## The Mythic Period

# 10

# The Coming of the Goddess

Robert Graves, who had been forced to leave Majorca in 1936 by the outbreak of the Civil War, wandered around Europe in Miss Riding's company until the spring of 1938, when they went to live in Pennsylvania. They soon parted company and have never met since. A month before the outbreak of World War Two, Graves returned to England, remarried, and, after being rejected for active service because of age, settled in a small Devonshire village, Galmpton-Brixton, where he continued writing as prolifically as ever. His work during the war years was primarily given to prose: *Sergeant Lamb of the Ninth* (1940) and *Proceed, Sergeant Lamb* (1941) were historical novels about a member of the Royal Welch Fusiliers during the Revolutionary War in America; *The Long Week-end* (1940), written with Alan Hodge, was a "Social History of Great Britain, 1918-1939"; *The Reader Over Your Shoulder* (1943), also with Hodge, was a "Handbook for Writers of English Prose"; and *Wife to Mr. Milton* (1943) was an iconoclastic study of the relationship between Milton and Marie Powell from which—characteristically, for Graves—Milton emerged as the villainous oppressor of young womanhood. He wrote fewer poems during this time than he had in the five preceding years. *No More Ghosts* (London: Faber and Faber, 1940) consisted chiefly of pieces previously published in *Collected Poems, 1938,*

and contained only four new poems; and fourteen new pieces
were printed in *Work in Hand* (London: The Hogarth Press,
1942), a small volume in which Graves's work appeared side-by-
side with poems by Norman Cameron and Alan Hodge.[1]

Two of the new poems in *No More Ghosts* reveal that Graves's
tranquil mood of the late Thirties was already beginning to dissi-
pate, and that once again the more violent emotions were con-
trolling his imagination. Both of these poems indicate, moreover,
that Graves now chose to give a freer rein to his fondness for
magic and myth than he had heretofore done. In "The Beast,"[2]
for example, we find what seems to be a myth created for the
purpose of the poem:

> Beyond the Atlas roams a love-beast.
> The Aborigines harry it with darts;
> Its flesh is esteemed, though of a fishy tang
> Tainting the eater's mouth and lips.
> Ourselves once, wandering in mid-wilderness
> And by despair drawn to this diet,
> Before the meal was over sat apart
> Loathing each other's carrion company.

The Beast is, of course, Graves's old enemy, Lust; and here it is
depicted as a loathsome creature whose flesh is attractive to
savages, but repellent to the poet and his lover, who, though compelled to eat, yet despise each other for having eaten. The whole
poem is thus no more than a vivid recasting, in a framework of
myth, of Graves's old theme of love versus lust.

The second poem, "A Love Story" (*No More Ghosts*, p. 41),
finds Graves once again using landscape as a symbol for emotional
states. We are first given the sort of highly charged setting which
was shortly to become a dominant characteristic of Graves's
"magical" poems:

1. An Authors' Note to this volume explains that the three poets were publishing their works together "for economy and friendship"; and there is no suggestion that—as Cohen (*Robert Graves*, p. 87) proposes—the younger men were in
any way Graves's "disciples." (Graves's comment on this note: "They were in fact
disciples of Laura Riding's.")

2. *No More Ghosts*, p. 40; retitled "The Glutton" in *Collected Poems, 1955*. This
poem is not to be confused with earlier "Beast" (cf. pp. 123-24).

> The full moon easterly rising, furious,
> Against a winter sky ragged with red;
> The hedges high in snow, and owls raving—
> Solemnities not easy to withstand:
> A shiver wakes the spine.

This frightening scene recalls to the poet a similar one in his youth, when he had

> fetched the moon home
> With owls and snow, to nurse in my head
> Throughout the trials of a new Spring,
> Famine unassuaged.

Thus internalized, the Moon symbolized for the youthful poet an ideal, unattainable love; in the midst of spring his hunger for love went unrelieved, and the coldness of winter persisted in his heart. But, we learn in the third stanza, the youth did at last fall in love; and, while he retained the image of the moon as the "ensign" of his love,

> snows melted,
> Hedges sprouted, the moon tenderly shone,
> The owls trilled with tongues of nightingale.

In the fourth stanza, however, the poet admits that the spring his new love had awakened was illusory, that it was "all lies": the woman's image had soon "turned beldamish," the nightingales had become once again only owls, and

> Back again came Winter on me with a bound,
> The pallid sky heaved with a moon-quake.

It had been dangerous, he concludes, to "serenade Queen Famine"; for now he was compelled to surrender the warmth and happiness that his illusory love had brought him, and to return to the bleak emptiness of his first setting.

> In tears I recomposed the former scene,
> Let the snow lie, watched the moon rise, suffered the owls,
> Paid homage to them of unevent.

Graves had by now ceased for the most part to generalize in his poetry, so it is probable that he is here not speaking of the inevitable course of all love affairs, but only of one ill-fated experience. The poem is effective enough as it stands, but the central figures in it—the moon, the owls, and the snow—will all take on added significance when we consider them as integral parts of the symbolic system Graves was shortly to develop.

In "Mid-Winter Waking" (*Work in Hand,* p. 63), one of Graves's best love poems, we find a happy sequel to "A Love Story"—and also perhaps a symbolic recognition of his recovered poetic powers. Here there is the same struggle between spring and winter in the poet; but now we find the poet, again in love, rejoicing that he has awakened from "long hibernation" to find himself "once more a poet," and looking forward eagerly to the spring which he is to enjoy with his lover, his new muse:

> Be witness that on waking this mid-winter,
> I found her hand in mine laid closely
> Who shall watch out the Spring with me.
> We stared in silence all around us
> But found no winter anywhere to see.

The overall theme of the few poems that Graves wrote during the period between 1939 and 1942 was love between man and woman, sometimes happy, sometimes not; and, despite the foreshadowing that we detect here, and that which we had discerned in the final poems of Graves's third period, it was not until 1944 that this theme became specifically related to the love of a special man—the Poet—for a special woman—the Muse.

The origins of this metamorphosis lie in Graves's *Hercules, My Shipmate,*[3] his 1944 novel about Jason and the Argonauts in their quest for the Golden Fleece. His research for this work, like that for all his historical novels, was exhaustive: before he began writing, he consulted the works of Homer, Hesiod, He-

---

3. New York: Farrar, Straus and Cudahy, 1944. Originally published the same year in London as *The Golden Fleece.*

cataeus, Aeschylus, Sophocles, Euripides, Herodotus, Pindar, Apollonius Rhodius, Diodorus Siculus, Strabo, Pausanias, and many other Greek and Roman poets and historians. By the time Graves had finished this research, he was able to trace in *Hercules, My Shipmate* the complete voyage of the Argo; to provide a complete roster of the Argonauts, with full biographies of each man present; and to determine—to his own satisfaction, at least— everything that had occurred during the adventure, from the initial loss of the Fleece by King Athamas of Minya, to the death of Jason years after the voyage. But Graves found something in his investigations of ancient Mediterranean history that seemed far more interesting to him than the story of the Argonauts: in every source he consulted, there were frequent references to a Mother-Goddess who appeared to have been worshipped, in any number of her varying forms, throughout all of the then known world. This was not Graves's first acquaintance with the Goddess: he had known of her since his schoolboy exposure to the Homeric epics, had encountered her often in his reading of the anthropological investigations of Jane Harrison and Sir James Frazer—and most especially in his encounters with her as Isis in *The Golden Ass* of Apuleius, in which she is described with great attention to detail:

I had scarcely closed my eyes before the apparition of a woman began to rise from the middle of the sea with so lovely a face that the gods themselves would have fallen down in adoration of it. First the head, then the whole shining body gradually emerged and stood before me poised on the surface of the waves. . . . Her long thick hair fell in tapering ringlets on her lovely neck, and was crowned with an intricate chaplet in which was woven every kind of flower. Just above her brow shone a round disc, like a mirror, or like the bright face of the moon, which told me who she was. Vipers rising from the left-hand and right-hand partings of her hair supported this disc, with ears of corn bristling between them. Her many-coloured robe was of finest linen; part was glistening white, part crocus-yellow, part glowing red and along the entire hem a woven bordure of flowers and fruit clung swaying in the breeze. But what caught and held my eye more than anything else was the deep black lustre of her mantle. She wore it slung across her body from the right hip to the left shoulder, where it was caught in a knot resembling the boss of a shield; but part of it hung in innumerable folds, the tasselled fringe quivering. It was embroidered with glittering stars on the hem and everywhere else, and in the middle beamed a full and fiery moon.

In her right hand she held a bronze rattle, of the sort used to frighten away the God of the Sirocco; its narrow rim was curved like a sword-belt and three little rods, which sang shrilly when she shook the handle, passed horizontally through it. A boat-shaped gold dish hung from her left hand, and along the upper surface of the handle writhed an asp with puffed throat and head raised ready to strike. On her divine feet were slippers of palm leaves, the emblem of victory.[4]

But in spite of such striking descriptions, it was in his fiction about the Argonauts that she first fully captured his imagination; and *Hercules, My Shipmate* soon became not so much the story of Jason and his adventures as it was a study of the Goddess cults in the second and first millenia B.C.[5]

Following generally the theses of Frazer and Miss Harrison,[6] Graves proposes in his novel that all religious systems prior to the middle of the second millenium were entirely matriarchal—that male deities were unknown until the thirteenth century B.C., when the Achaean and Dorian invaders of what is now Greece brought with them their patriarchal religion, dethroned the Goddess, occupied her temples, and set up the familiar Olympic

4. Apuleius, *The Golden Ass*, translated by Robert Graves (New York: Farrar, Straus and Young, 1951; New York: Pocket Library, 1954), pp. 237-38 (Pocket Lib. edition).

5. In "The White Goddess," a lecture given at the YMHA Center in New York on 9 February 1957, and subsequently published in *5 Pens in Hand* (New York: Doubleday, 1958), pp. 55-72, Graves stated: "The fact is, while working on my Argonaut book, I found the figure of the White Goddess . . . growing daily more powerful, until she dominated the story."

6. See Frazer, *The Golden Bough*, 13 vols., 3d ed. (London, 1923), esp. vols. V and VI; and Jane Harrison, *Prolegomena to the Study of Greek Religion* (Cambridge, Engl., 1908), *Ancient Art and Ritual* (London, 1913), and *Themis: A Study of the Social Origins of Greek Religion* (Cambridge, Engl., 1927). Graves has written me that he cannot recall when he first read these works; but he refers to *Ancient Art and Ritual* in *Poetic Unreason* (p. 275), which would establish a date for his reading it at least as early as 1924.

pantheon, presided over by Zeus. From this time on, according to Graves, Goddess-worship was broken into isolated cults which were, over the centuries, gradually hunted down and destroyed by the followers of the patriarchal religions, until the once-supreme Goddess became almost totally replaced by the new gods.

*Hercules, My Shipmate* is set in time about two generations before the fall of Troy, in a period when, according to Graves, the White Goddess was by no means yet evicted from the Mediterranean; and Graves sees the adventures of Jason and the Argonauts as a series of clashes between the old and new religions, in which the forces of the Goddess consistently triumph over the forces of the Olympians. The Fleece is stolen because King Athamas insists on venerating Zeus; Jason is invulnerable only because he is championed by the White Goddess of Pelion; and the Fleece is regained because the Argonauts are aided by Medea, the Goddess' priestess at Colchis. At the conclusion of the novel, the Goddess is still all-powerful, although she continues to suffer the indignities imposed on her by Zeus, whom she regards as a foolish and wayward son.

The precise nature of this Goddess is only hinted at in *Hercules, My Shipmate;* but Graves devotes himself to a study of her in *The White Goddess,* the exotic, often bewildering, but undeniably brilliant "Historical Grammar of Poetic Myth" he wrote this same year.[7] This work, which "will take its place beside *The Anatomy of Melancholy* as an eccentric classic of English literature,"[8] is a curious blend of fact and fancy, an often impenetrable wilderness of cryptology, obscure learning, and apparently *non sequitur* reasoning brought to bear on a thesis that has its roots partly in historic fact, partly in generally accepted anthropological hypotheses, and partly in pure poetic intuition. The most careful reader of *The White Goddess* will have difficulty

---

7. Although the first draft (tentatively entitled *The Roebuck in the Thicket*) was completed in 1944, the finished work was not published until four years later, by Faber and Faber. It was revised and enlarged in 1952, when it was republished by the same company. Subsequent references to this work are to the Vintage edition (New York, 1958).

8. Martin Seymour-Smith, *Robert Graves*, Writers and Their Works, No. 78 (London, 1956), p. 15.

in determining where fact leaves off and imagination begins, and
it is perhaps for this reason that scholars have refused to treat
the work seriously.[9]   But this neglect appears not to have disturbed Graves very deeply: in *5 Pens in Hand* (p. 57) he states
that *The White Goddess* was intended not as a scholarly docu-
ment, but as a manifestation of poetic faith; and that, as a poet, he
was seeking neither to compete with professional scholars, nor to
solicit sympathy from them.

In this same essay Graves recalls the genesis of *The White
Goddess*:

In 1944 . . . I was working against time on a historical novel about
the Argonauts and the Golden Fleece, when a sudden overwhelm-
ing obsession interrupted me.   It took the form of an unsolicited
enlightenment on a subject I knew almost nothing of. . . . I
began speculating on a mysterious "Battle of the Trees," allegedly
fought in pre-historic Britain, and my mind worked at such a
furious rate all night, as well as all the next day, that my pen
found it difficult to keep pace with the flow of thought. . . . within
three weeks, I had written a 70,000-word book about the ancient
Mediterranean Moon-Goddess whom Homer invoked in the
*Iliad* . . . and to whom most traditional poets ever since have paid
at any rate lip-service.   (*5 Pens in Hand,* pp. 54-55)

This mysterious enlightenment, Graves goes on to say, began one
morning when he was re-reading Lady Charlotte Guest's translation of *The Mabinogion,* and came across "a hitherto despised
minstrel poem" called *Hanes Taliesin (The Song of Taliesin).*

I suddenly knew (don't ask me how) that the lines of the poem,
which has always been dismissed as deliberate nonsense, formed
a series of early medieval riddles, and that I knew the answer to
them all, although I was neither a Welsh scholar, nor a medi-
evalist, and although many of the lines had been deliberately
transposed by the author (or his successors) for security reasons.

9. The most authoritative scholarly work on the subject, E. O. James's *The
Cult of the Mother Goddess* (New York, 1959), does not even give passing reference
to Graves's work, although there is in fact little contradiction between Graves's and
James's theories of the origin and nature of the Goddess-cults in the Mediterranean
area and in Western Europe.

He knew also (again, without knowing how) that the answer to these riddles must in some way be linked with an ancient Welsh poetic tradition of a *Câd Goddeu* ("Battle of Trees"), the subject of a thirteenth-century poem recorded in *The Red Book of Hergest,* a collection of early Welsh verse. The story of the Argonauts now temporarily forgotten, Graves dove into his father's collection of Celtic literature, and in a short time came up with the "facts" that supported his intuition. The *Câd Goddeu* and *The Song of Taliesin* were both, he concluded, intentionally garbled accounts of an ancient struggle between rival priesthoods in Celtic Britain for control of the national learning. These priesthoods were those which worshipped respectively the God-dess Danu (the Celtic version of Danäe of Argos) and the solar god Beli (originally the Egyptian god Bel). Danu-worship had been brought to Ireland and Britain in the middle Bronze Age by the Tuatha dé Danaan, a tribe of nomadic Grecians; and Beli-worship had been imposed on the British Isles by the Celtic invaders of the first millenium B.C. Thus, Graves concluded, the *Câd Goddeu* and *The Song of Taliesin* were symbolic accounts of a conflict between matriarchal and patriarchal religions—the same conflict that had begun hundreds of years earlier in the Mediterranean.

The bulk of *The White Goddess* is given to Graves's intricate explanation of the reasoning that had brought him to this conclusion, and deals chiefly with the nature of a pair of secret Druidic alphabets and the ways in which they served as sacred calendars for the old religion. It seems that these alphabet-calendars were, like the eighteen-letter Greek Orphic alphabet which preceded that of the Classical Greek period, tied in with tree-worship; and that tree-worship was throughout the Bronze Age, from Palestine to Ireland, associated everywhere with veneration of the pre-Aryan Triple Moon-Goddess. Once he had made this connection between the religions of the British Isles and the Mediterranean, Graves could proceed with great confidence to draw a multitude of correspondences between Greek and Celtic myth, and to assert that both of these mythic systems were, like his mysterious Welsh poems, nothing more or less than symbolic representations of the ancient battle between the Goddess and the usurping male deities.

Although most modern anthropologists would agree that goddess-worship was the earliest form of Western religion, there is much about Graves's audacious thesis that seems, even to the anthropological layman, to rest on shaky foundations. There is little reason to believe, for example, that the Tuatha dé Danaan were ever more than supernatural characters in Irish fairy-tales; or that Graves is correct in asserting that the Picts were originally from Thrace, and were driven from their original homes by the Achaean invaders. When discussing gnosticism, Graves does not make it clear that this earlier heresy was not held by a single sect, but sprang from at least three sources: Jewish (Essene and Kabbalist), Greek, and Oriental. In several places he seems to rely on information derived from sections of *The Golden Bough* which have since been disproved by anthropologists—as in his assumption that the Egyptian god Osiris was a less powerful and important personage than his spouse, Isis. There is, apparently, no evidence to link the Druids with any pre-Celtic element in British prehistory, as Graves does; and there is even some question that the earlier of Graves's Druidic alphabets—on the authenticity of which much of the argument of *The White Goddess* depends—is in fact authentic.[10] But if the work has caused academicians to view Graves as "a dangerous amateur, possibly even a charlatan, who imposes upon reality a world of private fantasies,"[11] it is still of immense value to the reader who is content to accept it as a supremely imaginative attempt to define the precise nature of poetic inspiration by relating it to classical and pre-classical myth, and specifically to the ancient veneration of the great Triple Goddess, the Magna Mater.

In the pre-historic matriarchal societies, says Graves, a queen who was the temporary incarnation of the Goddess took to herself

10. See R. A. S. Macalister, *The Secret Languages of Ireland* (Cambridge, Engl., 1937), p. 29. Graves appears to have relied very heavily on this book in his *White Goddess* discussion of Celtic languages, and of the old Ogham texts.

11. George Steiner, "The Genius of Robert Graves," *The Kenyon Review*, XXII (Summer, 1960), pp. 340-65.

periodically a king, who had to be sacrificed before his strength decayed, to preserve the fertility of the land. This Goddess is that familiar and traditional figure, the Muse, the religious invocation of whom is the function of all true (that is, "inspired") poetry. She is the female principle in its three archetypal aspects: as the Mother who bears man, the Nymph who mates with him, and the Old Crone who presides over his burial. She is thus instrumental in effecting man's creation, fulfilment, and destruction. She is simultaneously the Goddess of Happiness and Life, and of Pain and Death, and to ignore her in any of her manifestations, is impious and dangerous. Her ambivalent nature is reflected in the adjective "White" which is often part of her title: "In one sense it is the pleasant whiteness of pearl-barley, or a woman's body, or milk, or unsmutched snow; in another it is the horrifying whiteness of a corpse, or a spectre, or leprosy" (*The White Goddess,* p. 485). Thus she may appear in Welsh mythology as Olwen, the lily-white May-queen, or as Cerridwen, the fearsome white sow-goddess. In Greek myth she may be Hera, the mother; or Aphrodite, the love-nymph; or Hecate, the crone—or Cotytto, or Demeter, or Cybele, or Persephone, or Pasiphaë, or any of countless other figures. In Ireland she is Bride; in Egypt, Isis; in Syria, Ishtar; and in Jerusalem, Rahab.

Whatever she calls herself, however, she is almost always represented in mythic iconography as "a lovely, slender woman with a hooked nose, deathly pale face, lips red as rowan-berries, startlingly blue eyes, and long fair hair," who is capable of transforming herself suddenly into "sow, mare, bitch, vixen, she-ass, weasel, serpent, owl, she-wolf, tigress, mermaid, or loathsome hag" (p. 12). She is often referred to as the "Triple Goddess" not only because of her concern with birth, procreation, and death, but also because as Goddess of the Earth she is involved in the three seasons of spring, summer, and winter, and because as Goddess of the Sky she is the Moon, in her three phases of New Moon, Full Moon, and Waning Moon (p. 428). Most importantly, for Graves, she is also the Muse of Poetry.

In many mythic icons she is represented as granting her favors alternately to a pair of lovers—the God of the Waning Year, and the God of the Waxing Year.  In the more violent Goddess-cults, the parts in this seasonal drama were originally taken by the chief priestess and two men chosen from the tribe; and at the mid-summer celebrations the man acting as the God of the Waxing Year was lamed, crucified, dismembered, and ultimately eaten, in order to insure the health of the crops; and the man acting as the God of the Waning Year then became the consort of the priestess—until the mid-winter rites, when he in turn was sacrificed.

For Graves, all "true" poetry (which he now defines by citing A. E. Housman's famous test: does it make the skin bristle and the hairs stand on end if one repeats it silently while shaving?) is religious invocation of the Muse-goddess, and as such it may have only one theme.

The theme, briefly, is the antique story, which falls into thirteen chapters and an epilogue, of the birth, life, death, and resurrection of the God of the Waxing Year; the central chapters contain the God's losing battle with the God of the Waning Year for love of the capricious and all-powerful Threefold Goddess, their mother, bride, and layerout.  The poet identifies himself with the God of the Waxing Year and his Muse with the Goddess; the rival is his blood-brother, his other self, his weird.  All true poetry—true by Housman's practical test—celebrates some incident or scene in this very ancient story, and the three main characters are so much a part of our racial inheritance that they not only assert themselves in poetry but recur on occasions of emotional stress in the form of dreams, paranoiac visions, and delusions.  The weird, or rival, often appears in nightmare as the tall, lean, dark-faced bed-side spectre, or Prince of the Air, who tries to drag the dreamer out through the window, so that he looks back and sees his body still lying rigid in bed, but he takes countless other malevolent or diabolic or serpent-like forms. . . .  The test of a poet's vision, one might say, is the accuracy of his portrayal of the White Goddess and of the island over which she rules.  The reason why the hairs stand on end, the eyes water, the throat is constricted, the skin crawls, and a shiver runs down the spine when one writes or reads a true poem is that a true poem is necessarily an invocation of the White Goddess, or Muse, the Mother of All Living, the ancient power of fright or lust—the female spider or the queen-bee whose embrace is death. (*The White Goddess*, pp. 11-12)

When the Goddess-cults, which had spread across the Mediterranean into the Iberian Peninsula, and thence to Northwest Europe, were forced to go underground, her faith survived for a time among the peasants (who continued to celebrate her traditional festivals at the summer and winter solstices, as well as at May Day and Hallowe'en) and later among the anti-Christian witch-cults which persisted until the eighteenth century.[12] Since then, however, except among certain primitive and isolated matrilineal societies, the Goddess has been venerated only by the few poets who have chosen to make her their Muse. These are, for Graves, the only true poets: their imagery is drawn either consciously or unconsciously from the symbols of the Goddess-cults, and the magical quality of their poems largely depends on their familiarity with her mysteries. They may be called "romantic" poets, but Graves is careful to state that all members of the Romantic Movement in England were not necessarily true poets:

"Romantic," a useful word while it covered the reintroduction into Western Europe by the writers of verse-romances of a mystical reverence for woman, has become tainted by indiscriminate use. The typical Romantic poet of the nineteenth century was physically degenerate, or ailing, addicted to drugs and melancholia, critically unbalanced, and a true poet only in his fatalistic regard for the Goddess as the mistress who commanded his destiny. (*The White Goddess*, p. 12)

In English literary history, there have been few really true poets. Among them are John Skelton, "who wore the Muse-name 'Calliope' embroidered on his cassock in silk and gold" (p. 476); John Donne, whose *Songs and Sonets* are the record of his love

---

12. Graves's thesis here agrees generally with that of Margaret Murray, a prominent (if occasionally suspect) scholar in the history of witchcraft. See her *Witch Cult in Western Europe* (Oxford, 1921), and *The God of the Witches* (New York, 1960).

affair with the woman who served as his Muse;[13] John Clare, who believed in "a beautiful presence, a woman deity" (p. 477); John Keats, who saw the White Goddess as his "Belle Dame sans Merci"; and Samuel Coleridge, "whose description in the *Ancient Mariner* of the woman dicing with Death in the phantom ship is as faithful a record of the White Goddess as exists" (p. 484).[14]

Shakespeare, too, knew and feared the Goddess. In *Macbeth* he introduced her as the Triple Hecate presiding over the witches' cauldron, and as Lady Macbeth inspiring her husband to murder Duncan (just as the ancient queens presided over the ritual murder of *their* kings). The "magnificent and wanton" Cleopatra, too, was a type of the Goddess (and, fittingly, died from the bite of an asp—the serpent sacred to Isis); as was "the damned witch Sycorax" in *The Tempest* (p. 476).

True poets have been rare in England chiefly because they have been forced to live in a patriarchal society; and a patriarchal society favors a different sort of poetry. Under Apollo, who became the God of Poetry after the suppression of the Goddess, an era of classicism arose, which has flourished whenever a society becomes rigid and academic and ruled by logic and by manners. According to classical, Apollonian doctrine, the test of a good poet is "his ability to express time-proved sentiments in time-honored forms with greater fluency, charm, sonorousness, and learning than his rivals" (p. 495). The classical poets use "old-fashioned diction, formal ornament, and regular, sober, well-polished metre, as a means of upholding the dignity of their office" (p. 495).

The true poet, according to Graves, must always be original,

13. In *5 Pens in Hand* (pp. 68-69) Graves explains that "By ancient religious theory the White Goddess becomes incarnate in her human representative—a priestess, a prophetess, a queen-mother. No Muse-poet can grow conscious of the Muse except by experience of some woman in whom the Muse-power is to some degree resident." Apparently Donne's Ann More was such a woman, as was Keats's Fanny Brawne.

14. Cf. *Ancient Mariner*, III, ll. 190-94:

> Her lips were red, her looks were free,
> Her locks were yellow as gold,
> Her skin was white as leprosy,
> The Night-mare Life-in-Death was she,
> Who thicks man's blood with cold.

but in a simpler sense than his classical counterpart. He must address only the Muse—not the King or Chief Bard or the people in general—and tell her the truth about himself and her in his own impassioned and distinctive manner: "The Muse is a deity, but she is also a woman, and if her celebrant makes love to her with the secondhand phrases and ingenious verbal tricks that he uses to flatter her son Apollo she rejects him more decisively even than she rejects the tongue-tied or cowardly bungler" (p. 497). If he is sincere in his protestations of love, the Goddess may smile on him for a time; but the poet is the God of the Waxing Year, and he must expect that the Goddess will ultimately destroy him, savagely and remorselessly. The poet's "death" is, of course, a metaphoric one; what really happens is that he loses his vision of the Goddess, which means that his poetic inspiration must die: "The woman whom he took to be a Muse, or who was a Muse, turns into a domestic woman and would have him turn similarly into a domesticated man. Loyalty prevents him from parting company with her, especially if she is the mother of his children and is proud to be reckoned a good housewife; and as the Muse fades out, so does the poet" (p. 503).

Graves's attitude toward the Goddess is an ambiguous one. At one level in *The White Goddess* he is completely a rationalist: myth, for him, is primarily a dramatic shorthand record of such matters as invasions, migrations, dynastic changes, admission of foreign cults, and social reforms; and with disinterested precision he goes about making historical sense of them, and tracing the ancient Goddess-worship through its vicissitudes. As archetypes of central human experiences and emotions—in spite of what he says about the Prince of the Air in the passage quoted above—myths appear not to interest him at all. Jungian psychology, he has insisted,[15] has no place in his concept of the Goddess and her importance to society and the individual man.

On another level, however, the poet in Graves prevails; his Goddess is all-powerful, and he is capable of such passages as this:

15. *5 Pens in Hand*, p. 62.

Cerridwen abides. Poetry began in the matriarchal age, and derives its magic from the moon, not the sun. No poet can hope to understand the nature of poetry unless he has had a vision of the Naked King crucified to the lopped oak, and watched the dancers, red-eyed from the acrid smoke of the sacrificial fires, their bodies bent uncouthly forward, with a monotonous chant of "Kill! kill! kill!" and "Blood! blood! blood!" (*The White Goddess*, p. 502)

To a generation of readers who have been conditioned to this sort of thing by Sir James Frazer, Jane Harrison, Jessie Weston, and other cultural anthropologists, the theories expressed in *The White Goddess* will not necessarily appear absurd. We may, like Randall Jarrell, choose to see the whole work as a monumental sublimation on Graves's part of his personal experiences with women, especially with Laura Riding. Although Graves has emphatically denied this (*5 Pens in Hand*, p. 61), readers of his poetry and his autobiography may feel that Jarrell is at least partially correct. But Graves is very much a part of the literary environment of his childhood: he was brought up on the algolagnic heroines of Swinburne, the wan, hypnotic beauties of the Romantic poets, and the Fatal Women of Elizabethan tragedy; and his vision of the Goddess corresponds so closely to these stereotypes that it is impossible to see her solely as the product of his personal experience. What seems most probable is that Graves, in constructing his concept of the Muse, took the familiar female stereotype he inherited from centuries of romantic literature, and associated it with the antique Goddess who killed and devoured her lovers. He was seeking a name for the abstract concept which he felt lay behind all poetic inspiration, and he found the White Goddess, in all her awesome ferocity. Whether or not Graves believes in her as a true Goddess is irrelevant: what is important for us to realize from *The White Goddess* is that, for Graves, no poet is a true poet until he devotes himself utterly to the expression of his love for her. If he does not do this, then he will find himself writing the artificial, uninspired poetry of classicism. Once we have recognized this, we see that the fundamental ideas of Graves have not altered a great deal since the time of *On English Poetry*. The chief difference is that, in *On English Poetry* and *Poetic Unreason*, his defence of romanticism and his dislike for classicism were dressed in semi-Freudian attire; and that, in *The White Goddess*, the same points of view are expressed in a mythological, religious framework. He has simply traded one non-literary technique for another, and his basic beliefs have remained unchanged except in one respect: as he was to say one year after the publication of *The White Goddess*, "I now regard the poet as independent of fashion and public service, a servant only of the true Muse, committed on her behalf to continuous personal variations on a single pre-historic, or post-historic theme; and have thus ceased to feel the frantic strain of swimming against the stream of time. . . ."[16] The disdain for the public that he had felt during his second and third periods continues, then; poetry is for Robert Graves in the fourth period of his career still a purely personal matter—a private dialogue between the poet and his Muse, in which the reader can only be an eavesdropper.

16. *The Common Asphodel: Collected Essays on Poetry, 1922-1949* (London: Hamish Hamilton, 1949), p. x.

# 11

# The Goddess in the Poems

Although Graves is careful to point out that his White Goddess has her gentle moments, there is a great deal of justice in Martin Seymour-Smith's complaint that Graves "tends to overemphasize the cruelty of the Goddess at the expense of her gentleness."[1] As I have suggested, the reason for this preoccupation with the grislier side of the Goddess's sharply ambivalent nature may lie partly in Graves's literary heritage, and it seems probable also that Graves's temperamental inclination toward things disgusting or morbid has also played a part in defining his vision of the Goddess. An incident reported by Seymour-Smith would seem to support a contention that Graves finds it difficult to conceive of his Goddess as anything but bloodthirsty:

Once, when asked by a friend for an example of a gentle aspect of the Muse, he frowned for some time and then named a woman character in his re-handling of the story of Jason. . . . This character, though gentle certainly in speech, nevertheless causes somebody to be chased down a defile and stoned to death.

Graves's first poems about the Triple Goddess and her cults appeared scattered throughout *Hercules, My Shipmate* and *The*

1. *Robert Graves,* Writers and Their Works, No. 78 (London, 1956), p. 14.
2. *Ibid.,* p. 15.

*White Goddess,* and many more were printed in the three volumes of verse that he published between 1944 (the time that he began his full-scale investigation of the myths) and 1952 (the year in which he revised and enlarged his "Historical Grammar of Poetic Myth"): *Poems, 1938-1945* (1946), *Collected Poems, 1914-1947* (1948), and *Poems and Satires, 1951* (1951). It is certainly true that these Goddess-poems reflect Graves's fascination with the crueller side of her nature. In the poem which serves as his dedication to *The White Goddess,*[3] Graves sees himself as a lonely pilgrim who, full of scorn for the "saints" and "sober men" who revile her, has sailed out to find his Goddess,

> Whose broad white brow was white as any leper's,
> Whose eyes were blue, with rowan-berry lips,
> With hair curled honey-colored to white hips.

It is winter, and, though he seeks her out

> at the volcano's head,
> Among pack-ice, or where the track had faded
> Beyond the cavern of the seven sleepers,[4]

he can find no signs of her. But even in November, months before her reappearance in spring, he is gifted "with so huge a sense/ Of her nakedly worn magnificence" that he "forgets cruelty and past betrayal," and presses his pursuit of her, "careless of where the next bright bolt may fall"—that is, so eager for a glimpse of her that he gives no thought to the torment that such a glimpse will bring.

When the Goddess does appear, she may do so as a woman, but she is just as likely to assume the shape of any of the creatures that are sacred to her. In "Return of the Goddess,"[5] she is seen

3. This poem, slightly altered, was subsequently entitled "The White Goddess" and included in *Poems and Satires, 1951* (p. 1). I quote from the earlier version.

4. The cavern is that of Ephesus, in Ionia; significant here not so much because of the Christian myth of the seven sleepers, but because of the cavern's earlier use as a shrine to the wolf-goddess Artemis. Cf. Graves, *The Greek Myths,* 2 vols. (New York: Geo. Graziller, 1957), I, p. 354.

5. *The White Goddess,* p. 540; subsequently published in *Collected Poems, 1914-1947,* p. 240.

as "a gaunt, red-wattled crane" (we are told in *The White Goddess*, p. 538, that the crane was commonly associated with Kali,
the murderous Indian goddess), and the men who are to be her
victims are depicted as the frogs who hide, quaking in terrified
anticipation of the crane's coming, in an alder thicket.

> The log they crowned as king
> Grew sodden, lurched, and sank.
> Dark waters bubble from the spring,
> An owl floats by on silent wing,
> They invoke you from each bank.

Graves concludes *The White Goddess* with a prophecy that the
Apollonian religions (of which Christianity is a type) will ultimately fall, and that the Goddess will regain her original power.
This poem is obviously a symbolic restatement of that prophecy:
the Christian deity is, like the frogs' King Log, dumb, sodden, and
fast-singing; and the Goddess will soon return, like the crane, to
reclaim her wayward subjects:

> At dawn you shall appear . . .
> She whom they know too well for fear,
> Lunging your beak down like a spear
> To fetch them home again.

The imminent return of the Goddess is again foretold in "The
Twelve Days of Christmas" (*Poems, 1938-1945*, p. 27), in which
the Goddess is now seen as Hera, and the doomed god as Zeus,
her unruly and loutish son, who

> stole the axe of power,
> Debauched his virgin mother
> And vowed he would be God the Father;

who strangled Hera's lion twins (Graves is recalling here that the
goddesses of Crete and Pelasgia were often shown in icons as accompanied by a pair of lions) and hung her, with anvils tied to her
ankles, from a cloud; who "whipped her daughters with a bull's
pizzle" and "forced them to take the veil" (i.e., turned Hera's

capricious and promiscuous priestesses into chaste nuns). Hera
for a time will tolerate such disrespect; but Zeus, for all his bully-
ish power, is doomed: he will grow senile at last, and go

> Into the kitchen where roast goose,
> Plum pudding and mince-pies his red robes grease,[6]

while the Goddess, her dignity restored, looks on benignly (like
the ornamental angel perched at the top of the Christmas tree):

> She, from the tree-top, true to her deserts,
> With wand and silver skirts,
> Presides unravished over all true hearts.

As the Goddess destroys—or at least disgraces—her royal con-
sorts, she will no less surely turn on the poets who dedicate themselves to her. One of Graves's most striking poetic treatments of
this practice of hers is "Darien" (*Poems and Satires, 1951,* pp. 18-
19), in which he asserts that

> It is a poet's privilege and fate
> To fall enamoured of the one Muse
> Who variously haunts this island earth.

The poet here is a type of Adonis, and the Muse is the sea-nymph
Aphrodite who, "presaged by the darting halcyon bird" traditionally taken as her emblem (*The White Goddess,* pp. 193-94), and
carrying over her shoulder the Cretan axe with which she dis-
patches her lovers,

> Would run green-sleeved along her ridges,
> Treading the asphodels and heather-trees
> With white feet bare.

6. Graves is referring to another, later solar demi-god, St. Nicholas, who was
once the patron saint of scholars and children, but who has degenerated into the
white-bearded and buffoonish Santa Claus, who "in the early morning of Christmas
day, clad in an old red cotton dressing-gown, . . . fills the childrens' stockings with
nuts, raisins, sugar-biscuits, and oranges; and, while the family are at church
singing hymns in honour of the newborn king, presides in the kitchen over the
turkey, roast beef, plum pudding, brandy butter and mince pies; and finally . . .
goes out into the snow—or rain—with an empty sack and senile groans of farewell"
(*The White Goddess,* p. 507).

The poet tells how, once at full moon by the sea's edge, he came
upon her as she stood silent, "her axe propped idly on a stone."

> No awe possessed me, only a great grief;
> Wanly she smiled, but would not lift her eyes
> (As a young girl will greet the stranger).
> I stood upright, a head taller than she.
> 'See who has come,' said I.

> She answered: 'If I lift my eyes to yours
> And our eyes marry, man, what then?
> Will they engender my son Darien?
> Swifter than wind, with straight and nut-brown hair,
> Tall, slender shanked, grey-eyed, untameable;
> Never was born, nor ever will be born
> A child to equal my son Darien,
> Guardian of the hid treasures of your world.'

Darien is, of course, the Divine Child, the God of the Waning
Year; and the poet realizes that he, as potentially the old king,
must die if Darien is to be born:

> I knew then by the trembling of her hands
> For whom that flawless blade would sweep:
> My own oracular head, swung by its hair.

But he is nonetheless eager for the Goddess to choose him as her
lover:

> 'Mistress,' I cried, 'the times are evil
> And you have charged me with their remedy.
> O, where my head is now, let nothing be
> But a clay counterfeit with nacre blink:
> Only look up, so Darien may be born.

> 'He is the northern star, the spell of knowledge,
> Pride of all hunters and all fishermen,
> Your deathless fawn, an eglet of your eyrie,
> The topmost branch of your unfellable tree,

> A tear streaking the summer night,
> The new green of my hope.' Lifting her eyes,
> She held mine for a lost eternity.
> 'Sweetheart,' said I, 'strike now, for Darien's sake!'

There is more to "Darien," however, than a dramatization of the true poet's willingness to be destroyed: for, as the new king was supposed to be in a sense a reincarnation of his predecessor, so here the middle-aged poet seems to be longing for the sacrifice of his old self at the hands of the Goddess in order that he might be reborn as the youthful and vigorous Darien. He might thus be able, like the Greek Orpheus and the Welsh Bran (both types of the doomed god), to continue to sing after his decapitation.

The Goddess will not, however, grant her delicious but fatal favors to any poet who woos her. She is something of a critic, and is quick to reject any suitor whose poems displease her. In "Advice on May Day" (*Poems and Satires, 1951,* p. 13), Graves cautions his fellow Muse-poets that if, in their hymns to the Goddess, they make the mistake of singing the same song twice, or of singing a song "clean through," or of sermonizing, she will grow angry, turn on them, and rend them. She is best pleased, it seems, by fresh, brief, and simple statements of devotion.

The poems that Graves has written to his Muse are certainly original, and usually brief, but they are seldom very simple. Although their language and imagery are as precise and clear as anything Graves has written, and although the reader who is uninitiated into the Gravesian mysteries will still be able to receive almost the full emotional impact of the strange stories told by the poems, a complete understanding of them almost invariably requires a careful study of both *The White Goddess* and *The Greek Myths,* the intricately detailed compendium he wrote in 1957 partly to relate the myths, and partly to explain them in terms of his own singular theories.

As a brief paraphrase will show, a good example of this need for a familiarity with Graves's prose investigations is "To Juan at the Winter Solstice" (*Poems, 1938-1945,* pp. 28-29), which hap-

pens also to be perhaps the best of all Graves's magical poems.[7]
The winter solstice is the traditional birthday of all the solar
deities of antiquity, such as the Greek gods Apollo, Dionysus,
Zeus, Heracles, Adonis, and Hermes; the Syrian Tammuz; the
Irish demi-gods Lugh and Cuchulain; the Egyptian Horus; and
the Welsh Merddin (King Arthur's Merlin) and Llew Llaw
Gyffes. Graves chooses this solemn occasion to explain to young
Juan, his seventh child, that

> There is one story and one story only
> That will prove worth your telling,
> Whether as learned bard or gifted child;
> To it all lines or lesser gauds belong
> That startle with their shining
> Such common stories as they stray into.

The one story is, of course, that of the White Goddess and her
changing relations with her lovers; whether told by "learned bard"
or by "gifted child" (Graves is referring here to the myth of
Taliesin in the *Mabinogion,* in which the erudite old court poets
are outshone by Taliesin, the divine child whose verses are en-
coded paeans to the Goddess), it alone will pass Housman's test
for true poetry.

> Is it of trees you tell, their months and virtues,
> Of strange beasts that beset you,
> Of birds that croak at you the Triple will?

> Or of the Zodiac and how slow it turns
> Below the Boreal Crown,
> Prison of all true kings that ever reigned?

When a poet sings, like Taliesin or the anonymous author of the
*Câd Goddeu,* of the magic properties of trees; or of fabulous beasts
(the chimaera, unicorn, phoenix, or siren—all members of the

7. Graves provided some explanatory notes to this poem in Kimon Friar and
John Malcolm Brinnin's *Modern Poetry: American and British* (New York, 1951),
pp. 500-1.

Goddess' symbolic bestiary); or of prophetic birds like the crane, the vulture, and the owl; or of the Zodiac, in which the monotonously circling constellations symbolize the crucial events in the year's cycle of life; or of the Corona Borealis—originally the crown of the Cretan goddess Ariadne—which, "in Thracian-Libyan myth, carried to Bronze-Age Britain, was the purgatory where Solar Heroes went after death";[8] he is describing aspects of the single poetic story.

> Water to water, ark again to ark,
> From woman back to woman:
> So each new victim treads unfalteringly
> The never altered circuit of his fate,
> Bringing twelve peers as witness
> Both to his starry rise and starry fall.

The sun-hero always made his annual reappearance at the solstice as a child, floating in an ark; and the course of his life took him inexorably through his associations with the Goddess in her successive roles as Mother, Lover, and Layer-away. The twelve peers who observe his passage through life are, variously, the twelve Zodiacal signs, the twelve companions of the Celtic oak-king, the twelve scattered limbs of the dismembered Osiris, the twelve judges of the Teutonic god Balder, Charlemagne's twelve peers of France, Romulus and his twelve shepherds, the twelve knights of the Round Table—and even the twelve apostles of Jesus.

> Or is it of the Virgin's silver beauty,
> All fish below the thighs?
> She in her left hand bears a leafy quince;
> When with her right she crooks a finger, smiling,
> How may the king look back?
> Royally then he barters life for love.

The Goddess is here conceived of as Aphrodite (and, secondarily, as the Hebraic sea-goddess Rahab, the "fish-tailed queen of heaven"), who rose from the sea, ready to offer her sacred quince

8. Graves's note in Friar and Brinnin, *Modern Poetry*, p. 500.

to the doomed king who must sacrifice his life in return for her
love.

> Or of the undying snake from chaos hatched,
> Whose coils contain the ocean,
> Into whose chops with naked sword he springs,
> Then in black water, tangled by the reeds,
> Battles three days and nights,
> To be spewed up beside her scalloped shore?

The serpent is Ophion, who—according to the Orphic and Pelas-
gian creation myths—was created out of chaos by Eurynome, the
original Goddess of All Things, and who joined with Eurynome to
form the earth and the great ocean that surrounds it. The hero
who fought in Ophion's chops—that is, against the teeth of
the serpent—is Jason, who did so in order to capture the Fleece,
and who later fought in the brackish and reedy waters of the
Black Sea near the mouth of the Danube, in order to escape from
the Colchians.

> Much snow is falling, winds roar hollowly,
> The owl hoots from the elder,
> Fear in your heart cries to the loving-cup:
> Sorrow to sorrow as the sparks fly upward.
> The log groans and confesses
> There is one story and one story only.

The imagery of this stanza recalls that of "A Love Story," in which
the landscape was used to create an atmosphere of terror. The
winter scene, with the prophetic hoots of the owl (traditional
messenger of the death-goddess Hecate) from the doom-tree, the
elder (the ritual tree of the winter solstice, traditionally taken to
be the Crucifixion tree, and that from which European witches
took the wood for their magic horses), presages the coming of the
Goddess in her most fearsome aspect—as the remorseless destroyer
of the king. The lamenting log is that which was—and is still—
burnt in the Yule-tide festivals throughout Western Europe.

> Dwell on her graciousness, dwell on her smiling,
> Do not forget what flowers
> The great boar trampled down in ivy time.
> Her brow was creamy as the long ninth wave,
> Her sea-blue eyes were wild
> But nothing promised that is not performed.

Young Juan may concentrate on her gentler aspects (as his father has not), but he must not forget that the Goddess will turn murderous in the October saturnalia at the end of the doomed hero's reign, when Death (symbolized by the great boar, who kills practically all the great solar gods) will come at the hands of the Goddess' Maenads, who will have intoxicated themselves by chewing ivy leaves. The wild-eyed and fair-skinned (the ninth wave is always the whitest one) Triple Goddess is cruel; but she is just, and always keeps to her bargain: the solar heroes who seek her love do so in full awareness of the fate that awaits them; but they can be confident that, as surely as the Goddess will kill them, she will give them her love freely and honestly during the nine months of their reign.

As powerful as Graves's magical poems are, they exist, like "To Juan at the Winter Solstice," mostly on one level: that of awed celebration of the Goddess and her mysteries. Graves in his fourth period is generally even more effective when he avoids direct reference to the Goddess, and concentrates instead on examining the Single Theme as it applies to less exotic love affairs. Sometimes these relationships are given a framework from the classical myths; sometimes they involve only the poet and the woman he loves. In any case, these poems provide ample evidence that Graves's devotion to the White Goddess was bringing to his work a consistently greater degree of richness and subtlety than one finds in the preceding periods of his career.

Typical of the mythical treatments of the Theme is "Theseus and Ariadne" (*Poems, 1938-1945*, p. 25), in which we find Graves achieving an effect of irony through shifts in time and point of view. Theseus, having been aided by King Minos' daughter

Ariadne in killing the Minotaur and escaping from the Cretan
maze, has promised to marry the girl. But instead he abandons
her on the island of Naxos, and sails off to other adventures.
Now, years later, married to Ariadne's sister Phaedra, Theseus remi-
nisces about his old romance:

> High on his figured couch beyond the waves
> In dream recalling her set walk
> Down paths of oyster-shell bordered with flowers
> And down the shadowy turf beneath the vine.
> He sighs: 'Deep sunk in my erroneous past
> She haunts the ruins and the ravaged lawns.'

But Theseus' dream is inaccurate: Ariadne is no forlorn ghost,
wandering disconsolately among the ruins of her once-great kingdom.

> Yet still unharmed it stands, the regal house
> Crooked with age and overtopped with pines
> Where first he wearied of her constancy.
> And with a surer foot she goes than when
> Dread of his hate was thunder in the air,
> When the pines agonized with flaws of wind
> And flowers glared up at her with frantic eyes.
> Of him, now all is done, she never dreams
> But calls a living blessing down upon
> What he would have rubble and rank grass:
> Playing the queen to nobler company.

As Graves tells us in *The Greek Myths* (I, p. 347), Ariadne did not
die on Naxos, but was rescued by the god Dionysus, who married
her, made her a queen, and gave her many children. Theseus'
egotism has led his imagination to construct a fantasy which has
no basis in reality: he first recalls Ariadne's "set walk" along the
flowered paths in the days when—he supposes—she was filled with
love for him, and then pictures her as she "haunts" her ruins. The
ironic effect is achieved when we learn in the second stanza that
Ariadne (whom Graves identifies in *The Greek Myths* as a type

of the Moon Goddess) has not—as Theseus egotistically supposes—pined away for love of him, but has in fact forgotten him completely, and now walks "with a surer foot" the very paths that he imagines must be overgrown with weeds. Furthermore, it appears that her feelings for Theseus were governed not so much by love as by a fear of him so great that it seemed to her to be shared by the trees and flowers around her.

In both stanzas of the poem there is a time-shift (between things as they once seemed to be, and things as they are now); and between the two is a change of viewpoint—from that of Theseus to that of Ariadne. Such shifts are characteristic of Graves's manner in much of his best poetry, and are in fact his favorite way of showing the frequent discrepancy between reality and appearance. As Hayman says of "Theseus and Ariadne" in his *Essays in Criticism* article (p. 37), "The principle is simple, but the detail of the organization is complex; modulated echoes and modifying backward glances make suggestions of meaning reverberate through the poem and carry beyond it." The poem is related to the Single Theme in that Theseus emerges as a rather tarnished hero, while Ariadne, as the Cretan Moon Goddess, is triumphant. She has, Goddess-like, taken a new lover, and forgotten the old one.

The Theme recedes even further into the background in such poems as "Prometheus," "She Tells her Love while Half Asleep," "The Portrait," "Counting the Beats," and "The Survivor" as Graves begins first to use mythic situations to dramatize personal experiences, and then to compose love-poems in which only the somewhat gloomy atmosphere of his mythic mode is retained. In "Prometheus" (*Poems and Satires, 1951*, p. 21), Graves pictures himself as the rebellious Titan, condemned by Zeus to be chained forever to a rock, while a vulture feeds all day on his liver, which restores itself each night.

> Close bound in a familiar bed
> All night I tossed, rolling my head;
> Now dawn returns in vain, for still
> The vulture squats on her warm hill.

Yet it is not Zeus who punishes this Prometheus, but a woman
whose constancy he doubts; and the vulture that torments him is
his own jealousy:

> I am in love as giants are
> That dote upon the evening star,
> And this lank bird is come to prove
> The intractability of love.
>
> Yet still, with greedy eye half shut,
> Rend the raw liver from its gut:
> Feed, jealousy, do not fly away—
> If she who fetched you also stay.

This Prometheus, like his original, almost embraces his torture;
but where the original did so out of pride and a sense of justice
outraged, his modern counterpart does so because he has cast
aside his pride: he welcomes the vulture, jealousy, as long as the
faithless woman who has aroused it stays with him. Recognition
of the ironic contrast—that between the giant martyr of the myth
and his modern, love-enchained counterpart—depends, like that in
"Theseus and Ariadne," on a degree of familiarity with the myth
behind the poem; but, like the earlier poem, "Prometheus" can
stand by itself. "Theseus and Ariadne," with or without its background, is recognizable and moving as an illustration of man's distorting ego and woman's "lapsability" (to use Joyce's term); and
the reader of "Prometheus" does not need to consult Graves or
Bullfinch or Edith Hamilton before he can recognize that the
poem is a metaphoric treatment of a lover eaten up by jealousy.
    One of Graves's simplest—and loveliest—poems of this period
is "She Tells her Love while Half Asleep" (*Poems, 1938-1945,*
p. 22), and its only connection with myth is that Graves, in
*Hercules, My Shipmate* (p. 124), has Orpheus sing it to the Argonauts; after which he explains that the woman of whom Orpheus
has been singing is Euridice, his lovely wife, who had died trag-
ically years before. The background is totally unnecessary here,
in this little piece consisting of a brief statement and an illustra-
tive simile:

> She tells her love while half asleep,
> In the dark hours,
> With half-words whispered low:
> As earth stirs in her winter sleep
> And puts out grass and flowers
> Despite the snow,
> Despite the falling snow.

Once again, as in "A Love Story" and "Mid-Winter Waking," the woman's love is likened to the first tender signs of spring that appear in the midst of winter.

In "The Portrait" (*Poems and Satires*, 1951, p. 17), Graves does not mention the White Goddess or any of the myths in which she plays a part; but he does describe a woman in whom the mysterious power of the Goddess appears to reside. Throughout the poem this woman is contrasted with other, more mortal women, who seem to suffer a great deal from the contrast.

> She speaks always in her own voice
> Even to strangers; but those other women
> Exercise their borrowed, or false, voices
> Even on sons and daughters.
>
> She can walk invisibly at noon
> Along the high road; but those other women
> Gleam phosphorescent—broad hips and gross fingers—
> Down every lampless alley.
>
> She is wild and innocent, pledged to love
> Through all disaster; but those other women
> Decry her for a witch or a common drab
> And glare back when she greets them.

The poem is spoken, as we learn in the fourth stanza, by the girl's lover; and it seems obvious from his description of her that the poet takes her to be an incarnation of the Muse as a nymph or sprite: she is "wild and innocent," so unworldly that she makes all other women, who jealously brand her as either witch or slut,

seem gross and shrewish beside her. She is conscious of her
uniqueness, and wonders if her lover is a fitting consort:

> Here is her portrait, gazing sidelong at me,
> The hair in disarray, the young eyes pleading:
> 'And you, love? As unlike those other men
> As I these other women?'

If we are to judge from this poem, Graves sees the relationship
between the poet and the woman in whom the Muse-power dwells
as a rarefied thing, more spiritual than physical—or, at least, not
gross in the way that more mundane love-affairs are wont to be. In
the superb "Counting the Beats" (*Poems and Satires, 1951*, p. 3),
we learn that Graves still sees even this sort of love as limited by
time (as we might expect from his statements in *The White Goddess* about the way in which the affair between the poet and his
Muse must end unhappily). As in the earlier "Between Dark and
Dark" (cf. Chapter Nine, p. 138), passion and pleasure are here
seen as transient; and the incantatory, repetitive movement of the
poem emphasizes the sense of urgency of the lover, who is attempting to concentrate his and his loved one's attention on the fleeting
moment.

> You, love, and I,
> (He whispers) you and I,
> And if no more than only you and I
> What care you or I?

> Counting the beats,
> Counting the slow heart beats,
> The bleeding to death of time in slow heart beats,
> Wakeful they lie.

> Cloudless day,
> Night, and a cloudless day;
> Yet the huge storm will burst upon their heads one day
> From a bitter sky.

"Where shall we be" when this storm (death, or the death of their
love) "strikes home?" the woman asks. He answers:

> Not there but here,
> (He whispers) only here
> As we are, here, together, now and here,
> Always you and I.

The emphasized words, *you, I, counting,* and especially *here* stress the immediacy felt by the lover in his anxiety over the passage of time, measured in terms of their beating hearts. The tone is, in fact, not far from the bleak near-despair of the love poetry Graves wrote in his third phase: acutely aware that their time is running out, the speaker seems to be trying almost desperately to convince his loved one—and, probably, himself—that they must place all their faith in the present.

J. M. Cohen suggests[9] that one of the causes of Graves's old neurosis was the self-reproach that he felt at having survived the war in which so many of his comrades died; and there are certainly enough poems in Graves's canon to support such a theory.[10] Now, in "The Survivor" (*Poems and Satires, 1951*, p. 21), we find Graves comparing the man who has lived through war with the man who has emerged more or less intact from a love affair. He first pictures the "scarred and bemedalled" veteran of combat, his old comrades long dead, standing at the head of "a new undaunted company," and then asks:

> Is this joy? to be doubtless alive again,
> And the others dead? Will your nostrils gladly savour
> The fragrance, always new, of a first hedge-rose?
> Will your ears be charmed by the thrush's melody
> Sung as though he had himself devised it?

The implication is that the veteran, his memory permanently branded by the horrors he has been through, and the friends he has seen killed, will never again be able to experience pure joy. Guilt (to go along with Cohen) has diminished the survivor's capacity for pleasure. Turning to the man who has survived the death of a love affair, Graves then asks:

9. *Robert Graves,* Writers and Critics, No. 3 (Edinburgh, 1960), p. 25.
10. See for instance "Corporal Stare," *Fairies and Fusiliers,* p. 79; "Haunted," *Country Sentiment,* p. 67; "An Occasion," *Poems, 1914-1926,* p. 63.

And is this joy: after the double suicide
(Heart against heart) to be restored entire,
To smoothe your hair and wash away the life-blood,
And presently seek a young and innocent bride,
Whispering in the dark: 'for ever and ever'?

Again, the implied answer to the question is negative. The bitterness and cruelty that necessarily accompany the destruction of love, and the survivor's awareness that his new love, like his old one, will soon end, all combine to diminish the joy of the new affair.

That all of the poems just discussed are quite serious is not at all intended to suggest that Graves in his fourth period has suppressed his old penchant for satire, playful or otherwise. Nothing could be further from the truth; for, from *Poems, 1938-1945*, to the present, he has written almost as many satires as he has straightforward poems. What is important to note, however, is that Graves is now careful to distinguish between satire and "poetry proper," and assigns to each quite different functions. Poetry proper (i.e., "inspired" poetry) is the constructive side of the poet's profession, and satire the destructive side.[11] Satire, which can be called "left-handed poetry," and which was used by the ancient bards to "blight crops, dry up milk, raise blotches on the victim's face, and ruin his character forever," is now used "to destroy whatever is overblown, faded and dull, and clear the soil for a new sowing" (*The White Goddess*, pp. 498-99). Poetry is to be written in veneration of the Goddess and in celebration of the poet's love affair with her or her mortal surrogate; and satire is to be the weapon with which the poet attacks her enemies. Moreover, because "to write poems for other than poets is wasteful" (presumably because only other poets are capable of recognizing the sincerity and intensity of his love for the Goddess), Graves has announced that he writes "poems for poets, and satires and grotesques for wits."[12]  If I have stressed his "poems proper" thus

11. "The White Goddess," *5 Pens in Hand*, p. 67.
12. Foreword to *Poems, 1938-1945*. Graves goes on to say, with characteristic scorn for the "plain reader," "For people in general I write prose, and am content that they should be unaware that I do anything else."

far, then, it is not because Graves is not a competent and prolific satirist, but because he usually saves his best efforts for his serious treatments of the Single Theme.

His satires during this period are generally informed by the same flip cynicism that characterized so much of his earlier work— and that often detracted from its effectiveness. Occasionally, however, his destructiveness is impelled not by humorous contempt, but by anger. In "Secession of the Drones" (*Poems and Satires, 1951*, p. 26), for instance—recalling the way in which drones sometimes desert their hives and their Queen to form an all-male colony, and to eat filth instead of honey—Graves launches into an attack on men who, drone-like, have turned their backs on their Goddess and set up male-oriented societies and religions:

> These drones, seceding from the hive,
>   In self-felicitation
> That henceforth they will throng and thrive
>   Far from the honeyed nation,
>
> Domesticate an old cess-pit,
>   Their hairy bellies warming
> With buzz of psychologic wit
>   And homosexual swarming.
>
> Engrossed in pure coprophily,
>   Which makes them mighty clever,
> They fabricate a huge King Bee
>   To rule all hives forever.

The misanthropy here is Swiftian in its degree of disgust for what Graves feels to be the perverted and ultimately self-destroying egotism of modern man, who has rejected the feminine, life-giving principle represented by the Goddess, in favor of tepid patriarchal religions and spiritless man-created and scientifically-oriented societies.

For the most part, however, Graves seems in his fourth period to save his seriousness for his love poetry, and to use his satires and grotesques as vehicles for his somewhat tart sense of humor.

The objects of his ridicule are usually psychiatrists, narrow-minded logicians, the more Blimpish of his countrymen, shrewish women, pedants—in general, any individual or group that seems to him foolish, inflated, or ignorant of what Graves considers to be the proper modes of conduct. Since there is very little about the modern world that pleases him, Graves's range for satire is wide; and his sympathy is likely to be extended only to those few who, like himself, steadfastly refuse to be included in any group, movement, or system—whether social, political, academic, or religious.

Because he takes them so seriously, Graves's mythic concerns rarely appear in his satires. When they do, as in "Homage to Texas" (*Poems and Satires, 1951*, p. 28), an untypically charitable piece of light verse, they obviously have only a minimal connection with the Theme:

> It's hardly wise to generalize
>     About a state or city;
> But Texas girls are decent girls
>     And bold as they are pretty.
>
> Who dared the outrageous unicorn
>     Through lonely woods a-leaping?
> Who made him halt and lower his horn
>     And couch beside her, weeping?
>
> Not Helen  (wonder of her sex)
>     Nor Artemis, nor Pallas;
> No, sir: a girl from Houston, Tex.,
>     Though some claim it was Dallas.
>
> He told her: 'Ma'am, your Lone Star State,
>     Though maybe short on schooling,
> Outshines the whole bright forty-eight'—
>     And so it did, no fooling.

This little tribute to the lively Vestals of Texas, an example of Graves's satire at its mildest, is certainly little more than skillful and polished doggerel; and if we hold it beside, say, "To Juan at the Winter Solstice," the great gap that Graves has set up between his poetry proper and his satire is immediately apparent. The two belong to entirely different orders of verse.

When J. M. Cohen, speaking of Graves's poetry between 1944 and 1951, says that "The emotion which had been missing since his nursery-rhyme period, and which had been rejected whenever it attempted to appear, now emerged in greater strength than ever,"[13] he is somewhat guilty of over-simplification; for, as we have seen, Graves's second and third phases were hardly devoid of emotional poetry, even though he was attempting during most of that time to concentrate on detached analyses of intellectual problems. But Cohen's main point is well taken: it is certainly true that, once Graves had formulated his concept of the White Goddess and dedicated his most serious poetic efforts to the Single Theme, his work quickly became charged with a greater emotional intensity than it had before possessed. He was as versatile as ever, and the old pessimism about life and the impermanence of love still remained; but he had gone into his fourth period with a restored faith in the existence—however ill-fated—of real love between man and woman, and his investigations of the Goddess and the myths associated with her had given him a rich fund of imagery and event with which to express that faith. And, what is more important, he had at last found a "cause" that was ideally suited to his temperament. The Goddess was awesome, mysterious, alternately loving and cruel—altogether a figure that commanded the utmost in respect, devotion, and fear. Moreover, the lore connected with her worship was arcane enough to satisfy Graves's fondness for the dark alleys of erudition. The poet who aspired to attract her favors needed a vast reservoir of learning, ingenuity, tact, and—most of all—independence of imagination and unconventionality; and Graves knew himself to possess all these qualities. As Graves conceived of her, she was scornful of science and the more logically oriented philosophies, as the barren products of a patriarchal society; and Graves had long been opposed to both of these. Furthermore, the dark and bloody rites that were so integral a part of Goddess-worship provided an ideal

13. *Robert Graves*, p. 103.

outlet for Graves's attraction to the horrible, the grotesque, and the supernatural. She was, in short, the perfect Muse for a poet with a taste for the idiosyncratic and bizarre; and she caught, held, and enriched Graves's imagination as nothing before had been able to do. Whether she manifested herself as Mother, Nymph, or Crone, the White Goddess stood for the feminine principle as superior to the masculine; and Graves was prepared to pay her—or her mortal representatives—all the homage due from a loyal and humble subject.

# 12

# Recent Criticism and Poetry

For the most part, Robert Graves's critical writings since the 1948 publication of *The White Goddess* have been of two sorts: defenses of his theories equating true poetry with religious invocation of the Muse; and attacks on those poets, both past and present, who have failed to pay the Muse her proper tribute. The defenses are remarkable chiefly for their attitude of calm, untroubled conviction—clearly, Graves has no doubts at all about the validity of his theories, or about their beneficial effect on his own poetry; but the attacks, while obviously the products of a lively, shrewd, and learned mind, are all so extreme and subjective that many of Graves's recent critics have thrown up their hands in consternation and horror when forced to comment upon them.[1] But however much Graves's criticism of either sort is vitiated by his personal idiosyncrasies, the fact remains that whatever he has said

1. Hazard Adams, for example, in his "Criticism: Whence and Whither," *The American Scholar*, XXVIII (Spring, 1959), pp. 226-38, calls Graves "a berserk of violents," and finds his attacks full of unfairness, irrationality, and professional jealousy. Adams admits at the same time, however, that Graves's violence is "art and sometimes criticism," and that it is valuable at least for the healthy fury it has engendered among other, more timorous critics of poetry. For similar commentary, see also the correspondence of John Cotton, John Davies, and F. W. Bateson in *Essays in Criticism*, V (July, 1955), pp. 293-98; and Edward Dahlberg and Herbert Read, "Robert Graves and T. S. Eliot." *Twentieth Century*, CLXVI (1959), pp. 54-62. Dahlberg's remarks are as strongly (and petulantly) anti-Graves as any I have seen.

in the past twelve years about poets and poetry is well worth reading; not only because a certain amount of iconoclasm in criticism is always useful as a restorer of perspective, but also because there is probably no other living poet-critic who can discuss the practical aspects of his art with more common sense and authority. One may not share Graves's enthusiasm for the White Goddess,[2] or agree with his assessments of other poets' work; but no one can deny that, when Graves talks about the business of writing a poem, or about the duties of the poet, he deserves attention.

In 1949 Graves submitted his earlier critical writings to the same winnowing process by which he has continually altered his poetic canon, and published whatever he found deserving of retention in a work entitled *The Common Asphodel: Collected Essays on Poetry, 1922-1949* (London: Hamish Hamilton, 1949). The psychological arguments of *On English Poetry* and *Poetic Unreason,* and the sociological and historical analogies of *Contemporary Techniques of Poetry* and *Another Future of Poetry,* seemed to him now to be full of contradictions and special pleading; and he accordingly retained from these volumes only their practical observations about the techniques of composition, which he still felt to be reasonably sound. Most of *A Survey of Modernist Poetry* and *A Pamphlet Against Anthologies* was allowed to survive, as were essays from *Epilogue* on Nietzsche, Coleridge and Wordsworth, Keats and Shelley, and others.

*The Common Asphodel* also contained several essays previously uncollected. The most illuminating of these was "How Poets See" (pp. 295-306), dated 1939, in which Graves talks first about his own visual peculiarities, then about those of Keats, Coleridge, Wordsworth, Milton, and Donne. From the nature of their imagery, Graves deduces that Keats was short-sighted, and had to rely primarily on how the objects of his description felt, tasted, sounded, or smelled; that Wordsworth had "all the ac-

2. D. J. Enright, who is usually quite sympathetic to Graves, has said of the White Goddess that "she sounds like a cross between a shrewish wife and a military dictator." Cf. his "Robert Graves and the Decline of Modernism," *Essays in Criticism,* XI (July, 1961), pp. 319-37.

curacy and completeness of visual description" of a landscape, but that he was not as sensitive to color as Coleridge; that Milton was pained by every color but green before his blindness, and obsessed with light afterwards; and that Donne made almost no use of his "outward eye," and depended for his imagery either on popular literature or on science.

Graves frankly admits in this essay that his own powers of sight are imperfect ("I never have clear visions of objects except in half-sleep or slight fever or great emotional stress"), and that his ability to perceive objects is hampered by his habit of concentrating all his attention on only the most outstanding features of those objects. His sense of touch, however, is abnormally acute:

I can remember the shape of any body or inanimate object I have once touched, and if I were asked to reconstruct the dimensions of a house in which I have lived for some years, I should imagine myself walking through it in the half-dark, and know just how the rooms stood in relation to one another, their size, the position of their furniture, and so on.

Although such statements as these would seem to support the contention of John Press that Graves "relies very largely upon his sense of touch in his dealings with the external world,"[3] Graves's poems do not in fact reveal any such emphasis on a single sense. He seems, rather, to give about equal attention to sight, sound, smell, and touch—as he does, for example, in "Intercession in Late October" (*Collected Poems, 1914-1947*, p. 233), another poem to the Goddess:

> How hard the year dies: no frost yet.
> On drifts of yellow sand Midas reclines,
> Fearless of moaning reed or sullen wave.
> Firm and fragrant still the brambleberries.
> On ivy-bloom butterflies wag.
>
> Spare him a little longer, Crone,
> For his clean hands and love-submissive heart.

3. *The Fire and the Fountain: An Essay on Poetry* (Oxford, 1955), p. 144.

But, as this poem illustrates, Graves usually employs imagery only partly for its sensuous effect. The appeals to our senses here may enhance the dramatic impact of the doomed king awaiting his sacrifice, but we should know as well that almost every concrete detail in the poem relates to Graves's interpretation of the myth of Midas, son of the Great Goddess of Ida and King of the Phrygians: from *The White Goddess* (pp. 102, 103) and *The Greek Myths* (I, pp. 281-83) we learn that Midas, in order to lose his golden touch, washed his hands in the river Pactolus, the banks of which promptly became golden in hue—hence "drifts of yellow sand"; and that it was a reed from this river that spread the humiliating news to the whispering waves that Midas had grown ass's ears— hence "moaning reed or sullen wave." Further, bramble and ivy are leaves sacred to the Goddess, and important to her autumnal rites of sacrifice (*The White Goddess,* p. 210). The conclusion seems to be that in Graves's poems (especially the mythic ones) imagery is used at least as much for intellectual as for sensuous purposes—that Graves's appeal is directed as much to the reader's mind as to his sense of sight, touch, sound, or smell.

Six years after *The Common Asphodel* Graves published *The Crowning Privilege,*[4] another collection of critical essays, the most important of which were the six Clark Lectures he had delivered at Cambridge the previous year. His chief point in these is that poets belong to no guild, group, society, or association, and owe their allegiance only to the Muse herself; and that if they are false to this "crowning privilege," they betray the cause of poetry. These lectures are typical Graves: witty, downright, learned, tough, and academically outrageous and perverse. On his theme he strings an enormous amount of erudition about the ancient bards and Druids drawn from the same Welsh and Irish sources he had used for *The White Goddess,* and presents a century-by-century survey of English poetic history, from its beginnings to the present, pausing briefly to assault the reputation of almost every literary giant he comes across. Throughout the series he

4. London: Cassell, 1955; New York: Doubleday, 1956. References here are to the New York edition.

returns again and again to the central motif: "To call the tune is the function of the Muse alone. Her demands are unforeseeable and ungainsayable; and her hand cannot be forced" (p. 31).

In the course of English literary history, there have been very few poets, Graves feels, who were sufficiently aware of their unique privilege. His old favorite, John Skelton, was one; John Dryden was not: "He earned the doubtful glory of having found English poetry brick and left it marble—native brick, imported marble" (p. 37). Marvell was one; Cowley was not. Because the Goddess insists on truth, and ridicules the idea of using argument or rhetorical charm to overbear her intuition of truth, Milton lost her favor "when he allowed his rhetorical skill, learned at Christ's, to dull his poetic sense" (p. 108). The whole period between Marvell and Blake is poetically barren, "except for a few resolute blades of green grass showing up here and there between the marble paving stones" (p. 42). In this age dominated completely by Apollo, the arrogant usurper of the Goddess' reign over poetry, only Swift, with his Stella, could boast a personal Muse; all the other neo-classicists were inspired only by self-love or by the desire to appear wittier than their fellow-poets. The greatest classicist of them all, Pope, was the greatest villain of them all—and "an extremely poor technician" (p. 45) to boot.

Of the Romantic poets, John Clare, who went mad in his quest for the Goddess, is ranked above Wordsworth, who began as a devotee of the Goddess, but who deserted his personal Muse— Annette Vallon—and ended as a fumbling servant of the public. As for Tennyson, he never had a Muse—"except Arthur Hallam, and a Muse does not wear whiskers" (p. 50). In the last of the lectures, entitled "These Be Your Gods, O Israel!" Graves scores the public for having deified such dubious poets as Yeats, Pound, Eliot, Auden, and Thomas. He announces at the outset that his purpose is not to destroy, but to revive the public's taste for poetry; but, whatever his intentions, the essay soon becomes a merciless outpouring of his resentment at what he feels to be the undeserved adulation of the five contemporary deities.

Yeats, while a man of industry and careful craftsmanship (except, presumably, for "The Lake Isle of Innisfree"), lacked divine "grace."

"Grace" is the presence of the Muse Goddess; but she does not appear unless her poet has something urgent to say and to win her consent a poet *must* have something urgent to say. Yeats had a new technique, but nothing to say. . . . Instead of the Muse, he employed a ventriloquist's dummy called Crazy Jane. But still he had nothing to say. (*The Crowning Privilege,* p. 123)

To publish poems strewn with references to which not one reader in ten million has the key, as Yeats did, is regarded as impudence by the Muse (although, it seems, it is perfectly acceptable to use obscure references if they all relate to myths connected with Goddess-worship); but to be obscure, and to misquote frequently as well, is an even more heinous poetic crime—and this, says Graves, is what Ezra Pound has done. His major work, the *Cantos,* is "sprawling, ignorant, indecent, unmelodious, and seldom metrical" (p. 130); and he is fond of salting his poems with tags from languages of which he knows little. His Chinese ideographs, Graves suspects, "may well have been traced from the nearest tea-chest" (p. 130).

Graves despises Pound so thoroughly that he never pretends to any objectivity where his works are concerned. The worst thing he says of Eliot is that he was too much influenced by Pound, although he suggests that it might have been better for Eliot to have stopped writing poetry after *The Hollow Men.*[5] In the Thirties, Eliot "made his peace with the Hippopotamus and . . . became a churchwarden, edited Kipling, and recanted his former aspersions on Milton" (p. 134). But Eliot had been, however briefly, a true poet, as some of the haunting blank verse passages in *The Waste Land* prove.

Auden, for all his skill in composing light verse, is nothing more than a synthetist of the styles of other, better poets. He is, says Graves, guilty of plagiarizing the work of Laura Riding, in every way a vastly superior artist. (Graves's obstinate champion-

5. Graves has written me of Eliot that "he died as a poet about 1927, as far as I was concerned."

ing of his former Muse, while perhaps in some respects justifiable, is often uncomfortably similar to the stubborn and ludicrous support of Mrs. Elizabeth Daryush by Yvor Winters, a critic whose crankiness frequently outstrips even that of Graves.)

Of the five idols, only Dylan Thomas is treated at all sympathetically by Graves, who nevertheless deplores Thomas' sacrific of intelligibility for the ends of mere musical explosiveness: "Dylan Thomas was drunk with melody, and what the words were he cared not" (p. 130). But Thomas was above all a romanticist, an anti-intellectual, and Graves likes him for this.

Although, as F. W. Bateson says in his *Essays in Criticism* letter (cf. *supra,* p. 189n.), Graves in the Clark Lectures "is undoubtedly more of a literary sniper than the scrupulous analyst of meanings and values," and although he is sometimes even guilty of carelessness in them (as when, in discussing Yeats's "Chosen," he mistakenly supposes that the narrator is a man, not a woman),[6] there is still a great deal of sound, practical commentary and advice in *The Crowning Privilege* to redeem Graves as a critic. He is perhaps at his best when outlining the responsibilities of the poet, both to his profession and to society. Sincerity, simplicity, and lucidity are the poetic virtues he emphasizes:

Personally, I expect poems to say what they mean in the simplest and most economical way; even if the thought they contain is complex. . . . [The Goddess] rejects all over-erudite references in the poems offered to her. . . . The poet's approach to the Goddess is a personal one: he comes as himself, not in fancy-dress or borrowed clothing; and does not rant at her as though she were a public meeting, but speaks gently, clearly, intimately—they are closeted together. (*The Crowning Privilege,* pp. 105, 106, 101)

Rhythm and metre are a necessary discipline in poetry, but the poet must be careful not to be led by its demands away from the original thought that had prompted him to write:

It is unprofessional conduct to say: "When next I write a poem I shall use the sonnet form"—because the theme is by definition

6. See Peter Ure, "Yeats and Mr. Graves," letter to *Times* [*London*] *Literary Supplement* (June 12, 1959), p. 353.

unforeseeable, and theme chooses metre. A poet should not be conscious of the metrical pattern of a poem he is writing until the first three or four lines have appeared; he may even find himself in the eleventh line of fourteen before realizing that a sonnet is on the way. . . . Theme chooses metre; what is more, theme decides what rhythmic variations should be made in metre.   (p. 92)

Although Graves continues to believe that a sort of magical inspiration lies at the roots of the creative process, and that a poem —in its initial stages, at least—must be worked out while the poet is in a trance, he seems now to stress more than ever the necessity for a careful and painstaking "secondary elaboration." Excellence in poetry, it appears, entails a certain amount of hard labor, especially with problems of prosody. As he had done so often in his earlier critical works, Graves once again holds up Robert Frost as his best example of the true poet, who combines inspiration with craftsmanship: "Frost's poems, which combine traditional metres with intensely personal rhythms, show the advantage of staying put and patiently working at the problem" (p. 94). The poet must neither bind himself too tightly to metrical and rhythmic patterns, nor—like the *vers librists*—fling off their yoke entirely; he must, like Frost, express his individuality by using his own natural speech rhythms as variations on a metrical norm.

About the moral obligations of the poet, Graves is no less explicit:

I have never been able to understand the contention that a poet's life is irrelevant to his work. . . . If it means that a poet may be heartless or insincere or grasping in his personal relations and still write true poems, I disagree wholeheartedly. . . . And though it may be argued that no acceptable code of sexual morals can be laid down for the poet, I am convinced that deception, cruelty, meanness, or any violation of a woman's dignity are abhorrent to the Goddess; and that she loathes the deliberate sexual perversion which has male self-sufficiency for its object, and which has never been more boldly pursued by would-be poets than today.   (pp. 33, 113)

Most importantly, the poet must allow no extra-literary activity on which he takes part, whether concerned with his livelihood or with his social duties, to interfere with his poetic practice. He must join no organizations, whether social, political, or religious, if he intends to serve the Muse as she demands.

A poet's integrity . . . consists in his not forming ties that can impair his critical independence, or prevent him from telling the truth about anything, or force him to do anything out of character. It consists also in his refusal to pay more respect to persons than decency demands, or their attainments permit. (p. 115)

Graves's criticism since *The Crowning Privilege* consists for the most part either of brief occasional essays or of addresses delivered to audiences at American colleges and universities. Most of these have been collected, together with miscellaneous stories, essays on general subjects, travelogues, historical anecdotes, and poems, in three recent volumes: *5 Pens in Hand, Steps,* and *Food for Centaurs.*[7] There is in none of these any significant advance beyond or alteration of the attitudes expressed in *The Crowning Privilege:* Graves, as we might expect, is too much at home in the role of iconoclastic lone wolf to allow himself to mellow much with age; and all the critical and popular acclaim that has at last come to him has made him not one whit more charitable toward either the critics or the public. Like most of his fellow-poets, they are still the objects of his scorn.

There are in these later essays several more denunciations of his old enemies Milton, Wordsworth, and Pound, all based on ruthless dissections of individual poems. In "Legitimate Criticism of Poetry," a lecture delivered at Mount Holyoke College in 1957 (*5 Pens in Hand,* pp. 33-53; and *Steps,* pp. 63-85), Graves first tears apart "L'Allegro" and "Il Penseroso" line by line to show that they are confused jumbles in which sense is sacrificed to Milton's fondness for Latinate diction ("Why pretend that English poetry is held in a Latin strait-jacket, from which one has to wriggle out with the artful aid of grammatical and syntactical license?"). After

7. The first two published in 1958 by Doubleday of New York and Cassell of London, respectively; and the third by Doubleday in 1960.

this he reduces to absurdity Wordsworth's "The Solitary Reaper," in which he finds a slender and rather foolish event bloated into "significance" (a word Graves abhors) by verbosity, vague and abstract terms, and fuzzy logic. None of these poems, Graves says, can match Frost's "The Mountain" or Ransom's "Ilex Priscus," both of which are notable for their "good sense," coherence, and verbal economy.

In "Sweeney Among the Blackbirds," a talk given at the University of Texas in 1958 (*Steps,* pp. 106-28), Graves returns briefly to Pound's *Cantos,* which he evaluates with even more eloquence than usual:

Architecturally, ethically, or musically they invite no serious criticism; being, by your leave, a random sequence of sighs, coos, Bronx cheers, rhetorically garbled scraps of history, quotations from foreign tongues, falsetto screams, and indecent eructations.

Then, having so neatly disposed of Pound, Graves turns his attention once again to Eliot, whose "Sweeney Among the Nightingales" (which Graves calls "Sweeney *and* the Nightingales") he mocks chiefly because the classical allusions in it are inaccurate: the wood at Mycenae was not bloody, but tranquil; Agamemnon was murdered in a bath-house, not in a wood; and, since classical authority gives January as the time of Agamemnon's death, there would hardly have been any nightingales about to stain his shroud with their droppings.

To those who would counter that this sort of criticism is pedestrian and carping, and that Eliot's use of classical allusion is for the communication of symbolic rather than literal truth, Graves would point out that symbolism which does not tally with fact is false symbolism. His point may be a valid one, but the fact remains that such analyses as this one of Eliot's poem are ideal weapons for destruction, but useful for little else: *any* poem, when its every detail is scrutinized sardonically and negatively, is likely to appear ludicrous and sloppily contrived. Such a technique as Graves's, while admittedly potent, is nonetheless a limited one; and Graves frequently leaves himself open to charges of malice and narrowness when he employs it—which he does frequently. He is, moreover, not always as accurate an analyst as he might seem—as when, discussing "Sweeney Erect," he speaks of Sweeney's "wife" shrieking in the bedroom, when it is obvious that the woman is a prostitute.[8]

Where Graves's recent essays become most interesting to the student of his poetry is in those passages in which he very shrewdly and frankly discusses his own career. Occasionally he does so directly, as in his "Prologue to a Poetry Reading at Massachusetts Institute of Technology" (*5 Pens in Hand,* pp. 333-38), when he says that

> In the present confused state of literature, I would probably rank as a traditionalist; but not in the sense that I oppose innovations in poetic technique. . . . I am a traditionalist only in so far as I believe that certain principles of poetry cannot be violated without poetry turning into something else.

He is speaking here, of course, about his oft-repeated insistence that metre is essential to poetry, both as a discipline to the poet, and as a means of inducing a sort of hypnosis in the reader which will allow him to become aware of "larger symbolic sense of poetry"—the sense that prose, or free verse, must lack.

In "Sweeney Among the Blackbirds" Graves professes to be perplexed at the way in which, in his sixties, he has continued to write "in a vein that I should have finished with at least thirty years ago"; and in "Preface to a Reading of New Poems at the University of Michigan" (*Steps,* pp. 231-38), in a mood of self-criticism and humility rare in his prose, he contrasts himself, as an aging romanticist, with younger, fresher poets:

> The old poet knows too much; he prefers to take Pegasus around through a gap in the hedge, or along by a lane; yet keeps up with the hounds, and is usually in at the death. But this cannot be called hard riding; and the poet should, I think, ride hard or not at all. In fact, the poems I now write tend to be far too cunning. Not that, like most poets who have reached my age, I resort to

8. This discrepancy was first pointed out by D. J. Enright, "Robert Graves and the Decline of Modernism," p. 332.

rhetoric, traditional forms, musical metres, and classical references; but I have become such an obsessionist about getting a
poem right, that the product is usually too much of a *tour de force*.
I would have welcomed a little exuberant inexperience—short of
galloping rudely ahead of the pack and trampling the fox to death.

Usually, however, although always quick to state that his
poems are far from perfect, Graves appears to be reasonably satisfied with the course his career has taken; and it is obvious from
these essays that, when he speaks of the "true poet" and the sort
of poetry such a man must write, he has himself in mind. In the
essay just quoted from, for instance, Graves outlines the things a
man must do if he is to keep alive as a poet, and gives us what
amounts to a picture of what he has himself tried to be. To survive, he says, one must isolate himself from "the mainstream of
social life" in order to avoid everything that is untrue, pretentious,
dull, or anti-poetic. If one can do this, then

anger and scorn will die in him after awhile and be succeeded by
a wry humour. He will blame no one for the inequalities, lies,
pretences, tragedies and muddles that surround him, but accept
those as unavoidable adjuncts of the age into which he has been
born. Having worked out his own potentialities and limitations,
he will clear himself a small corner where no discrepancy divides
theory from fact: his private poetic world, where he can move
freely and without offense.

Graves has, in fact, never been able so completely to dissociate
himself from the outside world—except perhaps physically, by
virtue of his retreat to Majorca (where, since 1946, he has continued to live when not traveling and lecturing in England and
America); and, although a "wry humour" does inform a great
deal of his poetry and criticism, there is still enough anger in him
to disturb the more pacific of his readers. But few would deny
that he has succeeded in creating his own private poetic world,
where he is free to devote himself to the writing of his highly
personal love poems to the Goddess. And these poems provide
ample evidence that Graves is capable of taking the advice he has
offered to others in his essays: almost without exception they make

"sense; good sense; penetrating, often heart-rending sense" *(5 Pens in Hand,* p. 34). In spite of his obsession about "getting a poem right," they seldom seem overfine (although they are certainly as polished as anything being written today); and they are, for all their terseness and economy, full of the urgency and individuality and impassioned honesty that mark the true love-poet.

This perfectionism has had no effect at all on Graves's productivity: during the last decade he has also written over one hundred poems, almost all of which have been published in six volumes of collected verse: *Poems, 1953* (London: Cassell, 1953), *Collected Poems, 1955* (New York: Doubleday, 1955), *The Poems of Robert Graves, Chosen by Himself* (New York: Doubleday Anchor Books, 1958), *Collected Poems, 1959* (London: Cassell, 1959), *More Poems, 1961* (London: Cassell, 1961), and *Collected Poems, 1961* (New York: Doubleday, 1961).[9]

An examination of these collections will show that, qualitatively speaking, there has been no very great change in Graves's poetry since *Poems and Satires, 1951:* everything he writes bespeaks the same tart individuality, the same polished simplicity, the same directness, of his best work. From his serious poems (that is, those concerned with the White Goddess, or with the nature of love), most of which are grouped in *Poems, 1953,* and *More Poems, 1961,* one learns that Graves still holds true to the Single Theme; and from his satires and grotesques, which predominate among the new pieces of the 1955, 1958, and 1959 collections, it appears that he still retains his scorn for those who have not been so fortunate in their avoidance of sham, pretence, and subservience to unworthy causes.

If there is any change to be noted in the recent poetry, then, it must be one of degree, not of kind. Graves has taken no new stands, has espoused no new causes; but he seems now (quite naturally, for a man in his late sixties) to be more conscious than

9. He has, moreover, published also during this period no less than fifteen works of prose (excluding the critical miscellanies mentioned above): two novels; seven translations from Spanish, French, Latin, and Greek; three investigations of Biblical subjects; a critical anthology of English and Scottish ballads; and a collection of humorous stories.

ever of the swiftness with which all things—even love—pass. His mythic poems concentrate for the most part on the doomed god as he reaches the time of his destruction; and in his love-poems his attitude ranges from dismay at the inevitable death of love, to bewilderment and even exultation at the fact that his capacity for an intensely-felt love has not diminished with the advance of years. As Cohen says, the portrait presented by the recent poems "is of a man who knows the worst, yet has preserved a young heart."[10]

Of the seven poems in the 1953 collection that are directly concerned with mythic situations, "Dethronement" (p. 17) is certainly the best. Here Graves addresses the king who is about to die, advising him on the proper attitude to adopt toward the queen who supervises his ritual destruction.

> With pain pressing so close about your heart,
> Stand (it behooves you), head uncovered,
> To watch how she enacts her transformations—
> Bitch, vixen, sow—the laughing, naked queen
> Who has now dethroned you.
>
> Hymns to her beauty or to her mercy
> Would be ill-conceived. Your true anguish
> Is all that she requires. You, turned to stone,
> May not speak or groan, will stare dumbly,
> Grinning dismay.

The time for poetry, then, is past: once the queen has decreed death, the king's role in the drama requires him to flee, stag-like, so that he may be pursued by her "red-eared hounds" and her "swan-feathered arrows," as she now manifests herself as Diana, the huntress. The king's flight is a hopeless one, but he must not on that account slacken his pace, for to do so

> Would be ingratitude, a sour denial
> That the life she bestowed was sweet.
> Therefore be fleet, run gasping, draw the chase
> Up the grand defile.

10. *Robert Graves*, Writers and Critics, No. 3 (Edinburgh, 1960), p. 113.

The hounds will overtake the king, and rend him with "half a hundred love-bites"; but he must not despair, for his blood will make "an acceptable libation" for Persephone—Goddess of the Underworld—in whose demesne the king shall once again find peace.

"Dethronement" is typical of the mythic poems of this period, in that it depicts the Goddess, not as the mother or the lover, but as the destroyer of the poet-king; and we must conclude from it that Graves still is either unwilling or unable to portray the Goddess in any but her cruellest aspects. Once again, it is the king's necessary death that fascinates Graves; he does not in his mythic poems attempt to show the love that is so strong that the king will consent to be murdered in order that it might be granted him.

When in the 1953 collection Graves *does* turn to love, we find that here, too, he is thinking mostly of the time when love must die. In "The Straw" (p. 2), for instance, the speaker is a man who fears that his loved one may be regretting the pledges she had made to him:

> Peace, the wild valley streaked with torrents,
> A hoopoe perched on his warm rock. Then why
> This tremor of the straw between my fingers?
>
> What should I fear? Have I not testimony
> In her own hand, signed with her own name
> That my love fell as lightning on her heart?
>
> These questions, bird, are not rhetorical.
> Watch how the straw twitches and leaps
> As though the earth quaked at a distance.
>
> Requited love; but better unrequited
> If this chance instrument gives warning
> Of cataclysmic anguish far away.
>
> Were she at ease, warmed by the thought of me,
> Would not my hand stay steady as this rock?
> Have I undone her by my vehemence?

The straw quivers, of course, because the man holding it is himself quivering—having sensed suddenly that this love, in spite of (or because of) his vehemence and her submissiveness, is doomed. However willing she might be initially, Graves believes, it is not possible for a woman to be constant—not, at least, if she is a woman who has been touched by the Goddess.

In "The Foreboding" (p. 3), similarly, we see a man as he learns from a vision that his woman will desert him. This vision occurs when the man happens one day to peer in a window, and is shocked to see his own image, seated in his chair, with "gaze abstracted, furrowed forehead, unkempt hair." The man thinks at first that he is about to die, and that the vision is his farewell to his body—until the figure at the desk begins to write, on the paper before him, something which causes his tears to fall.

> He had written a name, yours, in printed letters:
>     One word, on which bemusedly to pore—
> No protest, no desire, your naked name,
>     Nothing more.

The eavesdropper realizes that the vision is intended not as a prophecy of his death, but as a sign that his lover will cause him grief in the near future. Aghast, he turns from the window.

> Why never a warning, either by speech or look,
>     That the love you cruelly gave me could not last?
> Already it was too late: the bait swallowed,
>     The hook fast.

But Graves does not by any means concentrate solely now on the inevitable unhappy ending of the love affair: in "Cry Faugh!" (p. 4), for example, he turns what has begun as a clever metaphysical disquisition on the problems of the man-woman relationship into a striking affirmation of romantic love. The first five stanzas are characteristic of Graves in his best satiric mood—witty, learned, and subtly scornful:

> Caria and Philistia considered
> Only pre-marital adventures wise;
> The bourgeois French argue contrariwise.
>
> Socrates and Plato burked the issue
>  (Namely, how man-and-woman love should be)
> With homosexual ideology.
>
> Apocalyptic Israelites, foretelling
> The Imminent End, called only for a chaste
> Sodality: all dead below the waist.
>
> Curious, various, amoral, moral—
> Confess, what elegant square or lumpish hamlet
> Lives free from nymphological disquiet?
>
> 'Yet males and females of the lower species
> Contrive to eliminate the sexual problem,'
> Scientists ponder: 'Why not learn from them?'

We know from his wry tone that the poet disapproves of all of these abstract and impractical ways of dealing with heterosexual love; but we are still happily surprised when the final two stanzas suddenly present us with a complete change in point of view and attitude. Now the poet turns from metaphysician to lover, and we see that what philosophies, religions, and sciences have said about love matter to him not at all:

> Cry faugh! on science, ethics, metaphysics,
> On antonyms of sacred and profane—
> Come walk with me, love, in a golden rain
>
> Past toppling colonnades of glory,
> The moon alive on each uptilted face:
> Proud remnants of a visionary race.

Graves may now be unreservedly pro-love, but he is against marriage—or, at any rate, against marriage when it turns love unnatural through being forced and rigid, or when it chains a supe-

rior woman to an inferior man. Such is the burden of "With Her
Lips Only" (*Poems, 1953,* p. 25), which is—like most of Graves's
poems now—very neatly and symmetrically constructed: a woman
unhappily fends off her lover and accepts her husband, in each
encounter assuaging her conscience by using her children as the
reason for her action:

> This honest wife, challenged at dusk
> At the garden gate, under a moon perhaps,
> In scent of honeysuckle, dared to deny
> Love to an urgent lover: with her lips only,
> Not with her heart. It was no assignation;
> Taken aback, what could she say else?
> For the children's sake, the lie was venial;
> 'For the children's sake', she argued with her conscience.
>
> Yet a mortal lie must follow before dawn:
> Challenged as usual in her own bed,
> She protests love to an urgent husband,
> Not with her heart, but with her lips only;
> 'For the children's sake', she argues with her conscience,
> 'For the children'—turning suddenly cold towards them.

In "Bitter Thoughts on Receiving a Slice of Cordelia's Wedding Cake" (*The Poems of Robert Graves, Chosen By Himself,*
p. 286),[11] Graves wonders

> Why have such scores of lovely, gifted girls
>     Married impossible men?

Why have they allied themselves with men "not merely rustic,
foul-tempered, or depraved," but with

> Imposible men: idle, illiterate,
>     Self-pitying, dirty, sly,
> For whose appearance even in City parks
>     Excuses must be made to casual passers-by.

---

11. Originally published in *5 Pens in Hand,* p. 355; after 1958 retitled "A Slice
of Wedding Cake."

Can it, be, he wonders further, that the supply of tolerable hus-
bands has fallen so low? Or might there be another reason for
this apparent discrepancy?

> Or do I always over-value woman
> At the expense of man?

The reader who is aware of Graves's attitude toward femininity
over the years might well be inclined to agree with the latter
hypothesis.

In "Call it a Good Marriage" (*Collected Poems, 1959*, p.
312),[12] Graves tells the story of a marriage that had in it every
element of success save sexual compatibility: the husband and
wife, with "interlocking views," never fought in public, always
acted circumspectly, and faced the world with pride.

> Thus the hazards of their love-bed
> Were none of our damned business—
>
> Till as jurymen we sat on
> Two deaths by suicide.

We see from this poem that Graves has apparently given up for
good the notion that there can be a love between man and woman
in which passion plays no part.

After the 1953 collection, Graves appears to have concentrated
for some time on occasional pieces and satires, most of which he
sold to *The New Yorker* and *The New Statesman*, and few of
which were first-rate Graves. There began to arise some doubt as
to whether he might not have reached his peak with the poems
of the late Forties and early Fifties, and been in a steady decline
since then. But *More Poems, 1961*, a slim volume containing
only thirty-nine pieces, proved conclusively that Graves was indeed a poetic anomaly: a man who, well into his sixties and considerably battered by experience, was yet capable of writing
romantic love poetry of a consistently high quality.

These new poems were also evidence that Graves shows thus
far no signs of ending his affair with the White Goddess, as he had

12. Originally published in *Steps*, p. 258.

discarded his psychological and metaphysical hobby-horses in the earlier stages of his career. She is still the woman to whom Graves writes his love-poems, and she continues to provide him with a rich supply of "metaphors for poetry." The chief difference between these new pieces and those which he had written between 1944 and 1953 is that they reveal what Ronald Gaskell has called "a gathering confidence in the handling of emotion";[13] that is, Graves now shows no reluctance in using a diction which is un-ashamedly romantic. Words of which we have learned to be suspicious in poetry—such as "slender," "moonlight," "shadow," "blossom," and "whisper"—he now employs without any trace of self-consciousness, without any feeling of uneasiness at moving counter to poetic fashion. He has not, it is true, mellowed a great deal in his attitudes toward love and society: he is still all for the former and all against the latter. But his new poems are those of a man who is quite sure of where he stands, and who no longer feels the need to defend his position against critical or public skepticism.

In his new magical poems, the Goddess is still the destroyer of her lovers: "Lyceia" (pp. 3-4), for example, portrays her as the cruel and merciless Artemis, who hunts with a pack of snarling wolves; and "Hag-Ridden" (p. 20) describes the way in which a man who has dreamed of the Goddess awakes

> in profuse sweat, arms aching,
> Knees bruised and soles cut to the raw.

But now Graves appears to accept with complacence and even eagerness the fate that awaits the poet who serves the Goddess. In "To Myrto of Myrtles" (p. 25) he expresses only surprise that she has come to him so late in his career:

> Goddess of Midsummer, how late
> You let me understand
> My lines of head, life, fate
> And heart: a broad M brand
> Inerasable from either hand.

13. "The Poetry of Robert Graves," *The Critical Quarterly*, III (Autumn, 1961), pp. 213-22.

Myrto, *The White Goddess* tells us, is another name for Aphrodite, the Love-Goddess to whom the myrtle was sacred, and who was known by several other names beginning with "M"—Myrrhine, Maia, Mariamne, Melpomene. By whatever name she is called, however, she is the Goddess in her manifestation as nymph, and the poet is amazed that she should have chosen only now to reveal herself to him.

Yet he feels no great regret at her lateness in coming, and can even forgive the inconstancy she is bound to show. In another poem ("The Falcon Woman," p. 11) Graves sees her as a noble and predatory bird, whose wildness is completely untameable; but he acknowledges that, as hard as it is for the man who loves such a creature, it is no less hard

> To be born such a woman
> With wings like a falcon
> And in carelessness of spirit
> To love such a man.

Graves has written no better statement of his concept of love than "Under the Olives" (p. 7), a simple, almost austere poem in which he expresses his complete acceptance of the irrational nature of love:

> We never could have loved had love not struck
> Swifter than reason, and despite reason:
> Under the olives, our hands interlocked,
> We both fell silent:
> Each listened for the other's answering
> Sigh of unreasonableness—
> Innocent, gentle, bold, enduring, proud.

That the Goddess is wayward in her loves is only one aspect of her war against reason. In "Turn of the Moon" (p. 21), a poem which is—while somewhat more complicated rhetorically than its companions in this volume—as moving as any of the simpler love-poems, she is the Moon-Goddess, in charge of rains and the tide.

> Never forget who brings the rain
> In swarthy goatskin bags from a far sea:
> It is the Moon as she turns, repairing
> Damages of long drought and sunstroke.

Whereas the Sun (Apollo, the God of Reason) is absolutely regular in his habits, "shining fierce in summer, mild in winter," the Moon is not:

> Never count upon rain, never foretell it,
> For no power can bring rain
> Except the Moon as she turns; and who can rule her?

> She is prone to delay the necessary floods,
> Lest such a gift might become obligation,
> A month, or two, or three; then suddenly
> Not relenting but by way of whim
> Will perhaps conjure from the cloudless west
> A single rain-drop to surprise with hope
> Each haggard, upturned face.

She refuses to be taken for granted, as the Sun is; but once she has demonstrated her independence, she will grant her favors to the thirsty earth:

> But if one night she brings us, as she turns,
> Soft, steady, even copious rain
> That harms no leaf or flower, but gently falls
> Hour after hour, sinking to the tap roots,
> And the sodden earth exhales at dawn
> A long sigh scented with pure gratitude,
> Such rain—the first rain of our lives, it seems,
> Neither foretold, cajoled, nor counted on—
> Is woman giving as she loves.

That the Moon has withheld her blessings for so long, and has teased us with them so often, only makes her ultimate gift of them more delicious. So it is with woman's love, Graves feels: it cannot be depended on; it must only be gratefully received when it is granted.

When he depicts the manner of her coming to her lover, Graves does not hesitate to invest his poem with all the romantic trappings he can find. Such is the case with "The Visitation" (p. 8), a poem he could never have written twenty or thirty years ago with the same degree of conviction and unself-consciousness:

> Drowsing in my chair of disbelief
> I watch the door as it slowly opens—
> A trick of the night wind?
>
> Your slender body seems a shaft of moonlight
> Against the door as it gently closes.
> Do you cast no shadow?
>
> Your whisper is too soft for credence,
> Your tread like blossom drifting from a bough,
> Your touch even softer.
>
> You wear that sorrowful and tender mask
> Which on high mountain tops in heather-flow
> Entrances lonely shepherds;
>
> And though a single word scatters all doubts
> I quake for wonder at your choice of me:
> Why, why and why?

It would appear from poems such as these that Robert Graves has, after a long and rather stormy career, at last reached some sort of safe harbor—a place from which he might continue, in his proud and cranky way, to write his terse, highly individualistic tributes to the Goddess without concern for popular and critical neglect and misunderstanding.

But in consideration of his apparently undiminished productivity, it hardly seems safe even now to assume that Graves's literary career can be summed up with any degree of finality. A collection of eighteen new poems has just been released by Cassell, and they may well show us something about Graves that we have not yet seen; he is working on a study of the Hebrew myths; he has even made some motions toward doing a Broadway musical about Solomon and Sheba. His recent lectures at Oxford have not, it is true, indicated any radical departure from the old attitudes: they have proceeded along the same eccentric and explosive-laden path he had followed in his lectures at Cambridge in 1955. His old hero, Skelton, is still held up as an example of the true, muse-inspired poet; and he still refuses to give an inch in his condemnation of Apollonian pseudo-poets—of whom the chief examplar is now taken to be Virgil (". . . his perfect lack of originality, courage, humor, or even animal-spirits . . . were the negative qualities which first commended him to government circles, and have kept him in favor ever since"). But Graves's career has been nothing if not filled with surprises and sudden shifts in attitude; and he may have another phase or two left in him yet.

One of the biggest paradoxes in his poetic career is the way in which, just as Graves was becoming reconciled to being thought of as interesting but somewhat old-fashioned, the critics and the poetry-reading public began to discover that this grizzled veteran of early twentieth-century literary campaigns had been for years quietly and steadily writing poetry in a way that communicated far more to them than did that of the "Apollonian" poets who had dominated the literary scene for so many years. The generation of young English poets who began writing in the Fifties— members of "The Movement"—in particular found themselves turning to Graves as an example; and the most promising poets in England today—Thom Gunn, D. J. Enright, Philip Larkin, and Ted Hughes, to mention only the best-known—have sought in their verse to catch something of the tough, ironic Gravesian tone.

Thus it has happened that Graves, somewhat to his consternation, has found himself no longer the perennial outsider from the main stream of English poetry. He had been self-excluded for so long that his traditional metres, his sense of form and discipline, had come back in style, and made him both the figurehead and the reluctant leader of the revolt against the literary Establishment. As the result of his suddenly increased stature, the Establishment now seems willing to bring Graves into the fold. His election to the Professorship of Poetry at Oxford was probably the strongest indication of this change in Graves's status. But, as Graves has written me, "The truth is that I don't belong to any literary society or racket and that, since I can't be ignored any longer, the Establishment is trying to include me; which will be embarrassing for them."

And, to judge from what he says of the Establishment in "Established Lovers," one of *More Poems, 1961* (p. 40), Graves has no intention of meekly allowing himself to be made a member. Here speaking of those distinguished poets—many of them former true poets—who have been so honored, Graves says:

> Observe him well, the scarlet-robed academician
> Stalled with his peers, an Order on his breast,
> And (who could doubt it?) free
> Of such despairs and voices as attended
> His visits to that grotto below sea
> Where once he served a glare-eyed Demoness
> And swore her his unswerving verity.

Graves has been a maverick, a self-exile, and an iconoclast for too long now to be willing to become a public figure—at least not one of the sort he mocks in "Established Lovers."

This study, necessarily sketchy and inconclusive, has attempted to trace only two aspects of the long and variegated career of a singular literary figure. Of Graves as a novelist or translator, I have said almost nothing. And even of Graves as a poet I have not been able to cover enough ground: he has, from 1916 to the present, published almost six hundred poems, and I have been able to mention perhaps only a fifth of these.

What I have tried to do is to outline his development as a poet and critic: to show how he began as a romanticist in the bucolic Georgian style; how he was affected by the First World War; how for a time he attempted to objectify his naturally subjective poetry by writing verses which dealt with a number of problems in psychology, religion, and philosophy; and how, failing in this and almost despairing of his future as a poet, he fled England.

I have tried to indicate something of the nature of his literary partnership with Laura Riding—to show how she simultaneously helped and hindered his career—and I have gone briefly into the background of his mythic poems, to suggest what he is trying to do in this fourth period of his career, when he asserts that he is the loyal follower of the Great Triple Goddess.

I have attempted as well to trace his career as a practical and theoretic critic, and to relate this criticism to his poetry where it is possible to do so.

The man himself has, I am afraid, eluded me; but this is no biography, and the reader of Graves's poetry does not need one, anyway—for, except in his second period, he has never attempted to keep autobiographical elements out of his work. He has, one feels sure, himself written the best possible description of Robert Graves, in a recent poem called "The Face in the Mirror" (*Collected Poems, 1959*, p. 301):

> Grey haunted eyes, absent-mindedly glaring
> From wide, uneven orbits; one brow drooping
> Somewhat over the eye
> Because of a missile fragment still inhering,
> Skin deep, as a foolish record of old-world fighting.
>
> Crookedly broken nose—low tackling caused it;
> Cheeks, furrowed; coarse grey hair, flying frenetic;
> Forehead, wrinkled and high;
> Jowls, prominent; ears, large: jaw, pugilistic;
> Teeth, few; lips, full and ruddy; mouth, ascetic.
>
> I pause with razor poised, scowling derision
> At the mirrored man whose beard needs my attention,
> And once more ask him why
> He still stands ready, with a boy's presumption,
> To court the queen in her high silk pavilion.

Here he is as he must really be: a grizzled and tough old poet who, in pride and wonderment at the survival of his romantic instincts, asks only to court the Goddess—which means after all only to write careful, honest, and tightly disciplined poems which make "sense; good sense; penetrating, often heart-rending sense." And this, it must seem to anyone, is what Robert Graves knows how to do better than any other poet today.

# Afterword

I met Robert Graves for the first time in May of 1963, in Washington, D.C., where he had come to give a reading of his poems.  We talked in a general way for a few hours, chiefly about his most recent work, and he was very helpful in clearing up some of the unresolved problems of my book.  At one point in the conversation he suddenly smiled and asked me if he seemed, in the flesh, to be the sort of man I had expected him to be.  I thought for a moment, and then said yes, that he was precisely the man to have written "Rocky Acres," "To Juan at the Winter Solstice," and "The Face in the Mirror."  Graves seemed pleased and said that he had never known a real poet whose poetry had not been an accurate self-portrait.

The picture that Graves, the man, makes is certainly no less impressive than the picture in the poetry.  He is very tall, still quite well-built and vigorous, with a strong sense of *hauteur* about him: very imposing, and very aware of being imposing.  It would be impossible for a man of Graves's appearance to be anything but what he is: a poet of great skill, discipline, and strength of character—but, with all of these qualities, a determined and conscious streak of eccentricity (the Celtic streak in him, the literary ethnologists would say).  Graves is the sort of man who can, even when silent, dominate a crowded room completely. One would not like to be his enemy.

By the time of this meeting *Swifter than Reason* was already half-way into galley proofs; and Graves got considerable satisfaction out of declaring to me that the book was already obsolete— that he had, in the year since my manuscript had been completed, written many new poems, taken many new positions. He was right, in a way: certainly he had been prolific in the past year— had written so many new poems, in fact, that he was embarrassed over this sudden proliferation and was planning to publish a batch of them privately, out of sight of the public and the critics. But, as he revealed in his reading that afternoon, these new poems had not suffered from the speed with which they had appeared. They were as good as anything, almost, that he had written. Most of them were love poems and seemed to differ from the love poems in his recent collections perhaps only in their greater degree of tranquillity and resignation. More than ever, they seemed to be the words of a man who would be stoically and proudly loyal to the Goddess and to her human counterparts, even as they inevitably betrayed him.

My book had become obsolete for another reason, too. Graves is no longer so little known in the United States as he was a couple of years ago. His popularity appears, in fact, to have increased enormously: he is in great demand as a reader and lecturer, his poetry has won him many awards, his books are selling well, and —as I discovered that afternoon—there are suddenly a lot of people around who seem to know his work well. His audience that day was a large one, and as he read his poems it followed him intelligently and appreciatively. There were dozens of young women there, delighting in the praise accorded their sex by the poems; but I was most intrigued by observing, in the section of seats next to mine, four nuns, all in a row: each with her own copy of *Collected Poems, 1961,* and each raptly following Graves's reading, serene and secret smiles on each face.

# Bibliography

I. POETIC AND CRITICAL WORKS OF ROBERT GRAVES.

The following are arranged in chronological order.

*Over the Brazier.* London: The Poetry Bookshop, 1916. Second impression, 1917; reprinted, revised, and with a new preface, 1920.

*Goliath and David.* London: The Chiswick Press, 1916. Privately printed.

*Fairies and Fusiliers.* London: Heinemann, 1917; New York: A. A. Knopf, 1918.

*The Treasure Box.* London: The Chiswick Press, 1919. Privately printed.

*Country Sentiment.* London: Martin Secker, 1920; New York: A. A. Knopf, 1920.

*The Pier-Glass.* London: Martin Secker, 1921; New York: A. A. Knopf, 1921.

*On English Poetry: Being an Irregular Approach to the Psychology of This Art, From Evidence Mainly Subjective.* London: Heinemann, 1922; New York: A. A. Knopf, 1922.

*Whipperginny.* London: Heinemann, 1923; New York: A. A. Knopf, 1923.

*The Feather Bed.* Richmond, England: L. and Virginia Woolf, 1923.

*The Owl* (Winter, 1922). A periodical of miscellany edited by Graves and William Nicholson. [Contains two poems by Graves ("Full Moon" and "Knowledge of God"), and poems, plays, stories, and drawings by Edmund Blunden, Basant Mallik, W. J. Turner, T. E.

Lawrence, Siegfried Sassoon, W. H. Davies, Thomas Hardy, Philip Guedalla, Frank Dobson, and others.]

*Mockbeggar Hall.* London: L. and Virginia Woolf, 1924.

*Poetic Unreason and Other Studies.* London: Cecil Palmer, 1925.

*Contemporary Techniques of Poetry: A Political Analogy.* London: L. and Virginia Woolf, 1925.

*John Kemp's Wager: A Ballad Opera.* Oxford: Blackwell, 1925; S. French, 1925.

*The Marmosite's Miscellany.* (Published under the pseudonym of "John Doyle.") London: L. and Virginia Woolf, 1925.

*Robert Graves.* (The Augustan Books of Modern Poetry, No. 13.) London: E. Benn, 1925.

*Welchman's Hose.* London: The Fleuron, 1925.

*Another Future of Poetry.* London: L. and Virginia Woolf, 1926.

*Poems, 1914-1926.* London: Heinemann, 1927.

*Poems, 1914-1927.* London: Heinemann, 1927. (Published in a limited edition the same year as *Poems, 1914-1926,* including nine new poems not contained in *Poems, 1914-1926.*)

*A Survey of Modernist Poetry.* With Laura Riding. London: Heinemann, 1927.

*A Pamphlet Against Anthologies.* With Laura Riding. London: Jonathan Cape, 1928.

"November 5th Address," *X: A Quarterly Review,* I (June, 1960), pp. 171-76. (Footnote on p. 171 reads: "Apparently given in 1928 to the Teacher's Union in London, but I cannot recall the occasion. R. G.")

*Good-bye to All That.* London: Jonathan Cape, 1929 (originally announced as *Up to Yesterday*); reprinted: Jonathan Cape, 1931; revised and reprinted: New York, Doubleday Anchor Books, 1957.

*Poems, 1929.* London: The Seizin Press, 1929.

*Ten Poems More.* Paris: The Hours Press, 1930.

*Poems, 1926-1930.* London: Heinemann, 1931.

*To Whom Else?* Deyá, Majorca: The Seizin Press, 1931.

*Poems, 1930-1933.* London: A. Barker, 1933.

*Epilogue: A Critical Summary,* ed. With Laura Riding. Deyá, Majorca: The Seizin Press, and London: Constable and Co., Ltd. Vol. I: Autumn, 1935. Vol. II: Summer, 1936. Vol. III: Spring, 1937.

*Collected Poems, 1938.* London: Cassell, 1938.

*No More Ghosts: Selected Poems.* London: Faber and Faber, 1940.

*Work in Hand.* With Alan Hodge and Norman Cameron. London: The Hogarth Press, 1942.

*Poems, 1938-1945.* London: Cassell, 1946; New York: Creative Age Press, 1946.

*Collected Poems, 1914-1947.* London: Cassell, 1948.

*The White Goddess: A Historical Grammar of Poetic Myth.* London: Faber and Faber, 1948; New York: Creative Age Press, 1948; amended and enlarged, London: Faber and Faber, 1952; reprinted, New York: Vintage Books, 1958.

*The Common Asphodel: Collected Essays On Poetry, 1922-1949.* London: Hamish Hamilton, 1949.

*Occupation: Writer.* London: Cassell, 1950; New York: Creative Age Press, 1950; reprinted, New York: The Universal Library, 1950.

*Poems and Satires, 1951.* London: Cassell, 1951.

*Poems, 1953.* London: Cassell, 1953.

*Collected Poems, 1955.* New York: Doubleday, 1955.

*The Crowning Privilege.* London: Cassell, 1955; New York: Doubleday, 1956; London: Pelican Books, 1959.

*5 Pens in Hand.* New York: Doubleday, 1958.

*Steps.* London: Cassell, 1958.

*The Poems of Robert Graves, Chosen By Himself.* New York: Doubleday Anchor Books, 1958.

*Collected Poems, 1959.* London: Cassell, 1959.

*Food for Centaurs.* New York: Doubleday, 1960.

*The Penny Fiddle: Poems for Children.* London: Cassell, 1961.

*More Poems, 1961.* London: Cassell, 1961.

"Service to the Muse," *Atlantic Monthly,* CCVII (June, 1961), pp. 43-44. (Accompanied by all of Section XI from *More Poems, 1961,* with exception of "Lyceia.")

*Collected Poems, 1961.* New York: Doubleday, 1961. (Same as *Collected Poems, 1959,* with contents of *More Poems, 1961,* added.)

*Oxford Addresses on Poetry.* London: Cassell, 1962; New York: Doubleday, 1962.

*New Poems, 1962.* London: Cassell, 1962.


II. SECONDARY MATERIALS ON ROBERT GRAVES. The following are arranged in alphabetical order.

Adams, Hazard. "Criticism: Whence and Whither?" *The American Scholar,* XXVIII (Spring, 1959), pp. 226-38.

Aiken, Conrad. "The Mortality of Magic," *Skepticisms: Notes on Contemporary Poetry* (New York, 1919), pp. 193-98.

Algren, Nelson. "Sentiment with Terror," *Poetry,* LV (1939), pp. 157-59.

Anon. "A Personal Mythology," *Times* [*London*] *Literary Supplement* (June 5, 1959), p. 336.

Anon. "Signs of an All Too Correct Compassion: Laments for the Maker," *Times* [*London*] *Literary Supplement* (September 9, 1960), p. xiii.

Auden, W. H. "A Poet of Honor," *The Mid-Century*, No. 28 (July, 1961), pp. 3-9. Reprinted in *Shenandoah*, XIII, No. 2 (Winter, 1962), pp. 5-12.

Bogan, Louise. "Satire and Sentimentality," *Selected Criticism* (New York, 1955), pp. 316-18.

Bullough, Geoffrey. *The Trend of Modern Poetry.* London, 1949.

Campbell, Roy. "Contemporary Poetry," *Scrutinies, By Various Writers* (London, 1928), pp. 161-80.

Church, Richard. "Robert Graves, A Traveller in the Desert," *Fortnightly Review*, CLV (1941), pp. 384-91.

Cohen, J. M. *Robert Graves.* Edinburgh, 1960. (Writers and Critics Series, No. 3.)

Cotton, John, John Davies, and F. W. Bateson. Correspondence in *Essays in Criticism*, V (July, 1955), pp. 293-98.

Cowan, Louise. *The Fugitive Group.* Baton Rouge, 1959.

Creeley, Robert. "Her Service is Perfect Freedom," *Poetry*, XCIII (May, 1959), pp. 395-98.

Dahlberg, Edward, and Herbert Read, "Robert Graves and T. S. Eliot," *Twentieth Century*, CLXVI (1959), pp. 54-62.

Davie, Donald. "Impersonal and Emblematic," *Shenandoah*, XIII, No. 2 (Winter, 1962), pp. 38-44. Originally published in *Listen*, III (Spring, 1960).

———. "The Toneless Voice of Robert Graves," *The Listener* (July 2, 1959), pp. 11-13.

Dudek, Louis. "The Case of Robert Graves," *Canadian Forum*, XL (December, 1960), pp. 199-201.

Enright, D. J. "The Example of Robert Graves," *Shenandoah*, XIII, No. 2 (Winter, 1962), pp. 13-15.

———. "Robert Graves and the Decline of Modernism," *Essays in Criticism*, XI, No. 3 (July, 1961), pp. 319-37.

Fraser, G. S. *The Modern Writer and His World.* London, 1953.

———. "The Poet and His Medium," *The Craft of Letters in England*, ed. John Lehmann (London, 1956), pp. 98-121.

———. "The Poetry of Robert Graves," *Vision and Rhetoric: Studies in Modern Poetry* (London, 1959), pp. 135-48.

———. "The Reputation of Robert Graves," *Shenandoah*, XIII, No. 2 (Winter, 1962), pp. 19-32.

Fuller, Roy. "Poetry: Tradition and Belief," *The Craft of Letters in England,* ed. John Lehmann (London, 1956), pp. 74-79.

———. "Some Vintages of Graves," *The London Magazine,* V (February, 1958), pp. 56-59.

Gaskell, Ronald. "The Poetry of Robert Graves," *The Critical Quarterly,* III (Autumn, 1961), pp. 213-22.

Graves, Alfred Perceval. *To Return to All That: An Autobiography.* London, 1930.

Gregory, Horace. "Faithful to a Goddess and a Queen," *The New York Times Book Review* (July 16, 1961), pp. 1, 20.

———. "Robert Graves: A Parable for Writers," *Partisan Review,* XX (January-February, 1953), pp. 44-54.

Gunn, Thom. "In Nobody's Pantheon," *Shenandoah,* XIII, No. 2 (Winter, 1962), pp. 34-35.

Haller, John. "Conversations with Robert Graves," *Southwest Review,* XLII (1957), pp. 237-41.

———. "Robert Graves in Lecture and Talk," *Arizona Quarterly,* XV (1959), pp. 150-56.

Hayman, Ronald. "Robert Graves," *Essays in Criticism,* V (January, 1955), pp. 32-43.

Hoffman, Daniel G. "The Unquiet Graves," *Sewanee Review,* LXVII (1959), pp. 305-16.

Jarrell, Randall. "Graves and the White Goddess," Parts I and II, *The Yale Review,* XLV (Winter, Spring, 1956), pp. 302-14; pp. 467-78.

———. "Poets," *Poetry and the Age* (New York, 1955), pp. 200-14.

Lawrence, T. E. *Letters,* ed. David Garnett. New York, 1938.

Lucas, F. L. "Critical Unreason; or, Dr. Cottard's Saturday Night," *Authors Dead and Living* (New York, 1935), pp. 255-63.

Mais, S. P. B. *Books and Their Writers.* New York, 1920.

Monro, Harold. "Some Poets and Poetasters of Our Time," *Some Contemporary Poets (1920)* (London, 1920), pp. 172-74.

Muir, Edwin. "Robert Graves," *Transition: Essays on Contemporary Literature* (New York, 1926), pp. 163-78.

Press, John. *The Fire and the Fountain: An Essay on Poetry.* Oxford, 1955.

Quennell, Peter. *The Sign of the Fish.* New York, 1960.

Schwartz, Delmore. "Graves in Dock: The Case for Modern Poetry," *New Republic,* CXXXIV (March 19, 1956), pp. 20-21.

Seymour-Smith, Martin. *Robert Graves.* London, 1956. (Writers and Their Works, No. 78).

Sherman, Arnold. "A Talk with Robert Graves, English Poet in Majorca," *Commentary*, XXII (1956), pp. 364-66.

Simon, John. "Nowhere is Washing So Well Done," *The Mid-Century*, No. 16 (September, 1960), pp. 11-18.

Skelton, Robin. *The Poetic Pattern*. Berkeley, Cal., 1956.

Spender, Stephen. "Poetry for Poetry's Sake, and Poetry beyond Poetry," *Horizon*, No. 76 (April, 1946), pp. 221-38.

Steiner, George. "The Genius of Robert Graves," *The Kenyon Review*, XXII (Summer, 1960), pp. 340-65.

Swanson, Roy Arthur. "Graves's 'Hercules at Nemea,'" *The Explicator*, XV, No. 9 (June, 1957), p. 56.

Swinnerton, Frank. *The Georgian Scene: A Literary Panorama*. New York, 1934.

Tante, Dilly (pseudonym of Stanley J. Kunitz), ed. *Living Authors: A Book of Biographies*. New York, 1932.

Thwaite, Anthony. "Muir, Graves, and Empson," *Contemporary English Poetry: An Introduction* (London, 1959), pp. 125-39.

Trilling, Lionel. "A Ramble with Graves," *A Gathering of Fugitives* (Boston, 1956), pp. 20-30.

Untermeyer, Louis. *Modern British and American Poetry*. New York, 1923.

Ure, Peter. "Yeats and Mr. Graves," letter to *Times* [*London*] *Literary Supplement* (June 12, 1959), p. 353.

Ussher, Arland. "Robert Graves: The Philoctetes of Majorca," *Dublin Magazine*, XXXII (1957), pp. 18-21.

Waugh, Arthur. *Tradition and Change: Studies in Contemporary Literature*. New York, 1919.

Ward, A. C. *Twentieth-Century Literature, 1901-1950*. New York, 1957.

Wilkinson, Marguerite. *New Voices: An Introduction to Contemporary Poetry*. New York, 1927.

Williams, Charles. "Robert Graves," *Poetry at Present*. (Oxford, 1930), pp. 194-206.

# Index